M000207731

Genesis of a
Duck
Cop

Genesis of a
Duck
Cop
memories & milestones

Terry Grosz

Johnson Books
BOULDER

© 2006 by Terry Grosz

All rights reserved. No part of this publication may be reproduced or transmitted in any form or by any means, electronic or mechanical, including photocopy, recording, or any information storage and retrieval system, without permission in writing from the publisher.

Published by Johnson Books, a division of Big Earth Publishing, 3005 Center Green Drive, Suite 220, Boulder, Colorado 80301. E-mail: books@bigearthpublishing.com www.johnsonbooks.com

Cover design and photo shoot by Peter Streicher, shushu Design Composition by Eric Christensen

9 8 7 6 5 4 3 2 1

Library of Congress Cataloging-in-Publication Data
Grosz, Terry
    Genesis of a duck cop: memories & milestones / Terry Grosz
        p. cm.
    ISBN 1-55566-373-7
    1. Grosz, Terry. 2. Game wardens—California—Biography. I. Title
    SK354.G76A3 2006
· 363.28—dc22   2005035301

Printed in the United States of America

Contents

Dedication

In every work like this there are people standing in the wings whose hands and hearts have appreciably touched not only the words, theme, and very essence of the work but the heart of the author as well. This work is no different except in one beautiful and fulfilling instance. I was the recipient of a heaven-sent blessing early on in my life, a blessing that has remained to this day.

When Donna Larson walked through the door into our classroom in the eighth grade so many years ago, I was instantly struck with a revelation few in this world ever have the opportunity to experience. I knew at that moment that she would be my wife, lifelong soulmate, and partner! I knew in such a strong sense of the word that it was almost physical. That sense never wavered or left me, and in 1963 she became my wife, fulfilling the dreams in my heart and soul. Today, forty-plus years later, my love for her has never wavered or been stronger. She truly is my soulmate from a marriage made in heaven.

It is to this Renaissance woman, the mother of my children, my best friend, and always golden counselor, that I dedicate this final book of my series. I also rededicate my heart and soul in these lines for her to have and to hold until that magical force that brought us together moves us into the vast time of the great beyond. No man could have asked for a better love of his life or visionary partner who in so many ways walked side by side with him through many blessed years together. I am truly blessed.

Donna, I will love you forever and a day.

Preface

IN MY FIRST SIX BOOKS, the reader travels with me through thirty-two years of wildlife law enforcement and the changing times. These adventure books are constructed to personally involve the reader, giving him a sense of what the action in the world of wildlife law enforcement was *really* like. Along with the essence of the chase in these books, also comes the changing of the times. Those changing times saw many of the great north coast rivers of California almost empty of salmon and sturgeon because of siltation from logging, legal and illegal Indian gill netting, heavy amounts of water drawn down by the farming community, pollution, illegal snagging, over-fishing by the commercial fishing fleets, and the illegal sale of those sport-caught fish by humankind. This was a time when the great hoards of waterfowl diminished from the Sacramento Valley skies because of illegal and legal over-harvest, loss of winter habitat, loss of wetlands, and loss of breeding habitat, which were compounded by the long-term effects of droughts.

I saw native prairies even further diminished to today's pathetic fragments, along with the losses of associated wildlife. I witnessed the continuing, almost out of control drainage of wetlands in the states of North Dakota, South Dakota, and Minnesota by local dirt farmers hell bent on raising that last bushel of subsidized wheat. And with those drainage actions came diminished waterfowl and shorebird populations, not to mention endemic wildlife populations. I saw neo-tropical bird species common to North America's environment at the start of these adventures all but disappear some three decades later. Some disappeared because of habitat loss, transmission line strikes, continued use of DDT in Mexico, Central and South America (DDT that is still being produced in America), losses in oil pits, cyanide poisoning at heap-leech mining sites, and the like.

I witnessed major wildlife diseases such as chronic wasting disease, West Nile virus, whirling disease, and others, strike deeply into the free roaming populations of the birds, fish, and ungulates of the land. I witnessed the decline of the sage grouse and mule deer, more than likely due to the effects of overutilization of their lands by grazing interests. I saw bald and golden eagles die by the thousands from illegal poisoning, trapping, and shooting because sheep raising interests didn't like sharing *your* public lands with anything but their grassland-destroying sheep. I observed many other bird and animal species diminish or disappear from the public lands in the seventeen western states because of *severe* overgrazing by livestock interest leasing those lands at ridiculously low rates due to questionable western politics. I saw the start of the destruction of the world's last remaining temperate rain forest in Alaska because of short-sighted and destructive state and federal politics.

I have seen the destruction of over seventy percent of the oceans' fisheries due to over-fishing with drag nets, drift nets, long lines, purse seines, and every other form of man's intentions. I have seen seventy percent of the world's fresh water supplies become contaminated because of man. I have witnessed golf courses using as much water *per day* as man uses to drink *world wide* on a daily basis. I have observed Native Americans from Alaska destroying great numbers of marine mammals under the guise of cultural, religious, and subsistence purposes and then selling those products, which were unlawfully taken, for drugs. In my lifetime the rain forests have dangerously dwindled in size along with their wildlife populations. I have witnessed the federal government weaken federal conservation laws so the U.S. Military could freely destroy migratory bird populations and marine mammals in the course of their actions. I saw the conservation laws of the land in North America double to address the increasing resource-related problems, yet saw *no* appreciable increase in numbers in the wildlife law enforcement community . . . saw . . . ENOUGH!

This seventh and last book is a different read from all my others. In this book, the reader will discover from whence I came and the momentous bumps in the road leading to my life today. There are funny stories like "My First Bear Hunt" and "To Milk A Cow." Adventure abounds in "Forest Fires I Have Known," "Alaska," and "My First Deer." The crazy stories "To Bomb a Beaver Lodge" and "No Safe Takeoff" tell of pure and simple danger. History lies in the chapters titled "Andy Swingle," "To Cut a Tree, to Grow a Man," and

"Earl 'the Pearl' Dudley." A unique sadness is the centerpiece in the stories "The Chinese Graveyard" and "'Please Remove Baby.'" Life's lessons cross paths with reality in "My Arrival," "Growing Up Poor," and "A Very 'Special' Taxidermist." And where would a book of mine be without politics spreading its tendrils throughout in a story titled "The National Wildlife Property and Eagle Repository." There are fish and game related tales in "The Tule Lake Snow Goose Hunt" and stories of great introspection such as "The Value Of Training" and "To Shoot a Coyote." As one will see, there is something for everyone with a whole lot of variety throughout: a special moment, memory, or milestone in a life that hopefully made a difference.

In this book the reader will gain an insight into the author from day one, which was pretty rough in and of itself, to the current times—which are still exciting. The stories, in characteristic fashion, are full of twists, turns, blind curves, and lessons—guaranteed to make one think, smile, or wonder as to how I got as far as I did without being smashed flatter than a sail cat. There goes the assistance of those two guardian angels once again . . .

Enjoy the reads for what they are. Enjoy the history for what it represents and cry over that which is no more. For much, there truly is no more.

Acknowledgments

FOR OVER THIRTY-TWO YEARS I missed a lot of important family events because I was too busy trying to save those in the world of wildlife that had no voice. At the time, it seemed the right thing to do. My kids were little, had the guiding hand of a *great* mom, and the critters seemed more in danger than did the home front. As I progressed up through the ranks changing duty stations, the demands for my time from the animals continued to take on gigantic proportions, as did my work efforts. That translated into longer and longer stints away from home. The next thing I realized, I had almost adult-sized kids. By then, my involvement with everyday operations had become so huge that I could only give my hunting- and fishing-loving kids one weekend a year with their dad.

Assuming the Denver Special Agent in Charge position in 1981, I began to slow down, especially with the realization that my two sons and daughter were almost grown. Throughout all those previous years they "made do" with what little time they had with dad, but a lot was missed on both sides of the fence. Making the time, realizing I couldn't save all in the world of wildlife, I began creating more dad-related opportunities for my kids. In those few remaining years, all of my children turned out to be crack shots, excellent hunters and fishermen, outstanding woods people, excellent conservationists, and good human beings with great ethics. This was mostly due to their mom's influence and some from their "Johnny Come Lately" dad.

It is to Richard, Christopher, and Kimberlee that I acknowledge many of my life's successes—successes because they silently sat by, supporting their dad's vision quest at their own expense. Now grown, they have gone into society to make their ways. Richard, Kimberlee, and Christopher (until his sudden and untimely death on October 13, 2005) make it a point to spend a lot of time with your children. Thank you, kids, for making your dad proud!

PART ONE
Memories

1

My Arrival

MY LIFE HAS BEEN a wonderful series of "moments, memories, and milestones," starting with my arrival. It was your standard "bomber turn" event dealing with the birth of a child. Well, maybe not standard when you looked at all the facets. Mom was a tough North Dakota farm gal, born during some of the roughest times in American history and certainly living on some of the toughest lands in the lower forty-eight. She weathered many hardships, including long, fierce winters; the Depression; and the loss of her father at an early age. She had to carry more than her share of the load, helping her mother keep the farm solvent. When she turned eighteen, enough was enough. There had to be a better life out there, and she was bound and determined to find it. Taking a piece of fried chicken from the Sunday dinner, an orange, and $1.50 (which she stuck in her shoe), she told her mother good-bye. Her mother, washing clothes by hand in the North Dakota wind, never looked up or even answered. As I said, times were tough, and both the land and the people were harsh.

Mom hitchhiked to Yakima, Washington, where she got a job in the Tea Pot Cafe for $2 a day plus tips. A short time later she met a dashing young man who dressed in flashy clothes and danced like a whirlwind. The relationship blossomed, and soon they were married. As was usually the case in those days, I was promptly on the way.

Birthing usually was a normal sequence of events, but there were storm clouds on the horizon in my case. In my prime, I stood six feet four inches tall and tipped the scales at 320 pounds. Mom—well, if she was five foot three inches tall and weighed one hundred pounds, that was stretching it some. However, she always pulled her share of the wagon and worked at my dad's grocery store right up to the day she went into labor. When she arrived at the hospital, the doctors discovered they had a problem. Mom was running a temperature of 103 degrees, had jaundice, and tipped the scales at only 105 pounds! But by the looks of it, she was carrying one hell of a jumbo-sized baby.

For the next forty-eight hours, Mom was in hard labor. The hospital used ether to help with the pain, which caused Mom to lose all her hair and everything she had eaten (which wasn't much) and loosened all her teeth, making it very difficult to chew for months afterward. Finally the doctors told my dad the baby was too large to pass through the birth canal. And because they had waited so long, it was too late to do a cesarean section because of Mom's now very weakened condition. Dad was told they could save either the mother or the baby, but not both. Dad, to his credit (I would have done the same), told the doctors to save his wife. With that, the doctors returned to the ordeal. Using a large set of forceps, they grabbed me by the head and jerked! Out I came, slicker than cow slobbers ... messed up, but imagine what that did to my mother!

At that moment, my two guardian angels were assigned. I was still alive, as was mom. However, after they jerked me out like that, I was a mess. My head was black and blue from being pulled through the birth canal with such force. Both eyes were swollen shut, and my lips looked as if someone had hit me squarely in the mouth. There were several deep cuts on the side of my head where the forceps had dug into the flesh, and I was bleeding like a stuck hog. My left shoulder and arm were also twisted and misshapen. But we were both still alive on June 22, 1941. Years later, Mom told me that when they brought me in for her to nurse, she tried to turn me away. She told the nurses that wasn't her baby all cut up and beat to hell. But it was—all nine pounds, twelve ounces! No wonder Mom had had such a problem with my delivery ...

For years my left arm and shoulder were kept in a sling device to slowly twist everything back into normalcy. And it worked. Today you can still see by the way I carry my left arm and shoulder that I was injured at birth. But I pitched hay as a kid, worked as a logger, played six years of high school and college football (as a lineman), hunted, fished, and spent over thirty-two years working in state and federal wildlife law enforcement. To be frank, those thirty-two years were pretty rough-and-tumble at times. But the arm and shoulder were good enough for me to pass all the physicals they could throw at me, and here I am. The only thing I ever had to pass up because of those birth injuries was a stint at the U.S. Naval Academy (I passed the written test but flunked the physical) and, while I was in college, the naval air cadet program. However, I did serve my country and its people, though not as a military man, and my service as a conservation officer was just as important to our national heritage and the lives of those yet to come.

Mom is gone now, and I am in the twilight of my life. I have lived a great life to date and will continue to do so until called for my next assignment. So I would say my arrival, despite its problems, was one of those sterling moments in my life.

2

My First Bear Hunt

IN 1946 MY MOTHER and father split the sheets over his womanizing, drinking, and gambling. Soon afterward Dad was caught stealing money from the till of the store where he was the general manager. Mom left for the high ground with two little kids to raise, and Dad went to San Quentin. With no other means of support, the three of us were taken in by my uncle Lanoie and his family until Mom got a job and could support herself.

I was only six years old, but to help at my uncle's I hauled firewood, cleaned out the woodburning stove, washed dishes, cleaned my room, and helped in many other ways that were not very interesting for a kid like me. I wanted action! Sometimes my uncle would take me down to the shop where he worked as a heavy-equipment mechanic for a local lumber company. Now, that was the stuff. There were parts everywhere, nuts and bolts and just about everything under the sun a kid could get into, all permeated by the smell of solvent and diesel fuel. My uncle was a great man, good with kids and supportive of his family, who helped anyone in need within arm's reach. He was just what the doctor had ordered for a kid like me, adrift without a dad.

In that shop filled with broken-down logging and lumber trucks and huge D-8 caterpillars was the genesis of my first bear hunt.

There were six other mechanics in the shop, and all were avid hunters and fishermen, as were most people in those days. In addition, they were all "big talkers" about their avocations. I used to sit for hours by the glowing potbellied stoves, roaring out their heat in that cavernous, drafty old building, listening to stories of big fish, loads of ducks, big bucks, blue grouse so numerous they could be killed with sticks, and the mighty black bear. More than likely those stories were stretched a tad for my young ears, but they had the desired effect. I couldn't wait to grow up and take my place among such men, slaying powerful bears, shooting hordes of ducks and Canada geese, or coming home with long stringers of trout. But for me, the stories about the dangerous black bear took the front seat. Now, *that* was a critter to be reckoned with in my big-as-a-garbage-can-lid eyes and wildest dreams!

The men used to talk about using packs of baying hounds to run down the bears, shooting them out of trees, being attacked when their quarry was cornered, and the many good meals that came from a successful hunt. The more I listened, the more eager I became to partake in a bear hunt, regardless of the dangers or my age. The itch finally got so bad that I began begging the fellows to take me along. Most of those grizzled old men just laughed and said I was too young to go on such a dangerous venture. That only whetted my appetite even more, and I became relentless in my pursuit of the chance to go on a hunt for the mighty black bear. I was big for my age and could handle the danger, I thought.

Not making any headway with those fellows, I turned my begging toward my uncle. As I said earlier, he was a good man, and I figured he would recognize my potential as a great bear hunter. So I continued my loud vision quest. I wanted a bear hunt with no holds barred, in which I would single-handedly tree and kill the "bar" just like Daniel Boone! At first my uncle's good nature put up with my constant pestering. As I persisted, he lost patience and was not amused. However, I was going to get a bear, and he was going to help me, come hell or high water! More of the latter, as you will soon see. ...

Over the next several months, I am sure Uncle had about all he could take. One evening after dinner he casually mentioned that he was going bear hunting that evening. *Holy cow,* here was my chance, I thought. I instantly began with the "please take me, I can help, I want to go, I can help drag 'im" and other such nonsense. I could see that I was wearing him down, so I poured it on. I couldn't let this chance slip through my fingers. Finally he gave in! Hot dog! I knew my six-year-old negotiating skills would pay off! "Get all your chores done and we will go tonight," he promised with a grin. Boy, talk about a fireball. I roared around the house until all my chores were finished.

At last the hallowed hour arrived. It was about nine in the evening and darker than Billy Hell. But that was all right; I would be with my uncle, and between the two of us, *we would get our bear.* Mom got me dressed for the cold of the evening, and Uncle went out into the woodshed to get the gear we would need. Soon I was ready to go, and with a kiss from Mom for good luck, out the door I went into the first real outdoors adventure of my young life. I don't think my feet even touched the ground! Visions of a plump bear roast in a Dutch oven with mounds of carrots, spuds, celery, onions, tomatoes, and cloves of garlic danced in my head.

Meeting Uncle in the woodshed, I got my first surprise. He didn't have any packs of mean black-and-tans or bluetick hounds to run the bear.

"Uncle," I said, "how are we going to get the bear without any dogs?"

"No problem," he replied. "I put some bait out to attract the bears. Driving home tonight, I saw a bear's eyes shining in the headlights as he ate the road-killed deer I put out. Don't worry; he will be there."

My uncle was a good man, so if he thought that was all right, so did I. Then I saw that he didn't have any kind of rifle.

"Uncle," I asked, "do you want me to go get your rifle?"

"Naw," he replied. "Shooting them just ruins the meat. We are going to catch him another way tonight."

Now I was really confused. No dogs to run the bear up a tree and no gun to shoot him out of that tree. That did not compute even in my six-year-old mind. However, my uncle knew what he was doing, so I didn't worry (too much).

"Here, hold this," my uncle said as he handed me a gunnysack.

"What's this for?" I asked.

"To hold the bear," he replied.

Oh no! I thought. I don't remember any of the men around the stoves talking about putting a live, savage black bear into a damn little old gunnysack! A little unsure now about this bear-hunting excursion, I said, "How does this work?"

"It works very well, Terry. I will get you to hold the sack behind our bear-bait station, and I will go out in front and scare the bear toward you. When he gets close, you run him into the sack and whack him with this." He then handed me a stick of firewood. By now I had a set of eyes the size of garbage-can lids!

"Are you sure?" I asked in a wobbly voice, trying not to show my terror at being left holding the bag.

"Oh, hell, yes. I have done this a dozen times, and it always works slicker than cow slobbers," he replied. Even at age six, I saw that this plan was not so good. It wouldn't have taken much for me to abandon ship at that point, but this might be my only chance to go on a bear hunt and I wouldn't want to miss it for all the world. So I toughened up. ...

With my gunnysack, stick of firewood, and heart up in my throat, out the door of the woodshed I went into the inky blackness of the Plumas County winter night, wishing we had a few hounds and at least *one* rifle. Uncle led with the flashlight, and I stumbled along behind as we walked up the hillside behind his house. Soon we were in a dense thicket of small pine trees, and he stopped and listened carefully. "Hear that?" he said.

"Hear what?" I said with a loudly thumping heart.

"The bear! I can hear him down there on the bait station tearing the deer carcass to bits with his *huge, sharp* teeth and long claws."

Man, that did it! We were so poor in those days that Mom couldn't afford to get my hair cut. Have you ever seen ten inches of long hair standing straight up?

"Here," said Uncle, "get your sack ready like this." He opened the sack with the mouth facing toward the bear-bait station. "Now, hold it steady like this, and when I scare him, he will run up the hill and right into the sack. When he does, you close the sack and whack him a couple of times on the head with that big stick. When I get here, the two of us will carry him home and butcher him so we can have some bear steak for dinner tomorrow night."

It was a good thing it was dark as the inside of a dead cow. Otherwise Uncle would have seen a six-year-old absolutely scared to death, hair standing straight up, a set of eyes the size of thirty-six-inch culverts, and a hind end so tight it couldn't pass an ounce of wind! Before I could say anything, Uncle was gone into the dark of the night with the flashlight to confront the savage bear loudly tearing the deer carcass apart (I was sure I could now hear it!).

My tongue was so thick, I couldn't even call after Uncle and ask him to come back so we could reconsider the plan. Then, horror of horrors, his light disappeared! I stood there with every tooth chattering in my head and every bone quaking in my body, and it was obvious that those symptoms were not caused by the cold. ... Then *I really heard it!* Something was coming my way. The sound wasn't loud at first, but by damn, something was coming toward me through the dark timber.

"Uncle," I whimpered. Nothing! *"Uncle,"* I whispered a little louder as the approaching noise got louder! *Uuhrrrrrr* went the "bear," and *aahhhhhhhhh* I went screaming down the hill, tossing my gunnysack and stick high into the air. *Wham*, I plowed right into a tree my size, running right over the top of it in abject terror. Hitting the ground with a thud, I roared back to my feet. I was flying down the mountain now. Then I slammed headfirst into a dense stand of manzanita brush, hitting so hard that I just bounced back, falling flat on my back! *Aahhhhhhhh*, I screamed, knowing for sure the bear had tried to grab me and somehow I had managed by the grace of God to escape. That added more fuel to my engine, and I came off the mountain like a P-51 in a shallow dive—right up a steep bank and off into nothing ... *kaplush!* Unfortunately, on the other side was a mud puddle about a foot deep, which I hit full force and face down. Leaping up out of the cold water (I had broken the ice, bloodying my nose in the process), I let out a scream for my mother that could have been heard clear to the moon. Still fearful that the bear was in hot pursuit, I hit high gear and broke the sound barrier. As I ran by a neighbor's house, one of his mean dogs took chase and bit me in the ass! That did it! Lights started going on in the houses as I screamed my way through the neighborhood.

When I got to my uncle's front door, I couldn't turn the handle fast enough and mashed my bloody nose again. My mom and aunt were sitting at the kitchen table, and I ran full-tilt into Mom, knocking her clear out of the chair and onto the floor. It took a few moments to get me cooled down and to wash the blood off my face, which I was positive the bear had caused. I figured that bear had come within inches of getting me! About then Uncle arrived through the back door all out of breath. "Did you get him?" he asked.

I just stared back, wide-eyed and still terror-stricken.

"Damn, Terry, I ran him right by you. Did you get him?"

"No," I sheepishly replied.

"Boy, he was a big one. I was hoping when I got there you would have him," he replied with a big grin.

I wasn't sure what to believe, but I knew one thing for sure: I was lucky to be alive! That bear had swatted at me, thrown me high up into the air, causing me to land in a freezing pond of water, and tried to eat me in the manzanita brush! It would be a cold day in hell before I would go bear hunting again.

Things settled down a bit after that, but it was hours before I could get to sleep. The only good thing about it was that I was able to take my rightful place by the roaring potbellied stoves the next day and recount my tale of close escapes on my first bear hunt. All the men listened and confirmed with serious looks that I was lucky to be alive. All of them had seen that same bear feeding on the deer carcass earlier and swore it was at least twelve feet tall and weighed at least a ton! Man, I thought, I really *was* lucky to be alive. ...

Over the years I have hunted in many places in the United States, for ducks, geese, dove, sage grouse, cranes, deer, elk, wild hogs, coyotes, and everything in between. However, I have never gone on another bear hunt, nor will I! I escaped with my life by the barest (no pun intended) margin and do not wish to take such a chance ever again.

Uncle is gone now. He passed away on February 25, 2004, and God could not have called back a better or more generous man. His death made me think back over the many years to my first bear hunt on that cold winter evening. He sure was a brave man to run that bear right to me carrying nothing but a flashlight. ...

3

Growing Up Poor

IT WAS DEEP WINTER in Plumas County, the kind of winter many old-timers remembered in the days before global warming and long-term droughts became a reality. There was six feet of heavy wet snow on the level in the Sierra Nevadas, and the angry-looking dark gray clouds sliding in from the northwest portended more to come.

It was 1946, and Mom, Sis, and I had moved in with her brother and his family in a little lumbering town named Sloat. Their home was simple lumber-company housing, and cramped to say the least, especially after the addition of us three. But we all pitched in and made do. Mom had recently divorced my dad (almost unheard-of in those days) because of his drinking and penchant for messing around with other women. Mom was a tough North Dakota farm gal who lived by the philosophy, "You made your bed, now lie in it." However, when the "demon rum" started making him abusive, that was the end of the line for the marriage in her eyes. "Lie in your bed" or not, she wasn't going to take his beatings every time he came home drunk! Having nowhere else to go, she asked her younger brother Lanoie if he could help our little family until she could get back on her feet. Hence our trip from the Bay area of California, through the beautiful, historic Feather River Canyon to that little mountain town of Sloat, nestled on the eastern side of the Sierra Nevada Mountains.

Finding meaningful work in those little lumbering towns was tough in those days, and it was even tougher for a woman. In that neck of the woods a woman's place was still in the home, especially with the service-men still coming home from the war and looking for work. However, that mind-set was slowly changing, especially after the positive contribution made by women during the recent war effort. They had wedged their feet in the door of opportunity, and many didn't want to go back to their old ways. Mom finally landed a job tailing off behind a clete machine in a box factory owned by the Meadow Valley Lumber Company in Quincy, another small mountain lumbering community like many in the Sierra Nevada Mountains in those days, some fifteen miles from Sloat. We moved from the warmth and comfort of my uncle's home into an adventure that left many marks on my carcass that remain to this day. Many of those marks are deep, but I learned from them all.

In those days boxing material for just about everything of any size was wood, not cardboard. Fruit, machinery, nuts, cheese, fresh vegetables, canned goods, candy—you name it, and it came and went in wooden boxes. Everything else came in gaily printed cloth bags, bottles, steel cans, or small paper containers. A clete machine is a piece of machinery holding four to six saws protruding vertically from a steel platform and partially covered by a steel hood for user protection. Into those saws were fed two-by-six or two-by-eight boards of a prescribed length. The saws transformed those boards into four to eight one-inch-square posts, each six to eight inches long. The posts were then used as corners for all manner of shallow wooden boxes, to which the slats and end pieces could be nailed. The taller the wooden box, the longer the boards run through the clete machine. Mom's job as tail-off was to sort out the posts as they emerged from the saws, stacking the good ones to her left in a prescribed-size bundle and tossing the bad ones into an open chute alongside her work station. Those scrap pieces were moved on a conveyor belt to an outside burner, where they were burned (a process that is no longer legal because of air pollution; today those scraps are made into valuable pressed boards). It doesn't sound like much of a job but let me tell you, it was a son of a gun! Usually men fed the machines and women tailed off. Time was really money in those days, and the boards were fed into those machines end to end as quickly as possible. If you couldn't keep up the pace, you were fired. I used to watch my mom when I worked in the same box factory some years later (illegally at age fifteen—you were supposed to be eighteen to work at such a dangerous profession. However, George Dean, the plant manager, knew I was trying to put away money for college and let me work). Her hands moved at a blurring speed, sorting the good materials from the bad. Blemished posts (those not square or able to hold a nail) literally flew into the "hog" (disposal chute), while those passing inspection were hurriedly stacked into bundles on a belt of rollers to her left. Once the appropriate size was reached, each bundle was shoved down that roller belt into a tie-up machine that compacted

the posts, wrapping them tightly with one or two wire strands. From
there they were rolled along another conveyor belt into the waiting hands
of a stacker who stacked the different-sized bundles coming from as
many as six feeder-machine stations onto pallets placed in organized con-
fusion on the floor. Once a pallet was filled to the correct height, usually
ten to thirteen bundles high, it was picked up by a fork lift and loaded
into a boxcar next to the building or sent to the warehouse to fill future
orders. This level of boring, blinding work was carried out for an eight-
to ten-hour day (with two ten-minute breaks per day). In Mom's case, all
at the glorious pay rate of seventy-five cents per hour (before taxes).
Along with the job came the ever-present danger of knots flying off the
rapidly spinning saws, sometimes with such velocity that they could
knock down people several feet away. Wood slivers could also fly off rapidly splintering posts from the saws whirling at a murderous speed. Many
a night as a six-year-old I dug inch-long slivers out of my mom's bloody
hands and forearms with a sharp knife or needle. She never said a word,
just took the pain in typical North Dakota farm-girl silence. Then she
would soak her hands in salty water so the swelling would go down before the next day's shift.

Our first place to live in Quincy after moving from my uncle's home
in Sloat was a long single room over a two-car garage. No heat, running
water, or toilet facilities, and two single-pane windows at each end for
light. It was just a spacious loft with a small tin woodburning stove on
stubby legs in the middle of the room. The room was not even insulated! But it was all Mom could afford, so there we were, able to look
through the wide cracks in the floor at the open garage and winter
snows below. The landlady took pity on the three of us and supplied
two old military cots for sleeping and a few pots and pans for cooking
to go with Mom's four blankets. Hell, we thought we were in seventh
heaven with those treasures! Scrounging around in the garage, I found
an unused one-gallon water pail and an empty paint bucket. I would fill
the water bucket twice daily from an outside spigot for cooking, cleaning up, and washing dishes. We used the old paint bucket as a "honey
bucket" (if you have to ask …). You may be wondering what had happened to our other family possessions such as beds, clothing, cooking
utensils, and the like. Well, my dad had liked to gamble in addition to
drinking and chasing the ladies. After losing heavily, he had sold most
of the household goods to pay his debts. Except for the few things
Mom had had in storage after our earlier move from Idaho to the Bay

area, he had left us with nothing but the clothes on our backs, and of course Mom had no money to get those things out of storage after the divorce settlement. All she had wanted from the divorce was her freedom; hence the total lack of support, which was not uncommon in those days. My biological dad probably wouldn't have been able to pay alimony or child support anyway because shortly after the divorce he was incarcerated in San Quentin for embezzling funds from the supermarket he had managed. But Mom was tough, and we made do after she struck out on her own.

If the county welfare people had been aware of our plight, my sister and I probably would have been taken away from Mom. That was how it was in those days. If your parents couldn't provide, you were removed from your family with a simple court order, sent to the county home, and adopted if someone would have you. Therefore, Mom never went to the welfare people for any kind of help because she believed that if they realized we were living in such squalid conditions, we kids would have been out the door and into the orphanage. Mom made it very clear to us that we had to work together to stay together and that times would be tough. However, we would still have each other if we worked through the tough times, and that was all that mattered.

I can still remember the intense cold in that room over the garage. Neither my sister nor I had any decent winter clothing. Hell, as I said before, we mostly had just the clothes on our backs! Mom wasn't much better off. She had a ragged man's jacket she had picked up from the trash to keep her warm, a pair of man's jeans, and cheap shoes that were so lightly constructed, she used to stuff cardboard in them to fill the holes worn through the soles (she had to walk two miles to work and back each day—we had no car, and Mom never learned to drive). I remember Mom finally calling my grandparents, who lived in Mott, North Dakota, and asking to borrow $50 so she could get us kids some winter clothing. My grandparents, old-fashioned Germans, called my dad to see what he thought about the request. Still bitter over the divorce, he told them we didn't need any help, so my grandparents called Mom back and refused the loan. So we froze most of that winter. Colds, runny noses, earaches, swollen tonsils, and sore throats were the norm, but a doctor or medicine was out of the question, so we just lay near the warm stove (when we had fuel) and bawled. If Sis was too sick to go anywhere, I stayed home from school to take care of her while Mom worked. Then I usually caught what she had, and on it went.

Mom would come home every day with a bundle of slats and sticks from the box factory to use in our old tin stove for cooking and what little warmth it provided. Mom would fire up that old stove, hurriedly fix what little dinner we had (pinto beans mostly), wash dishes from the bucket heating up on the back of the stove, and then hustle us off to bed. Heaping the last few remaining precious wooden slats into the stove, she would shut the fire door, set the damper, and hurry to bed herself. Within half an hour, the cold seeping up through the cracks in the floor and down from the snow-covered, uninsulated roof would turn the room into an icebox (bet many of you today don't even know what that is!) as the fire burned low, then finally went out. Even with old newspapers laid on the cot for extra insulation, it didn't take long for the cold to creep into our bones, and by midnight we just lay there and shivered.

Food was another major issue. We didn't have much, and that is one experience still buried deeply in my soul. Even today I always make sure there is plenty of food on hand and don't mind sharing my blessings with others, even if I have to cut short my own rations. I remember what it was like being hungry, and it wasn't a whole lot of fun. We usually had stomach cramps, blurred vision, and headaches from lack of food, and it was especially difficult for a growing boy who was always hungry.

Mom got paid every two weeks, and with each little bit of money we held on until the next paycheck. I still remember the disaster surrounding her first check. In order for her to work at the box factory, she had to be a member of the local union. Instead of taking the initiation fee and the year's monthly dues a little bit at a time over each paycheck so we could have something to live on and pay bills, *they took it all in one chunk!* That left very little, and as a result we froze and went hungry over the next two weeks. I remember being so hungry during that time that I ate several handfuls of allspice from a canister Mom had on hand for canning. Try that sometime; I guarantee you won't do it again, no matter how hungry you are!

At six years old, I did the shopping for our family because Mom was always working (I also baby-sat my sister, who was two years younger, when we were not in school). Many moms today will just gasp at that— a six-year-old caring for a child two years younger! But I was old for my age, and maturing rapidly even then. ... Come to think of it, my two guardian angels must have been on duty even then.

Mom would spend just $25 each month for groceries. If we ran out, we went hungry; it was that simple. I remember walking down to the old Boyd's Super Market, holding my sister's hand, and doing the shopping at that young age. I knew from a list Mom gave me *exactly* how much to spend on each item, and if it cost more than the few pennies I had to spend, I didn't buy it! Those were the days for a wide-eyed, always hungry kid. Supermarkets were *nothing* like they are today, but it was still a glorious place to walk the aisles, wishing I could have some of this or that, and it was usually warm inside. I would buy a large cloth sack of flour, one of dried pinto beans, dried maccaroni, and sugar (when the sacks were emptied, Mom would make us kids T-shirts and underpants from the material). With those staples, Mom could work wonders; she was one of the best cooks and bakers I have ever known. Then I would purchase a four-pound box of cheese (ten cents), a gallon tin of lard (twenty-nine cents), a nickel's worth of margarine—white with an orange dot of food coloring in the middle (you squeezed the one-pound plastic sack back and forth until the orange dot had turned all the contents yellow), powdered milk (ugh!) (fifty-nine cents for a twenty-pound sack), one pound of hamburger (twenty-nine cents; there was only one grade in those days) that would be split three ways *once a week*, and a one-pound tin of Folger's coffee (the only size they sold in those days; nineteen cents). If fresh fruit was in season, I would carefully select a lug of peaches and tomatoes for $1 each (when is the last time any of you paid $1 for a twenty-pound lug of peaches or tomatoes?), and I'd usually purchase a few feminine things for Mom. Then I would troop up to the counter and pay our bill, making sure they charged me what Mom had written on the shopping list for each item. After that I would struggle home in three or four trips with armloads of groceries (the huge sack of flour was the worst because I couldn't set it down in the dirt, especially when the ground was wet). When Mom got home that evening, she would carefully go over every purchase to see that I had purchased the right things and to make sure I had spent the correct amount for each item. If I had purchased the wrong thing, I was sent right back to the market to make things straight. For instance, I remember that I was once seven cents short in the change I had received. I was sent right back to get that seven cents … and I did.

Every day before Mom got home, down the steep outside stairs I went with the empty water pail to get fresh water for cooking and washing. I remember many times being so weak from hunger that I couldn't make it all the way back up with that heavy bucket without resting. After making a quick check on my sister, I would head back down the steps with that damned old honey bucket, dumping its contents into the vacant lot next door, then taking it to the outside water spigot to wash out the evil-smelling thing. Then back up those stairs, putting it back at the end of the room so the smell wouldn't run us out of our "home." One day, when I started down those steep outside stairs to empty the honey bucket, it was *really* full, and the smell kept me dry-heaving (even today my stomach will let go on certain things — such as changing baby diapers). Trying to navigate those steep, narrow stairs with no hand rail, carrying a pail that weighed just about as much as I did, I slopped some of the liquid on the front of my school pants. I overreacted, shoving the pail out farther to avoid any further wrecks, which threw me off balance, and over the side of the stairs I plunged. I fell fifteen feet, landing on some old boxes of trash under the stairs, and lay there for an instant trying to regain my wind. The empty honey bucket flopped down right beside me, quickly followed by all its former contents, sloshing squarely onto my head and shoulders!

I jumped up and promptly slipped in the "soup," falling back into it in fine style, messing up the other side of my school clothes! Man, you talk about a mess! I was covered from head to toe in all the honey bucket's glory. ... Getting up and rubbing my back, which was sore from that landing in the trash boxes (a wonder I wasn't killed), I hobbled over to the outside water spigot, gagging every step of the way. Taking off my smelly clothes down to my "bare nakeds," I began washing them in the ice-cold water. Here it was December, with snow on the ground, and I was outside without any clothes, washing off the stink before my mom got home. I knew she would be upset if I was a mess because she wouldn't have the time to wash my clothes for school. So I did the washing myself (if you could call it that without any soap). Talk about cold! I finally got my clothing somewhat washed out, then washed myself under the spigot as well and, not having anyplace warm to dry out, put the wet clothes back on and sloshed my way upstairs to check in on my sister. Another disaster awaited my eyes! My sis was sitting on the floor, happily eating granulated sugar by the handful. I guess she was hungry too. Somehow she had reached up into the apple crate serving as a cupboard and pulled the sack of sugar down onto the floor. Man, was I upset. That sugar had to last another week, and there was precious little left. Taking Sis and putting her on the cot, I attempted to scrape up what I could of what was scattered on the floor. I was able to scrape up about a cup, losing the rest through the cracks.

There I stood, soaking wet, smelling like a sewer pond, with only a cup of sugar left and the sound of my mother climbing the stairs after a hard day's work. Man, you talk about bawling. My whole world sure looked bleak at that moment. My poor mom must have thought the world had ended when she saw the wet, shriveled thing standing before her, smelling like all get-out, with a forlorn-looking single cup of sugar held out as if an offering for screwing up. Bless her heart (may she rest in peace), she tiredly put down the bundle of firewood and, realizing what must have happened, gave me a big, much-needed hug. Then she sent me off into the adjacent woods to gather pine cones from around the bases of the trees (the deep snow hid most of the cones that had fallen farther from the trees). By the time I got back, ice had formed on my wet clothing and I was shaking like a dog passing peach pits. But at least she had the water heating up, and the little tin stove glowed a warm red. With my sack of pine cones, she was able to wash my clothes as well as cook our dinner of pinto beans and bread. That gave me an idea, and from then on she had a ready sack of pine cones every day. She hung my clothes above the stove on some nails in the rafters, and I soon had some better-smelling, warm, and dry things to wear. Today I look at my closets full of clothes and just marvel at the "good old days"!

Soon Mom had saved some money, and we moved from the room over the garage to a very small one-room trailer house made of quarter-inch-thick plywood laid over a frame of two-by-fours. Again, there was no insulation, but this place had a big cast-iron stove, two rickety beds, a big old floppy cloth chair that looked and smelled as if a bear had slept in it, a linoleum floor with no cracks to let in the cold air, and *a bathroom!* Well, a sort of bathroom ... it was a small wooden shack about fifty feet from the house with three holes in the seating board (why there were three holes was beyond me—I wouldn't want to plop my big behind alongside someone else, much less two somebodies). The outer board across the back of the sitting area was missing, allowing the winter winds and snow to howl in. More than once I had to shovel snow off the seat before I could take care of business. That missing board also allowed everybody to see your bare hind end in all its glory when any of the holes was being used ... but it was a damn sight better than having to carry that stinking honey bucket up and down the steep stairs on a daily basis. *Well, sort of ...* I was always careful to look down each hole to see whether a monster lurked below when I had to "see a man about a horse." I didn't want a hand to come up out of that dark, smelly place and grab me by the hind end! I made sure I wouldn't have to dally there, hanging defenseless over that dark and mysterious place. ... Maybe that was one reason why I grew up to be such a fast runner for my size.

The new place, like the old one, didn't have any locks on the front and only door. In those days, you didn't really need locks on the doors, and we didn't have anything worth stealing anyway. People didn't lock the doors to their vehicles either, and many of those vehicles didn't have ignition keys but just a button on the dashboard that you pushed to start the motor, or a starter pedal on the floor. Yet nobody seemed to worry about a vehicle being stolen. It was the same when shopping; you could go to several different stores and leave your groceries in the back of the pickup. No one ever took the groceries, no matter how long you stayed away. Times were simpler and different then. Try that today, and the back of your truck will be cleaner than a black-and-tan hunting dog's chow bowl after a long, exhausting day in the field.

There was a woodpile alongside our new trailer, put there by the landlord for our use. That was great because Mom no longer had to lug wood home daily for cooking and washing. With that boon, my household chores changed again. At six years old, I was taught how to make a fire in the stove and lectured on the inherent dangers in playing with matches. In fact, Mom gave me only one match, and if I didn't have a good hot fire going when she got home, there was hell to pay. I never missed! With that old stove and the woodpile, it was now possible to have breakfast instead of going hungry as we had in our first place because we never had firewood in the morning (having used it up the night before). However, breakfast consisted of the same thing each morning: oatmeal with no milk or sugar ... *ugh!* I hate that sludgy damn stuff to this day. But Mom could get a twenty-pound sack of oatmeal for twenty-eight cents, and to be frank, that yuck stuck to my ribs for most of the day, so it must have had some redeeming value. You may be wondering how I remember prices on those things from so long ago. Hell, that was only fifty-eight years ago! And when it is driven into your head that there is just so much money to spend and you had better buy only items you can afford, you learn the costs forever! Also, being in such dire straits, we ate the same things over and over for years because they were all we could afford. And prices didn't change much in those days, especially when you were eating the same food mules ate.

Things sure got better in the days following the acquisition of that big wood stove. I could keep my sister and myself warm all day when we weren't in school. I learned to soak pinto beans overnight and the next day would leave them to slow-cook on the back of the stove for our dinner that night and lunch the next day. Mom would provide the seasoning because what little she had was too expensive to chance to a six-year-old's methods of application. When pintos got to be a drag, I would dig out the sack of macaroni (hoping the mice hadn't been into it), and that would be the menu for a while until we got tired of it. It didn't take long to get tired of just "mac," salt, and a slice of bread. Then came the occasional Sunday, and it would be heaven in our household. Mom would spring for a whole frying chicken, which I would kill, scald, gut, and pick. Our neighbors, the Kliens, raised a flock of Rhode Island Reds and would sell a young rooster to Mom for nine cents a pound, live weight. Let me tell you, that whole chicken was eaten, down to the cluck (even the feet were washed and fried)! Mom would roll the pieces in seasoned flour and fry it crispy in hot lard (I know it sounds bad now, but it was *oh so good* in those days). With a side of pinto beans smeared in chicken gravy or cooking lard from the frying pan, I was alive again, and for once my empty gut would almost be filled. However, that frying chicken was made to last all week for the three of us ... and it did! Mom usually ate the back, neck, and wings so Nancy and I could have the meaty pieces. I guess moms routinely do that, don't they?

There were other advantages to living in that old trailer house with the cast-iron stove that always made the place warm and smoky inside. Bathing now became a routine—well, if you can call it a routine. On wash day I would haul water until I was blue in the face. Mom would heat it on the back of the stove until it was scalding hot, then dump it into a big zinc washtub on the floor. I would hustle out and get another pail of cold water, which she would dump into the washtub to make a nice warm bath. I would rush back out for another pail of water and set it on the hottest burner to heat while Mom slipped her tired body into the tub for a few moments of bliss. When she was finished washing and dried off, the most recent pail of water would be scalding from the roaring stove. Into the tub with the somewhat dirty water would go that pail of hot water, followed by my sister. She would squeal and snort as she happily played in the water. Meanwhile, out the door into the night I would run for another pail of water from an outside communal spigot. Back I would come, and onto the stove it would go. By now Nancy would be getting a good going-over by Mom with the washcloth. Then out she came, and as Mom dried her off in front of the stove, I poured the next pail of hot water into the now really gray water in the tub (remember, we used a crude, soft lye soap in those days—none of that scented crap for us). Off would come my clothes and into that great tub of warm water I would thankfully slip. By that time, the water smelled a little "used," especially on the memorable occasions when my sister had peed or pooped in the tub before I got to it! Well, it was still a damn sight better than having the spilled honey bucket dropped on my head!

The bathing ritual was performed only on Friday nights and for the rest of the week, we went dirty and stunk like everyone else. I remember that some of our neighbors washed only once every two weeks! They claimed that to wash any more frequently than that would not be good for one's health, and that was in the days when deodorants were few and far between and seldom used. When I am in the shower each night, letting the hot water run over my tired carcass, I think of those zinc-washtub days. Sometimes the good old days just don't seem quite so good. ...

That old trailer, like our first place of residence, was not without its problems. First of all, it was full of mice. They would jump on our heads all night long and nibble on our fingers, and what they didn't treat that way, they pissed on. It seemed as if our clothes always smelled of mouse urine one day after Mom had washed them. If we didn't have our food in metal containers or hung from the ceiling, the mice got into it. We couldn't afford mousetraps in those days (a nickel each), so we just put up with the problem and swept the mouse droppings from the floor and countertops each day.

Since the trailer was not insulated, it was colder than Billy Hell in the winter once the fire went out and the heat left that old cast-iron stove. So Sis and I slept together in one bed and Mom in the other. Between us, we still had only four flimsy blankets. Mom would give us three, and she would sleep in her clothes with her one blanket wrapped around her for warmth. Her old rickety bed, having seen better days, finally gave out and sagged so badly in the middle, that she couldn't sleep in it without getting a sore back. So out the door it went, and Mom slept in a big sofa-like chair (which was also full of mice and smelled). But things were looking up.

Right next door to our trailer sat an old house that had been built with railroad ties during World War I. The family living there moved on, and our landlord asked if we would be interested in moving in. Mom jumped at that suggestion. The rent went up from $15 to $20 a month but the place had a big kitchen with a sink and running water and two bedrooms. No bathroom (we still used the "three-holer" out back), but what an improvement—especially because the place was really warm! Those thick old railroad ties soaked in creosote (a carcinogen) were just the ticket. They not only held the warmth but kept out the cold, mice, and ants as well. However, before we could move in the landlord had to fumigate the place. It seemed a bedbug colony had moved in and raised hell with the last inhabitants. For two weeks the house was covered with plastic sheeting as toxic bombs set off inside did their magic (so there was even more poison in the house). Then the landlord painted the place inside, and we moved in. We felt like lords and ladies!

No more wood stove for us; Mom now had one of those newfangled propane stoves and gas heaters. No oven, mind you, but four burners on the stove. She bought a small collapsible tin oven that could be placed on top of one of the gas burners. With that, Mom made some of the world's best pies, homemade breads, and cookies. Then we got another break. Mom got a pay raise from $.75 per hour to $1.25 per hour because she was such a good worker! We were in seventh heaven! Believe it or not, Mom was now making enough money to stick some away in the hope that someday she could get what was left of her furniture, clothing, and other belongings out of storage. Those were happy days in the old tie house. It was clean, neat, and warm, and Mom made a nice home out of it for the three of us. But life was still looking up!

Summer was on the way, and the plant world came back to life. Plumas County is truly a beautiful place. In the heart of the old gold country and the still living history of the Forty-niners, it also had wildlife resources by the bucketful in those days. I now had the opportunity to make some money to help Mom out. I turned seven that summer, and boy, you talk about a whirlwind. I mowed (with the old push mowers) and raked lawns, pulled weeds, planted gardens, and stacked and split winter wood (I was big for my age and could do heavy work if necessary, including swinging a sixteen-pound mall to split logs). I dug septic tanks (ten feet deep and square), sold the *Grit* and *Boy's Life* newspapers, milked cows, and picked up scrap metal, selling it for a few more pennies to add to the pot. I probably brought home $6 to $10 per week from those efforts, which in those days, was a gold mine! We still struggled, but at least we could now eat meat more than once a week. In addition to all that work, Mom made me go to every Bible school in town to keep me out of trouble. And when the fruits and berries were ripe, she made me haul a ton home every day for winter canning before I could do anything else. It was all a set of quiet efforts to keep her growing boy out of trouble. In those travels to pick apples, steal corn from a farmer's field (Mom didn't know about that—just figured the farmer had given us some), or pick blackberries, I passed many good-looking trout streams.

Soon a whole new world opened up for me. That summer my dad came to see us and tried to win Mom's heart back. She was having none of that, and he left shortly thereafter, but not before leaving me a hand-crafted, split-bamboo fly-fishing rod! Mowing two lawns and raking another gave me just enough money to purchase some fishing line, split-shot sinkers, and two packages of number 6 Eagle Claw hooks (the best kind), and a little handiwork with a shovel next to a neighbor's leaking septic tank brought me some bait (the best worms in size and color and the easiest to get were in sewage-soaked earth—who worried about disease in those days?). The next day found me eagerly fishing Green Horn Creek, just a few miles east of where I lived, pursuing the local rainbow and German brown trout. Not knowing quite what to do, I soon learned the tricks of the trade from another fisherman on the creek. Hours later I was trudging home, wet and hungry but with fifteen (the limit in those days) of the prettiest slab-sided, pink-meated, twelve-inch rainbow trout you ever did see! That night we had a feast that was pure heaven. All of us discovered we *really* loved eating crispy fried trout (lard-cooked, again), especially Mom! From then on, trout graced our table as often as the other things I picked or scrounged throughout the county. Believe you me, that fishing rod caught at least a ton of fish in its lifetime. It finally exploded under the load of trying to land a thirty-two-inch German brown caught in a beaver pond. During those fishing trips, I kept my eyes open for other fishing grounds, and soon I was a master at knowing where to fish and the best bait to use in each area. In short, I became a damn good fisherman, and it is a sport I enjoy greatly to this day. But I unearthed another treasure during those fishing trips that became a lifelong pleasure and passion. In my lonely travels, I quickly developed a love for the adventures and great peace offered by the out-of-doors. I had no one to teach me how to appreciate or understand the environment, but I keenly watched and learned. I discovered where the best places in the valley were for trout fishing and where the big ones lurked, that German browns liked the warmer waters of the beaver ponds and the rainbows the faster, cooler waters. I learned that beaver ponds were the best places in which to jump-shoot ducks, especially mallard and wigeon. I learned where mountain quail territories were and how to call those birds into shot-gun range with just my mouth, and I learned how to locate and stalk the ever curious California mule deer (killing my first at age fourteen). Last but not least, in searching for old bottle dumps left by the Forty-niners and old logging shows, I discovered the oak forest spaces occu-pied by the elusive and very tasty band-tailed pigeons. I was slowly becoming a part of the land and the world of wildlife. I would say my two guardian angels were at work again, this time teaching me the breadth of God's wonders.

Summer sped by, and soon winter was again at the door, curtailing my fishing, wandering, and berry- and fruit-picking. However, I had done well, and our larder was full of good things from the land, thanks to Mom's abilities as a canner. How many moms today would let a seven-year-old (who couldn't swim, by the way) go out and about as I did? I walked many miles a day in the hills and along the streams of the county (among the rattlesnakes), and when I was tired just hitchhiked or walked home. Oh, what a glorious experience it was. But soon the snow came, and with it the drudgery of being confined at home when not in school.

School wasn't a whole lot of fun for me in those days. I didn't have much in the way of clothing and had to wear cheap $1.25 brogans (an ugly half shoe, half boot). They never fit my feet properly, and I hated how they looked. But they kept my feet dry, and they were the only shoes Mom could afford for a kid who was hard on everything he wore. Let me tell you, my feet have sure paid the price for wearing such shoes! My lunches weren't much in those days either: simple mayonnaise-and-mustard sandwiches with a wrinkled apple I had picked off some farmer's fruit tree months earlier. I am here to tell you, the other kids' meat sandwiches, especially homemade meat loaf, sure looked good!

But with the winter snows came a windfall! I could earn money shoveling people's walks, roofs (to keep them from collapsing—in 1952 we had ten feet on the level after one storm), and driveways, and I moved a literal mountain of snow before winter was done. At first I would borrow the owner's snow shovel, but when I had made enough

money, I bought my own. Then the snow really flew! Again, most of
the money I made came home to help out. Soon I was able to buy some
nicer clothes for school, and then my education took on new meaning.
I began to mature and to enjoy most of my classes, especially now that
I was dressed more like the other kids in my class.

Summer was once more upon us, and Plumas County seemed even
prettier than the year before. Again the trout caught hell, as did just
about every apple tree, blackberry patch, and chokecherry and elder-
berry bush. I now had a $5 used girl's bike that my Uncle Lanoie had
purchased for me, and I was in hog heaven. Being another year older, I
felt able to roam farther and farther until fifteen- to twenty-mile treks
were the rule of the day (my sis was now staying at a neighbor's house).
That was, until I broke the bike going down the side of a deep gravel
pit. When I hit the bottom at a high speed, I guess the bike had had
enough of me, and it split right in two. Boy, what a hell of a wreck that
was! I slid at least half a mile on the side of my face. After that it was
back to shank's mare or my thumb to get where I wanted to go. But I
had been bitten by the bug of adventure. Eat your hearts out, Tom
Sawyer and Huckleberry Finn. ... Surrounded by the mining history
of the land and the beauty of Plumas County in the high Sierras, I was
on a tear. What a wonderful world it was for a boy who was all eyes,
ears, and a floppy hat discarded by its previous owner, full of questions
and an empty gut. Streams I could drink from (don't try that today unless you want to get sick), pine-scented forests I could roam through
during the hot July days, and the ever-present wildlife at every turn if
I was looking.

Again, some moms will probably have a case of the vapors that my
mom would let me rattle around in the wilds and hitchhike home at the
grand old age of eight years old. In those days we had a lot of good
people around, and it wasn't the danger that it is today. Many times as
I got older, I would hitchhike to some far-flung place to jump-shoot
mallards or wood ducks, leaving at *three A.M.* Seldom did a car drive by
at that time of the morning that wouldn't pick me up, shotgun and all,
and take me where I wanted to go. Sure, sometimes I would get picked
up by someone who had been drinking, but when I realized it, I would
ask the driver to let me off at the next road, making up a story that I
had left my worms or shells behind. In later years, during high school,
I would bring my hip boots, hunting jacket, and shotgun to school,
leave them in the principal's office until the end of the day, then hike all

the backwaters home, jump-shooting ducks or pursuing the mountain quail to my heart's content! Try that today in our crazy society.

The other oddball thing about growing up in those times was shoes. Come summer, off they came to save shoe leather, and from that time on you ran on your bare feet! By the end of summer I could cross gravel at a dead run and feel no pain in my feet because of the calluses I had built up through my many miles of shoeless wanderings. Then came the first two weeks of school and the reintroduction of the old shoes. Your feet, unused to tight-fitting shoes again, really complained, but after a time everything settled down and was all right.

Thus ran my years until I reached eleven. I met a chap named Harold Tweedle from Quincy (three miles away), and the two of us became instant friends. We did a lot of fishing and hiking together, and then Harold introduced me to the world of guns and hunting, loves that remain with me to this day. Every day that I wasn't in school, berry-picking, or working to make money to make ends meet, I was fishing or hunting. At first I couldn't afford any gun of my own, but Harold lent me his double-barrel, 12-gauge Winchester shotgun and model 94 .32 Winchester special. I suppose in today's society that would be a violation of some idiot gun law. Hunting mountain quail (Mom's favorite to eat), jump-shooting ducks off beaver ponds or small streams, stalking the cautious mule deer, ambushing the mourning dove off a grain field, or sneaking up on the sharp-eyed band-tailed pigeons became my world and the love of my life (this was before my wife and best friend, Donna, happened on the scene).

It was now 1953, and Mom had been dating a fellow at the box factory who ran the tie-up machine. He too had been divorced and was looking carefully at the possibility of another marriage. His name was Otis Barnes, and he came from a pioneer family that had settled during the late 1800s in the next valley over from Quincy, near a small town called Taylorsville. Otis had been raised in that neck of the woods and in his middle years went to work in the box factory. As he and my mom saw more and more of each other, things began to get serious. I remember one of those sessions in which two people feel each other out when Mom told Otis she had just gotten rid of one "slop" and wasn't looking for another. And wherever she went, her kids went too. Also, if he was interested in any kind of relationship, he had to give up drinking, smoking, fighting (Otis was one hell of a street fighter—strong as a bull and with a very high tolerance for pain), chewing tobacco, and running around. He really loved Mom and us kids, so he did what she asked and married her in 1954. From that day on, things looked up. My new dad was an excellent father, a man of great ethics, and a hard worker. He saved his money from work (turning his paycheck over to Mom), and slowly, between the two of them, they paid off all their debts. We moved into a little house on the main street of East Quincy, and Mom finally got her furniture and other household items out of storage. Surprise, surprise, all our winter clothes no longer fit ... or were needed. And in this home, *we had a real bathroom!* No more monster lurking under the sitting board, waiting for an unguarded bottom. ... Several years later we moved one more time into a fairly nice home, for East Quincy, on Pine Street, where my parents remained until Dad died in 1985 and Mom in 1999. But not before the two of them, working blue-collar jobs, managed to save almost $200,000, which was passed on to their kids and grandkids after their deaths! Not bad coming from a one-room place with cracks in the floor to their last, very well-insulated, I might add, home. ...

My sister still lives next door to our old home with her husband, Dee, and probably will until they pass as well. I moved on to many a location after seven years in college, first as a California State Fish and Game warden in two locations and later as a special agent for the U.S. Fish and Wildlife Service in six different areas across the nation. Before my retirement in 1998, I settled with my bride of forty-three years (at the time of this writing), Donna (whom I have known and loved since the eighth grade), and our family in the foothills of Evergreen, Colorado. We were blessed with two sons and a daughter, all of whom went into public service. None of our kids ever went hungry. ...

Those early years before Dad "officially" became part of our family were tough. But they were good in many ways, toughening up my sister and me for that process called life. We learned about family values and where the true strength lies for living in this day and age: in one's religion (mine was the great outdoors), surrounded by the strength of the family unit working together. Early on, I was always hungry. I was big for my age and tried to help Mom every way I could, but I always seemed to be a quart low when it came to the amount and kind of grits registered in the boiler department. Another thing I remember was that I always seemed to be working hard, trying to earn money to help out the family or to set aside for college. From age nine on, I brought enough money into the family to pay for what I ate. From eleven on, I paid for everything that wasn't a personal gift, including my clothes, medical expenses, food, fishing and hunting equipment, summer camps, and any side trips I took. I take great pride in that achievement!

My labor history as a child is a story in itself. I herded milk cows for local dairymen. I hayed with some of the local ranchers from the time I was able to toss a bale of hay up onto a wagon or truck bed. I dug graves for the princely sum of $6.50 per hole. I didn't like that job at ten years of age because I figured a hand would come out of the ground next to where I was digging and get me! I mowed lawns, pulled weeds, chopped wood, sold Christmas trees, picked up copper wire from along the transmission lines and sold it to Gus Schott, the junkman, sold newspapers, shoveled snow, dug septic tanks, washed windows, sold frog legs (illegally) (until I realized how good they tasted), lied about my age and went to work at the box factory at age fifteen, lied about my age and went to work in the woods as a logger for Meadow Valley Lumber Company at age sixteen, dug ditches, fought forest fires, and did anything in between that would earn me money. By the time I went to college I had amassed a small fortune that put me through my first six years of college, up to my second year as a master's degree student.

Though I was without a dad for many years, I was blessed with neighborhood men who took me under their wings during some of those hard years before Otis arrived on the scene, including Bill Slaten, Ben Buss, and John Gray. During my preteen years, they showed me the way, teaching me right from wrong, and thankfully those teachings took. I also learned that there is always a way to get things done if you just put in enough back, sweat, and thought.

Those hard times prepared me for the rest of what was to come, which many times was not easy. The most important thing was that my mom always showed us love and care. She was a fighter and a hard worker, and she instilled both of those qualities in us kids, facets of our inner beings that remain with Nancy and me to this day. She also fostered in us the ability to care for others less blessed, even when we didn't have "a pot to pee in and a window to throw it out of" ourselves. From my stepdad, Otis, whom I fondly and meaningfully call my father, I learned many things: truth, honesty, hard work, ethics, the value of a man's word, the value of a man's handshake, caring for others, sharing a cold drink from a spring far off the beaten path, how to *really* catch trout and hunt the mule deer, and a strong sense of the history of the land and love for its resources. Those traits, coupled with what Mom taught me, were plainly and simply blessings!

4

To Milk a Cow

As I was walking home one day with a creel full of trout and an empty gut, an old red International pickup passed, slowed, and then stopped on the side of the highway in front of me. Emerging from the pickup was a large man whom I knew as Ernie Leonhardt, a local businessman and rancher from the valley surrounding my hometown of East Quincy. "Terry," he yelled, "want to make a few bucks helping me with the cows?"

Now, in those days, I was as poor as a church mouse. But I was a big, strong lad for my age and not afraid of hard work, especially if it involved raising a few dollars to help my struggling mom. "You bet!" I quickly replied. Walking up to Ernie, I shook his hand, following that up with a question: "What kind of work?"

"Well," he replied, "I need someone to move my dairy herd from the field into the barn in the evenings and then help me with the milking and slopping the hogs."

"Sounds good to me," I replied. "When do I start, and how much is the pay?" When you're poor, the bottom line is pretty damn important, so I wasn't shy about asking.

"I will pay you a dollar a day and pick you up for work around 5 P.M., then drop you off at your home each evening. How does that sound?"

"Sounds like you have a deal," I responded with a wide grin. Now, $1 a day was big money in those days, especially for a boy who was only eight years old. That dollar would do wonders in helping my mom with her daily struggle to keep my sister and me fed and clothed.

"Then we have a deal," he exclaimed. "I'll see you down the road a ways tomorrow afternoon." With that and a wave of the hand, he got in his battered old pickup and was gone like a dust devil. Man, my heart was singing for joy as I raced home with the good news. Mom knew

Ernie and, as I had expected, was happy at the prospect of letting me work and bring another dollar a day into the family coffers. That would more than pay for the month's rent if I worked for at least thirty days! I was happy to bring a smile to that tired but wonderful face. As I washed the wet grass from the trout (I had lined the creel with grass to avoid spoilage) and helped Mom prepare our dinner of pinto beans and fried fish, I could hardly believe my good fortune. Another job, and to be paid with a silver dollar at the end of each day's labor. Hot dog! I was going to be rich. (I wish I had all those Morgan silver dollars today for the collector's value!) Oh, well—you can wish in one hand and crap in the other, and the one that fills up first is what you will get. ...

The next afternoon I was standing on the side of state Highway 70 in East Quincy around 5 P.M. Presently, along came Ernie in his pickup, and away we went, driving east to Bell Lane and following that to his old home site, located on his ranch in the valley by Green Horn Creek. The ranch site was a historical one, settled in the late 1800s by some of the valley's early pioneers. It was a great little spread, surrounded by rolling mountains, with belly-deep grasses on the valley floor and creeks, streams, and beaver ponds scattered liberally throughout. Next to the house, which was also situated alongside a little creek, were numerous outbuildings and machine sheds. Central was a large old landmark barn, also constructed during the 1800s, large enough to hold a herd of dairy cows on the first level and many tons of hay in the mow. In later years I put many a ton of hay into that barn. It is still standing today and is more than one hundred years old. It seems that when people built things in those days, even with hard use, they were built to last!

Ernie let me off at the edge of a large natural hay field and told me to put on an old pair of rubber boots from the back of his pickup. After doing so, I was instructed to bring the cows in from that field and herd them toward the barn. Once on their way, they would know where to go and would walk by themselves into the barn. He mentioned that one of the cows was a little lame, so I should move her along slowly. Once in the barn, Ernie said each cow knew her own feeding stall and would move directly into it, remaining there to be locked in and milked. I was to set the neck locks so they could feed but not wander around in the barn before being milked. By then he would be there with the milking machines and would give me further instructions.

I drove the dairy herd of Holsteins across the field toward the milking barn. It was one of those typical Plumas County warm afternoons, and I allowed myself some dreaming as I moved the lame cow slowly along behind the other stock. Almost every stream on Ernie's ranch held some great fishing. Some were best fished with worms, some with salmon eggs, and all were excellent with the great little live bait called the Hellgrammite (Dobson fly aquatic larvae). A brush-covered hillside opposite the barn was the territory of a healthy covey of mountain quail, and in the beaver ponds below there always seemed to be at least one pair of mallards, if not a whole flock. The stately California mule deer called the entire ranch their home, and I would kill many such deer in later years during the annual fall hunting season. Letting my mind continue to wander as I considered which stream held the best and biggest fish, I was brought back to reality with the advent of the ramp into the dairy barn. Slowly pushing the lame cow up the ramp, I was greeted by the view of all the other cows feeding in the trough, with their necks in their respective stalls. The lame cow slowly moved into her stall, and I locked her neckpiece, then locked all the other cows into place as they contentedly ate their grain and oats from the trough.

About then Ernie entered from a door at the far end of the barn carrying an armload of milking machines. "Terry," he yelled, "go into the separating room and get a big pail of warm water and some rags. The rags and soap will be in a cabinet next to the faucets." With that, I hustled into the room where the milk would be separated from the cream and butterfat, filled the pail with warm water, poured in some granulated soap, grabbed a handful of old but clean rags, and trotted back into the milking part of the barn. Ernie had just returned with some more milking machines. Setting one alongside each cow, he said, "Terry, grab that pail of warm water and some rags and wash off their udders. I need to get some more milking machines but will be back shortly and we can get the milking going."

"Yes, sir," I replied as the vanishing figure of my new boss headed into the separating room to get the last of the milking machines. But now I had a problem! I was not sure what the hell an udder was and sure as shooting was not going to show my stupidity by asking for an explanation the very first day on the job! I considered myself smarter than the average bear and good at working through problems toward the correct solutions. I began the deductive process with my eight-year-old mind in high gear. Well, let's see ... obviously the soap and water were to wash dirt from the cows. That I had down pat. Now, as to the part of the cow needing the soap and water treatment—that was a horse of a different color. A quick look with my sharp set of eyes and I had the solution ... and off I went at a high rate of speed to impress my new boss regarding what a fine fellow he had just hired! No slouch, this fellow, I thought, dreaming of that silver cartwheel in my pocket at the end of the day for a job well done.

Ernie entered the milking barn with the last of the milking machines and with one look at me and my endeavors dropped the machines, doubled over, and began laughing uncontrollably. Stopping what I was doing, I just stared at him in disbelief. What the hell was his problem? I asked myself. I had done my job with the soap and water, washing down eleven cows and heading for the twelfth. I sure as hell wasn't lying down on the job, I thought. Regaining some composure, Ernie stood up and between bouts of hard laughing, said, "Terry, the udders. You need to wash the udders. *Not their hind ends!*" Well, crap (no pun intended). I had looked those damn cows over several times to identify what I considered dirty on their anatomy. Their hind ends were the perfect candidates for a cleaning, so that was where I headed! I was doing one hell of a good job, to my way of thinking. I did kind of think it was odd that when I lifted the tail of each cow to wash its hind end, they got a funny look on their faces! And their *moos* were a little odd and deep-throated when the warm water hit their soft hind ends! In fact, one was so surprised that it crapped a bushel on my hand and arm when the hot water hit the exit hole, filling my five-sizes-too-big boots in the process! Realizing that I had really screwed up, I stood there in midstride with a goofy look, a poop-covered hand, and wash rag, unfit for this world. But, not wanting to admit defeat, I thought he'd at least have to admire my work! I must say, those cows had the prettiest hind ends you ever saw. ...

Walking over to me with eyes moist from laughing, Ernie squared me away on what needed washing and the proper method. With that, I procured another pail of soap and water and hustled through twenty sets of teats and udders in a heartbeat. Man, you talk about embarrassed! I certainly had not started out well on my first day at work. And if that experience was not bad enough, the history of that episode was to follow me into another realm of my life some years later.

The next day on the job held even more surprises. It seemed as if the cows made their way into the barn from the field more easily than the day before. Even the lame cow seemed to have a little more steam and less of a hitch in her "giddy-up." Locking them into their stalls, I hustled into the separator room, loaded the bucket with soapy hot water, and returned posthaste. Time was money, and I didn't want to slow Ernie down this time in the milking process. Heading down to the end of the line, I started to wash off the teats and udders on the lame cow. All of a sudden I noticed that the eleven cows whose hind ends I had cleaned the evening before had stopped eating. They were looking around at me through their stalls with a wide-eyed look of anticipation, and every one of them, *to a cow,* had her tail uplifted as if expecting the same handsome treatment she had received the night before! Damn, you talk about feeling silly! That kind of behavior was exhibited for several more days until they lost hope and tired of the tail-lifting game.

In 1959 I assumed the position of student body president at Quincy Junior-Senior High School. As such, I was responsible for many duties, working for the school administration and managing various activities for the student body. One of those duties, I discovered, was going to the Rotary Club luncheon every first Monday of the month. There I would get to meet Quincy's businessmen, learn to mingle and mature, and bring those folks up to speed on school happenings. About eleven on the appointed day, the school principal, Hanlon Tharp, would gather me out of whichever class I was in and drive me down to the Rotary meeting. There he would introduce me to the folks in the organization and privately coach me on what he wanted said regarding the school activities from the previous month. I would nervously rehearse what I was to say and sweat bullets until my presentation was completed.

Come my first meeting with the Rotary Club, I was understandably nervous. I had little training in public speaking, and meeting with a bunch of men whom for the most part I didn't know was really not my bag of worms. I would rather have been fishing or frogging (that was in the days when we had bullfrogs). However, it came with the turf of being student body president, and I would do my best. As expected, I met a bunch of old guys with limp handshakes (my dad Otis Barnes had taught me to always give a handshake that spoke of a real man on the other end), managing to smile my way through the occasion. Then it was off to lunch with the group. We ate as the meeting progressed, and they finally got to the old business portion. Not really paying much attention, I all of a sudden heard a voice I recognized. It was Ernie Leonhardt speaking, and in the far-off recesses of my mind I heard the words, "When I first met Terry ..." Boy, that put me on high alert! Ernie went on to tell the story of the time when I had first worked for him and had washed clean the hind ends of eleven of his cows instead of their udders. ... You talk about a *riot!* Ernie was a good storyteller, and before long he had all the club members lying on the floor crying their eyes out. Man, you talk about being red in the face ... there was nowhere for me to hide my six-foot-four, captain-of-the-football-team frame, so I just stood there and good-naturedly took the best they could give. Oh well, I thought through my reddened ears, burning neck, and flaming face. You created the story through your own stupidity. Now you are going to just have to stand here, grin, and bear it. And I did ... somehow.

But the damned joke didn't end there! The next day in school, it seemed that all the teachers had heard the story from the principal, and laughter rang through the halls of the school whenever I hove into view. Then all the kids got involved in the joke, and of course gloried in the revelation. I finally wore out my smiling muscles on the hundredth telling, or upon hearing a loud *moo.* ... Come football practice that evening, I was able to take some revenge on those laughing at me during the day, if you get my drift. However, I began to learn to laugh at myself, a trait that has helped keep my head size normal and allowed me to appreciate the many joys and wrecks that normally come along in life.

You know, I can still see the faces of those damned cows and their collective looks of anticipation. I hope they all ended up as hamburger patties. ...

5

My First Deer

HUSTLING HOME from high school, I dashed into my room, removed my school clothes, and put on my grubbies. Reaching into the corner of my closet, I extracted a Winchester lever-action, model 94, .32-caliber Special from against the back wall. I dug six stubby cartridges (all I could afford at the time), my hunting license, deer tags, and an old straight razor (I had lost my knife) out of my sock drawer, shoved them into my pants pocket, grabbed a homemade oatmeal cookie from the cookie jar, and went out the door. I took off on my bicycle east down state Highway 70 with my rifle, a big grin, and a hatful of big ideas centered around a monster buck. Arriving at Louis Thomas's wooded property by the roadside cut near Ramelli's Ranch, I walked the bike into the trees along an old logging trail so if anybody came along, they wouldn't see and take it. Then I headed for a little-known buck-brush-covered draw normally frequented by California mule deer.

I had roamed and in recent years hunted all over this part of Plumas County. I was dirt poor and couldn't afford a rifle or shotgun of my own, so I had to borrow them from friends when I wanted to hunt. In those days just about everyone hunted, not only for recreation but to provide food for their families. Many a local resident pitched in to help others in their time of need, and that kind of assistance included the loan of firearms. It seemed that everyone understood the importance of such a loan and did not abuse the weapon or the system. That was just the way it was during simpler times—times I miss dearly!

The area I was hunting was the characteristic forest cover of the county: ponderosa pine, Douglas fir, incense cedar, sugar pine, and every kind of buck brush and growth in between. It was outstanding habitat for the excellent-eating California mule deer that were common in the area. Hunting season was open, and this was my first for deer, so

I was quite excited. I walked slowly up a game trail, careful not to make any noise as I paused to load the stubby cartridges into the rifle's tubular magazine. Quietly indexing a live round from the magazine into the barrel, I let the hammer down cautiously and was also careful to point the barrel in a safe direction in case of an accidental discharge (common in the hammer guns of that era if one was not careful). Carrying the weight of the rifle easily balanced in my right hand, I got down to the business of hunting. Walking slowly to avoid stepping on any dry twigs likely to announce my presence, I let my eyes scan the forest before me and on each side. I had seen many mule deer in this area in times past, especially several big bucks, while hunting mountain quail, squirrels, and band-tailed pigeons. I had lodged those moments and that information in the recesses of my mind until the proper hunting season rolled around, and now here I was, all bright-eyed and bushy-tailed.

That particular afternoon almost fifty years ago still remains clear as a bell and easy to recall. The woods were quiet except for the persistent scolding I received from a gray squirrel for being in his territory. Continuing on because he would alert any deer in the area, I crossed the paths of several little chipmunks carrying seed heads from grasses to their dens as part of their winter rations. The deer trail I walked that afternoon was loaded with old sign and the occasional fresh track, but all looked small, like does or fawns. Oh well, I sighed, that was why they called this sport hunting and not killing. ...

A quick movement thirty yards to the left revealed a doe and fawn feeding on the terminal buds in a stand of buck brush with their rumps toward me. I had been so stealthy in my approach that they didn't know I was there. Remaining still, I looked for any amorous buck that might be in the vicinity of the two. No such luck, as the two deer fed off along the hillside, totally unaware of the intruder and possible danger lurking some few yards away (poachers often took closed-season does — meat is meat to many a person). Making sure they had gotten well enough away so they would not catch my scent and spook, I quietly moved on. There is nothing worse when quietly stalking deer than to have a doe, crazed with fear at your presence, go crashing through one brush pile after another, alerting every other deer for miles. Continuing on, I met the usual little forest creatures, but not the massive buck a young kid always dreams of seeing through the sights of his rifle.

Slowly cresting the timbered ridgeline, I stopped and let my eyes scan every potential hiding place below the rim where my world-trophy buck could be lurking. I even went so far as to begin tasting the many fine meals he would provide for my family, especially the liver with onions, fried spuds, and some of Mom's homemade pie. Yum, I thought, remembering how hungry I was and forgetting for a moment why I was there. Quickly getting back on track, I let my eyes flow over the ridge to my left. Once I had approved and memorized the direction of travel that would best limit the sounds and disturbance I would soon make, I continued my stalk, continually looking below me for anything out of place that might indicate a big buck in hiding. Nothing. Dang, I thought, for all the deer I had observed in this place during my prior outings, it was sure coming up dry now. Stopping and resting from the climb in case a buck jumped out close at hand (I wanted to settle my breathing so I could aim better), I enjoyed the majesty of the brushy terrain below. It included a narrow ravine surrounded by conifers, loaded with tons of buck brush, and dusted throughout with the odd rock outcropping. The silver-gray buck brush was thicker than the hair on a dog's back and thorny as the crown Christ wore on his last day. It wasn't a place one could quietly walk, but a wonderful place to feed and hide if one were a buck deer during hunting season.

Several long, heavily timbered fingers ran to the northeast, then joined back together some one hundred yards away. There was a small brushy draw below where they joined with a high rocky overlook. That was my destination, and since I had some distance to go, I commenced quietly walking and looking in that direction.

"Mule deer" were given that name by early Western explorers who, seeing the deer for the first time, were impressed with their large, mule-like ears. With that type and size of ear came a remarkable ability to hear a pin drop many yards away—hence my quiet approach. Stopping several times and remaining dead quiet, I hoped to make my quarry nervous (they more than likely heard my approach regardless of how careful I was). That was Plan A: spooking a big buck out of his bed and into my rifle sights. Nothing happened! Damn, I thought. This deer hunting is harder than it looks! After a while I reached the small rocky point overlooking the brushy draw, which was about one hundred yards long and thirty-five yards wide. Quietly sitting down, I laid the rifle across my knees and waited. That was Plan B: wait them out. For an hour only the usual forest events occurred. Jays and magpies flying by took no notice of me. There were Townsend's chipmunks scurrying around at my feet, and one brave soul even ran up the outside of my pants leg and onto my shoulder for a better look. Nothing else with a heartbeat broke the stillness of the afternoon. Down below, through the dense timber, I could faintly hear the traffic on Highway 70, especially the constant stream of logging trucks groaning under their loads, destined for the area's many mills.

More small ground-feeding birds flew and flitted by, in and out of the brush, looking for an evening meal. Almost dozing in the warmth of the sun and stillness of the afternoon, I was brought back wide-eyed with an instantly pounding heart. *Snap* went a twig in the brushy draw below me. Now more than alert to my surroundings, I stared intently into the draw. Nothing! After a few minutes I figured I had been dreaming and relaxed as I leaned back against the rock face.

Holy crap! As if generated from the mists of time, there stood a statuesque buck California mule deer forty or so yards down the draw. For what seemed a lifetime, he didn't move. Then he began to carefully look all around. All around except *up* in the direction of the rocky point where I sat! Now, in those days in California, you could shoot a buck only if he was a forked-horn or better (two-point Western count, four-point Eastern count). I didn't own any binoculars to aid me in determining how many points he had, so I looked and looked, trying to make antlers where they didn't exist! It was obvious this buck had been lying down in the brush of the ravine all the time. He had probably heard me coming across the rim above the draw and decided his best defense was to lie still in the heavy cover. Then, when it got quiet for such a long period as I sat on my rock, he either got curious or decided it was time to get the hell out of Dodge. His head was turned so that I couldn't tell if he was a legal buck or not. But *he was a buck mule deer!* God how I strained my eyes, but to no avail! That should tell you he wasn't the massive "mossback" I had dreamed of killing. ... Then he slowly turned to look down the ravine, and the sun shone on his antlers just right! He was a forked-horn, legal by California standards! Hot damn! I thought.

Slowly, oh so slowly raising my rifle and not daring to breathe for fear he would hear me and run off, I finally got to the correct shooting position. Using my knees as a rest, I carefully settled the front blade sight into the notched rear sight. Sighting just behind the shoulder, I *slowly* squeezed the trigger. *Boom* went the Winchester, with the recoil against my small frame knocking me back a little. When that happened, I lost sight of the deer. Quickly levering another round into the chamber, I sighted back to where the deer had stood just moments before. He was gone! Oh no! I cried to myself. Had I missed? *I couldn't have, not at that range,* was the panic-stricken answer flooding through my brain. Jumping to my feet, I decided I had the best view from where I stood, so I would just wait to see what happened. For the longest moment, nothing occurred. Not a sound, not a bird call (especially after the loud report of the rifle), not a whisper of wind, nothing. My heart sank. Thoughts of how I could have missed at that range, whether he had gotten away, or whether a twig might have deflected my bullet bounced through my young, inexperienced mind like balls in a pinball machine.

Unable to stand it any longer, I slowly walked down off the ridge toward a small pine tree in the middle of the brushy thicket where I had last seen my buck. Walking slowly around each bush, trying to maintain a firing lane in case my deer jumped up and tried to flee, I crept up to the spot where I believed the buck had last stood. Maybe there was some blood sign, and then again, maybe I had missed. ... I walked slowly around the last brush pile by the little pine tree, and *there he was!* On the ground exactly where he had fallen lay a beautiful little forked-horn buck. The light was still going out of his eyes, and he lay without moving. Remembering that wounded deer could injure an unwary hunter, I carefully poked his head with the barrel end of the rifle. He was deader than a box of rocks. Moving around so I could examine my kill more closely, I saw a blood spot the size of a silver dollar in his beautiful fall coat behind his right shoulder. Hot dog! I thought. I had hit right where I had aimed. A spot behind the shoulder was guaranteed to ruin very little meat but was deadly in its placement. The bullet would do maximum damage so the animal would not suffer, or worse, escape crippled only to die slowly and become coyote food. I think even God heard my primal yell of success and heartfelt thanks. Sitting down, I drank in the view of my first buck, wanting to enrich and immortalize the memory for all time. He was not large by any standards, maybe 125 pounds once dressed. He appeared to be very fat, and his grayish coat was glossy as all get-out. Wood ticks were beginning to crawl from the hair of his coat even as I looked, in recognition of the fact that their host was now dead. His hooves were sharp and not worn, and his antlers, although small, were legal.

Holy cow! I suddenly remembered that the animal had to be tagged to be legal in the eyes of the law! I dug in my pants pocket, and out came my deer tags. In those days, California allowed a person to take two bucks and in some instances a doe during the hunting season. In the heat of the moment, I discovered I didn't know which tag to fill out. Not having a dad or brother to show me the right way, I was at a loss. But I read the tags as best as I could and finally decided which one to use on my deer. Then I realized I didn't have a pen or pencil to fill out the tag! Damn, I thought. My first buck and I will lose it to the game warden because I haven't filled out the tags properly. Then it hit me! Terry, the ends of your bullets are soft, exposed lead. That will do in a pinch. I racked out the live shell in the chamber, letting it fall to the ground by the deer. Then, letting the hammer safely down, I picked up the live round, and sure as shooting, I could write with it. Filling out my tags with the date and time of the kill, I knew the buck was now legally mine. Oh poop! I didn't have any string to tie the tag on the deer's antlers as prescribed by law. A quick look at my $1.98 tennis shoes provided the answer. They weren't much to look at, but they did have shoelaces. Minutes later and half a shoelace shorter, my deer was lawfully tagged.

Then came the real work. The animal had to be gutted to avoid spoilage. I realized I was in a quandary. I had never gutted an animal so big in my life. Dove, ducks, geese, and squirrels, but not a deer! However, I reckoned it couldn't be much more difficult than gutting any other animal—just bigger. Yeah, that was it. I would gut it out like a squirrel, and that should do it, I surmised. Boy howdy! Was I in for a surprise! Since I didn't have a knife, I dug out my old straight razor that a man named Jim Tesky had given me. When I opened it and looked at it, it sure didn't give me a whole lot of confidence given the size of the animal lying on the ground. ... The damn thing was for removing whiskers, not gutting a deer! However, it was all I had, so after laying my rifle safely off to one side and poking the deer in the eye one more time to make good and sure it was dead, I commenced. Starting in front of the testicles, I made a ventral cut through the hide but above the intestines (didn't want to cut those open, they *stink!*) forward to the brisket. The razor just was not strong enough to cut through the brisket, so I stopped my incision there. Digging down into the clean-smelling viscera with my hands, I checked out all that was attached and then began cutting away those parts from the body cavity in order to remove the insides. Suffice it to say, in later years I could have gutted out two deer and one elk in the time it took me to gut my first deer ... but what a joy and milestone in my life. *My first deer,* and all by myself!

Before I was done, I looked as bloody as my critter now did. Then came the first of a series of dilemmas. I knew I should keep the heart and liver, but what about those other things inside the cavity? Unsure, I kept almost everything except the intestines. Stuffing all those parts back into the deer's visceral cavity pushed me into another predicament. How was I supposed to keep all that stuff in the cavity of the deer when I dragged it home? Being a sharp kid, I looked around. It would take something big to keep them inside, I thought. There it was. Taking my old beater of a work coat, I stuffed it into the deer's cavity along with all the other body parts. No loss of the guts now, I thought with a mile-wide smile on my blood-smeared and tick-covered face.

Jacking all the shells out of my rifle, I put them back into my pocket for safekeeping. I let the hammer back down over an empty chamber, reached over and grabbed the deer by the antlers with my right hand, and began to drag it up out of the brushy draw toward the ridgeline and my bicycle. That proved to be easier said than done. The deer and I weighed about the same, so it took everything I had drag it to the top of the ridge. Man, was I pooped when I got there. I still had several hundred yards to go, albeit downhill, and I was already worn out. Then, on came the light! Hiding my deer in a brush pile, I grabbed my rifle and headed for my bicycle. Once there, I hid my rifle and pushed the bike back up the trail to my deer. Another half hour of wrestling and I finally had the animal carefully balanced on my bike. Slowly wheeling it down the deer trail to where I had hidden my rifle, I faced another quandary: how to balance a deer that seemed to weigh at least a ton on a bike and safely carry a rifle. Another brilliant idea soon hit me, and inside the deer's cavity went the rifle, wrapped in my T-shirt and outside shirt (blood will rust metal, so the covering was necessary). Then out of the woods and down the highway I went, with a bigger grin than before. That grin got even wider as local people driving by, seeing me wheeling that deer home, honked their horns in congratulations. Man, tired or not, I was in seventh heaven!

Soon I wheeled that little deer into my yard. Otis, my dad, looked up from some wood he was splitting and just stared. With a big grin, he walked over and helped me lift my deer off the bike. When he did, a load of guts fell out, including the rifle. I unwrapped the rifle to make sure it was all right (it was). Dad said, "What the hell is all this stuff?" as he looked at all the body parts I had saved.

"I wasn't sure what to save, so I saved it all," I lamely replied.

Grinning, Dad bent over and identified all the parts for me to remember in the future—in other words, what to leave for the magpies and coyotes. He showed me the heart and liver, indicating that we would save and eat those. We gathered up the other parts and placed them in the trash can. Then Dad took the heart and liver, filled a big bucket with cold water, and tossed them into it to cool out. Grabbing the deer by the hind legs, he dragged it to the garage and laid it on the cement floor. He took out his ever-present pocketknife (always even sharper than my razor) and cut a slit through the skin between the back leg tendons and leg. He fetched a meat hanger from the back room of the garage, grabbed the deer by one leg, and inserted the meat hook into the slit and then into a similar slit in the other leg. Tying a rope to the center ring in the meat hanger, he threw it over a rafter in the garage and hoisted the deer up off the floor. I was still sitting on the woodpile, exhausted from my hunt, when Dad turned and said, "Come on. Now is as good a time as any to learn how to skin a deer."

Getting up, I walked over, not realizing just how stiff I was, and dug the straight razor out of my pocket.

"What the hell is that damn thing?" he asked.

"A straight razor Jim Tesky gave me," I replied.

"Throw that damn thing away," he growled (I never did, and Chris, my younger son, has it today). Digging into his pocket, he brought out one of his large two-bladed folding knives. "Here," he said. "If you are going to hunt big game, you might as well have the proper tools." (Chris has this knife as well.)

Grinning at my newfound fortune, the two of us skinned the deer, I learning to do it right with Dad coaching. I even managed to leave the flank meat on the carcass instead of cutting it off with the hide (buck hunters will appreciate this detail). Then Dad showed me how to clean the carcass (dirty and bloodshot areas are not allowed because they will sour the meat) and trim out the heart and liver so they could be prepared for the wonderful meals to follow.

As Dad cut the head off the carcass, he looked strangely at the deer tag on the antler. Undoing the shoelace, he took another long, hard look at my tag. "Son, you have the wrong tag on this deer!"

God, after all I had gone through, I had ended up doing another thing wrong. *I had a damn doe tag on my first buck!* Dad quietly closed the garage door to avoid the neighbors' prying eyes as I dug out my deer tags and this time, with his help, attached the right one.

Over the next fifty years, I killed a lot of deer from coast to coast, elk in the Rockies, wild hogs in the mountains of Northern California, and other varieties of big game. I killed many with fine neck shots up to six hundred yards away with my .340 Weatherby rifle and many with close-in body shots in my later years, as my eyes dimmed and lost much of their sharpness. But none ever exceeded the thrill or provided the memories gathered by a fourteen-year-old boy on his first deer hunt in his beloved Plumas County outdoors, with his bicycle, borrowed rifle, straight razor, and an illegally tagged forked-horn buck.

6

The Chinese Graveyard

THERE IS A HILL covered with manzanita brush, Douglas fir, and ponderosa pine standing between the mountain towns of Quincy and East Quincy in Northern California. It is simply called Quincy Hill. But the events that occurred there were of such magnitude that they resided in the deepest recesses of my soul for the next fifty years, and probably will until I die. It was a place where I would lose my child-like innocence and forever know the true "color" of humankind.

In my younger days Quincy Hill was home territory to at least three if not four large coveys of the elusive mountain quail. The denseness of the brush cover, ready access to many small water seeps, and tons of grass seeds along with tangy manzanita berries made it a natural habi-tat for those shy little speedsters of the Sierra Nevada Mountains. Mountain quail are excellent table fare. In fact, they were my mom's favorite game bird; hence my relentless pursuit whenever I had the time during hunting season. In those days you could hunt just about any-where on anyone's land, and the sound of someone shooting did not send everyone into a limp-brained, abject tizzy as it does today. I'll tell you, the passing of that period when things were simpler is a real loss to our culture and speaks worlds regarding the sad "evolution" of the American citizen.

Quail season was open that particular year, and I had borrowed Harold Tweedle's double-barreled, 12-gauge shotgun. Harold was a close school friend and hunting partner who owned lots of firearms. To own a pistol you had to be at least eighteen, but you could own any other gun (except machine guns—restricted ownership since the 1930s) at any age (Harold was just twelve; I was eleven). And firearms, *includ-ing handguns,* could be ordered through the mail without any fanfare! However, I was so poor that I had to scrounge just to be able to purchase shotgun shells from Harold at ten cents apiece. (I couldn't afford a full box—when was the last time any of you sportsmen paid $2.50 for a box of 12-gauge, high-base shells?) But I managed, and was a good shot— and the quail caught hell for it.

One beautiful fall day I decided I would give Quincy Hill a go and see if I could surprise Mom with a quail for dinner. Throwing an old wrinkled apple into my pocket, along with a dozen shells, I walked the two miles with shotgun in hand to one of my favorite quail-hunting areas on Quincy Hill. Arriving, I loaded my shotgun with number 4 shot (quail are tough to kill, hence the heavier shot size) and quietly began my hunt (quail have great ears, and if you are not careful they will hear you coming and flee). Passing through all my usual haunts, I found nary a feather or dropping. Changing tactics, I started hunting higher on the hillside, hoping the birds might be there. I would stop and call with my mouth every forty yards or so (mountain quail have a rather plaintive, whistling call that is easy to mimic), then quietly listen for five minutes. Hearing no return calls, I would continue stalk- ing, all the while listening for their multiwhistle calls or the rustling in the brushy undergrowth signifying feeding quail scratching for goodies. This stalking-and-stopping technique went on for about another thirty minutes—then I heard it! A single quail calling. Somehow it had got- ten separated from the rest and was now calling the flock to determine their location. Listening carefully, I finally located the approximate area of the covey from the sounds of the return calls and began a patient and stealthy stalk in that direction.

Twenty minutes later, after much slow, careful stalking, I heard the telltale scratching in the duff (dead leaves, pine needles, grass seeds on the ground) almost dead ahead. Slowly raising the shotgun to my shoulder, I ever so slowly kept stalking. Moments later I saw my first quail, followed by a dozen others, busily scratching like chickens for their supper. Carefully, almost not wanting to breathe, I slipped the safety to the "off" position as I sighted on the heads of three quail feed- ing closely together on the ground. *Whooom* went my first shot into those three quail, and the brush literally exploded with rocketing birds fleeing the danger. *Whooom* went my second shot from the full-choke barrel at a quail just clearing the top of the manzanita brush. An explo- sion of feathers erupted (like someone dumping out a feather pillow) where the quail had been flying over the top of the bead on the shot- gun. Now, anyone who has hunted quail knows it might look like a clean kill, but you had better quickly follow up a shot or the crippled bird may manage to get away and be lost. As I said earlier, mountain quail are tough to kill. Anything but a direct hit could likely lead to a crippled runner that, without a mountain of luck, would eventually be lost to the other forest critters as a meal. Breaking open the action of the shotgun, I quickly emptied out the two spent paper shell casings (we didn't have plastic shells in those days) and stuffed two more into the barrels in one fluid, practiced motion. Snapping the action shut, I set the safety on and took off at a dead run for where I had last seen the flying quail that had exploded with my second shot.

Suddenly, stubbing my foot on what I thought was a rock, I fell face first into the duff. However, I remembered in time to carefully hold up my shotgun barrel with one hand so I wouldn't fill it with dirt or damage it. Fast thinking for an eleven-year-old kid, eh? Jumping to my feet, with my eyes still focused on the still partially drifting puff of feathers, I took off running once again. *Ka-plow,* down I went once again, only this time even more spectacularly! Damnit, I thought, what the hell am I catching my feet on? Looking down this time as I leaped to my feet, *I stopped dead in my tracks!* Not two feet away from where I had fallen was a grinning, toothless human skull! Scattered on the ground around the skull were many other bones that also appeared to be human. With a thumping heart and a bad case of the big eye, I let the shotgun's safety off just in case I had to shoot my way out of this one! Forgetting my quail for the moment, I looked around on the ground only to find myself surrounded by dozens of red bricks stuck vertically in the ground, all spaced in neat, orderly rows. There must have been fifty or so of the bricks, and I noticed that each one had what appeared to be thick black ink on its flat surface, written in Chinese characters! I was standing in the middle of a very old Chinese graveyard. It was so far off the beaten path and so well buried in dense stands of brush that it had to be from the days of the Forty-niners and the California gold rush. Even at my age (being an avid reader of history), I had a great appreciation for gold field history, including the role of Chinese laborers, and the history of the land, especially Plumas County. *This was my very own historical discovery!*

I was excited and elated (notwithstanding the skull), all in one breath! Looking around, I could see that I was at least a hundred yards from any sign of human disturbance. It was obvious that the old graveyard had long been unused and forgotten. Maybe even for a hundred

years! Man! Slowly sliding the safety back to the safe position, I just
stood there looking at a sight not seen by human eyes for who knew
how long. Weeds and brush were the only flowers heralding a number
of pioneers lying in eternal sleep beneath the soil. Yet the history exuding from this sanctified ground, at least in my eyes, was as vibrant as
that of any other moment from those dynamic and wild times during
which these folks had lived. Here was a piece of history as fresh and un-
touched as the day of the quiet and solemn event that had placed the
last person buried there in their grave, far enough away from the mining community at large to avoid desecration but close enough to visit
and mourn for a loved one. My heart swelled with the historical and
emotional significance of the moment, as seen through the eyes of an
eleven-year-old dreamer some one hundred years later!

Carefully stepping to one side so as not to disturb anything, I
stopped and again deeply drank in this little-known corner of history
long forgotten by humankind. This graveyard represented some very
direct connections with Plumas County and its rich gold rush history!
It was small in size, almost as if the people who made it had not wanted
to draw attention to this little corner of the earth and its rich cultural
history. There were fifty-seven red bricks laid out in orderly rows,
which I thought represented a very large graveyard as far as my knowledge of the Chinese and the history of such sites went. Looking back
at the point in the manzanita brush where I had stumbled into the semi-
cleared graveyard, I saw the cause of my mishap. I had stepped on and
fallen over two of the brick headstones, knocking them loose from their
resting places. The skull and bones were a different matter: a deep
gouge in the ground from some long-ago spring runoff had opened up
one grave, scattering the bones of the inhabitant who had never made
it back to his home and family in China. Many little creatures had
chewed on the bones for the calcium they offered— so in a small way,
the dead Chinese pioneer was again contributing to the well-being of
the county.

Standing in reverence for those souls who had ventured to the rough-
and-tumble gold fields, never to return to their mother country or
loved ones, had a profound effect on me then and now, as I write these
words some fifty-three years later. There were families in China who
never discovered what had happened to their loved ones when the
money or letters home stopped arriving. Families who never got to see
the final resting place of their loved ones who had died naturally or violently as a result of an explosion in the mines, by a bullet from a white

miner angry at a person looking different than he, from starvation, disease, robbery, or drug addiction. Or they could have died while building the Union Pacific Railroad up through the dangerous Feather River Canyon in the effort to link a growing and robust nation forever. The men who did that dangerous work lived on a handful of rice and six cents a day as one of "Crocker's Pets" under the most extreme working and living conditions. They were known as "pets" because no one could build and blast the railroad through the deep granite canyons like the Chinese, whose attributes Crocker was quick to realize and exploit. A Chinese laborer would hang in a basket over the deep canyons, drilling blasting holes by hand with a single jack in the mountain that needed to be removed to make a path for the railroad to follow. Then he filled the holes with blasting powder, set and lit the fuses, and hoped his comrades could bring up the basket in time before the blast went off, sending him into the land of his ancestors.

In those next few moments a multitude of thoughts continued flooding through my young mind. Chinese who came from the old country deep in the dank and smelly holds of ships. Chinese who, once they landed in San Francisco, were looked upon by whites as subhuman. Chinese who, because of their dress and long queues, were instant targets for the ignorant and unwashed (that is, most of the masses in that day and age). Chinese who were relegated to the lowest-paying jobs and most dangerous occupations (powder monkeys or blasting experts). Chinese who were not allowed by law to own property or firearms, work the best mines (they were restricted to the tailing piles), vote, or even enter the worst saloons of the day. Chinese who, under such burdens, bravely fought back in their own way through the Chinese Tong Society (a society of Chinese toughs and killers who protected their countrymen), which helped to level the playing field. Chinese who, under the great weight of prejudice and extreme living conditions, fell prey to opium dens and other destructive influences beyond description. Chinese who, through their great and quiet determination, eventually melded into American society and in so doing not only made history of their own but strengthened and enriched the fabric of America for all time—a land that did not want them but was blessed by their presence.

The quiet of the afternoon added even more majesty to the moment in my young mind, the quail now long forgotten. Laying down my shotgun, I carefully replaced the two brick headstones I had knocked over in my eagerness to locate a possibly wounded quail. Then, taking my knife, I fashioned a digging stick from a dead manzanita branch and dug a hole in the graveyard. Picking up the bones as if they were still alive, I carefully deposited them in their new resting place and, with a little exploration, located that chap's headstone at the bottom of the wash out. I firmly planted it in the soil at the head of the new grave, tamping the soft dirt around it with my feet. Stepping back, I took a moment and said a prayer for all who rested in this hallowed ground. Strange words coming from a white boy over those from a land so far away, but I am sure God heard and understood the meaning of the words just the same. With that piece of history now safely tucked into the recesses of my mind and soul, I returned to the day of the living.

Carefully looking for the quail I had shot many moments earlier, I located his beautiful little body hanging in another bush as if placed there by an unseen hand. It had been a clean kill, and he had never moved from his final resting place. My first shot had killed two of the three feeding quail on the ground, and for that I was happy (keep in mind, a kid will kill anything in just about any manner. Today, if I don't get a clean shot in the air, I don't shoot). Mom would have her quail for dinner and I would be the proud possessor of a wide grin at having brought her some pleasure.

Carefully marking the graveyard, using a distant sugar pine and in- cense cedar for landmarks, I left the hill for home and my chores, a much wiser and more introspective young man than when I had ventured forth in pursuit of the elusive mountain quail. That happens sometimes when you discover a little piece of history and, in a small way, become aware of your roots and what we are all *eventually* to become. ...

Over the next four years I continued to hunt Quincy Hill off and on for the mountain quail it offered. Even then I had learned that to hunt exclusively just one covey of quail would soon destroy their ability to survive and procreate. With that newfound knowledge, I made sure I took only a few birds from each covey and then moved on. However, every time I hunted Quincy Hill, I took time to visit my "friends" and discuss "cabbages and kings." I always found that my time at that little piece of history on Quincy Hill answered many questions and aided in the growth and development of a budding young man who would end up serving his fellow humans for over thirty-two years professionally and sixty-four years (at the time of writing) as what I came to believe represented a good human being and a Christian.

One day, hunting on Quincy Hill for a large mule deer buck I had seen drinking at one of the springs on the hill, I heard the grating sound of a heavy bulldozer off in the distance. Realizing that it was pure folly to pursue my antlered quarry with such a racket not far from where he usually bedded down, I moved toward the sound with questions in my heart. The noise was coming from a part of the hill not far from my Chinese friends' final resting place. Crossing the hillside, I soon came upon the bulldozer, and fear tore at my heart. It was digging off a side of the hill, making way for a new Quincy garbage dump, and it was not far from the graveyard. Picking up my pace, I broke out into a manmade clearing where two large bulldozers were working. One was leveling the dirt, while the other was scraping and gouging great chunks off the hillside. Between the two of them, they were making a level site for the dump. Walking over to where the bulldozer was cutting off chunks of the hill, I was shocked to see the driver working not ten feet from the edge of the graveyard! Running to my "friends'" resting place, I placed myself between their ground and the operator where I could be plainly seen.

"Hey," I yelled, "you can't cut away this bank any further."

"The hell you say," said the grizzled old cat skinner (term used to describe a 'dozer operator) as he lowered the engine to an idle so he could hear me. The deer rifle in my hand probably garnered just a little more respect for such a youngster as well.

"Yeah; there is a graveyard up on this flat. You can't just destroy it."

"Are you sure?" he asked in amazement. Bailing off the cat, the man scrambled up the bank to where I stood to take a look for himself. Taking him to my sacred place, I showed him the fifty-seven graves all neatly laid out for God and everyone to see. Pissed that I had lost the secret beauty of this place, I was nonetheless determined to avoid the loss of a historic place in exchange for a damned old garbage dump. "Well, I'll be damned! You're right, kid, there is a graveyard here!"

With those words, I allowed myself to become encouraged at the prospect for survival of my secret place. For several more quiet moments we both stared at the surroundings laid out in peace and quiet by those pioneers from so long ago. Then, with a streaming spit of tobacco juice landing squarely on a headstone, my cat skinner uttered, "Shit, it's only a graveyard full of goddamned Chinamen! Them bastards don't have any immunity when it comes to what I am doing. It is not like a *real* graveyard!" With that, he whirled, walked down the hillside, and got back on his 'dozer.

I just stood there in utter disbelief! Here was a sacred piece of ground treated as if it was a shit heap! In the inexperience of my youth, I could not believe what was happening. ...

"Get the hell out of the way, kid, or I will kick your ass. I have to have another thirty yards of this bank removed by nightfall, and some damn snot-nosed kid isn't going to stop me." With that, he put the cat into second gear and commenced gouging away the bank by the graveyard. Cutting through my momentary fog, I tried again to reason with the old cat skinner, but to no avail. Running over to the other cat skinner, I asked if he was the other man's boss.

"Hell, no, sonny. We are working for the county and have a lot of dirt to move on this project." I pointed out the location and origin of the graveyard to that operator, and he just looked at me like I was trying to protect a sack of cats. "Hell, sonny," he said, "them is just dead Chinamen from a long time ago. No one will miss them! Now, get the hell out of the way so I can get back to work."

Shocked, I stepped back from the twenty-five tons of metal and watched in horror as the red earth at the edge of the Chinese cemetery came away in big gashes. Then row after row of headstones came tumbling down. The red earth was mixed with the white flashes of human bones as yard after yard of dirt was moved from the hillside. It wasn't long after that the entire Chinese cemetery was gashed off the hillside forever and used as fill on the opposite side of the new garbage dump. I could not believe what I was seeing, but in essence it was a glimpse into my future and what I would see time and time again in my life to come, namely, destruction and loss of our heritage with zero remorse or understanding felt by those committing the acts of stupidity!

Going home that evening, I felt a sincere sense of loss. At that age I didn't quite know what the feeling was, but I knew something important and irreplaceable had been lost for all time. Something that should have been kept, if for nothing else, in the name of common decency. Going back the next day in the hope that something would be left, I was greeted with a great gash in the land and a brand-new shiny garbage dump. ... That day I took a different path off the mountain so I could think. I had lost something that I now realize was part of the heart and soul of my nation, and it did not sit well even with a fifteen-year-old. Stumbling down the hillside covered with heavy brush, I tripped over a rock in my blind haste to leave the area, never to hunt on or visit that ground again. When I looked down, I saw that the rock was a *red brick with black Chinese lettering on it!* Freezing in my tracks, I looked around only to discover about ten more graves in a different area, just downhill and east of the new garbage dump. That area looked even more ancient than the one that had been destroyed. With that discovery and a hatful of determination, I walked into Quincy set on never letting what had happened the day before with the bulldozer *ever* happen again.

Stomping into Sheriff W. C. Abernathy's office, I told him about the previous day's events and my most recent discovery. He was personally incensed over the loss of the first graveyard but pointed out that it was on county property and unregistered as a cemetery. As such, the county could do with it as it saw fit. However, he promised to see that the second graveyard was protected, and I took him at his word. Then the two of us ventured out to my newest discovery.

Today that site is fenced and protected on the side of Quincy Hill as a piece of Plumas County history. People go there every year to marvel at the little graveyard and guess about its inhabitants. I go there to cry inside about the loss of my first hidden Chinese graveyard, its permanent loss to our history, and the loss of my innocence, which ultimately raised a question in my heart and soul about the decency of humankind. I guess that is one of the reasons why, when I went into wildlife law enforcement at the state and federal levels, it didn't become just a profession. *It became a vision quest.* No more would a cat skinner bulldoze a piece of history or natural resources without thinking twice about his actions, if I had my say. ... The badge and the gun would be used if necessary to ensure that our heritage remained for those yet to come.

Years later, as a Fish and Game warden in the Hoopa Valley of Northern California, I stopped by a remote stream for a much-needed drink and some lunch. Walking down to the stream, all the while looking carefully for rattlesnakes, I was surprised to discover 153 headstones of all shapes and sizes. Walking among those stones, obviously removed from some pioneer graveyard and dumped in the remote recesses of the creek, was a revelation. Most of the stones dated from the 1860s to the 1890s! Two were just large boards with information about two soldiers killed by the Hoopa Indians in the 1870s! Someone discovering the old graveyard in the way of what he called progress had loaded up the headstones and quietly dumped them into this forgotten creek. Then he probably went about his business reclaiming the land previously occupied by those early California pioneers without a backward look at what he had just done.

I have seen worse over the years, and a lot of it! It is never-ending and without thought, heart, or soul. In short, a plague that follows most of humankind.

7

Andy Swingle

I WAS WALKING home from high school one day when a red Chevrolet pickup slowed as it passed, then stopped on the side of the road ahead of me. A slender, balding man with a wry smile stepped out and began hobbling toward me (I knew he had a bad knee from an angry mule's kick). "Terry," he said, "got a minute?"

"Sure, Howard, what can I do for you?" I responded. The man was Howard Larson from East Quincy, father of Donna Larson, the girl I had fallen in love with in eighth grade but had yet to come up with enough courage to ask out for a date. Howard was Quincy's only laboratory technician at the time, and one of the best according to the many people he treated. My mother always said Howard gave the best shots in town. Keep in mind that those were the days when needles were used many times over, and it was up to the technicians to keep them sharp. In Howard's case, you never felt the needle! He was very good at what he did and had an outstanding bedside manner.

Being a compassionate man, Howard was on a mission that day, a mission I was soon to share and that, in many ways, set the standard for how I deal with people to this day. A very old Quincy pioneer had fallen and broken his hip. The man's name was Andy Swingle, and he was in the old Quincy Hospital. Howard said that Andy was so old (ninety-eight) that he didn't have any living next of kin and was lonesome just lying there in the hospital bed day after day. Somehow Howard had learned that I had a great love for anything historical, including those early-day pioneers in Plumas County. He was right on the money. Any loose day I had, if I wasn't fishing, hunting, or working, I could be found digging in old garbage dump sites from the days of the Forty-niners for old bottles, crawling around in abandoned, partially collapsed mine shafts looking for treasure, or just hiking the county in quest of any other scraps of history. According to Howard, Andy used to drive stages from Quincy to La Porte (an old gold-mining town) and from Quincy to Marysville (a big historical gold-mining trading center). Now, until I heard that I wasn't really keen on being company to an old somebody I didn't even know, especially one that could be dying! However, when Howard said this guy had been a stagecoach driver during the early days of California history, my ears shot up like an elf's! I let Howard know I would be very interested in spending some time with Andy, but I had my chores and schoolwork to do first. After those were tended to, I would try to spend some time every week with the old fellow. A smile crossed Howard's face, and I could tell he was pleased. So was I. If Howard took a liking to me, maybe I would have a chance with his daughter, who had the world's greatest blue eyes.

The following week, with some trepidation, I went to the hospital. Walking in, I was greeted by the receptionist with, "Good afternoon, may I help you?"

"Yes, Howard Larson asked me to look in on Andy Swingle whenever I had the time. I have some free time and would like to see him if that is possible," I replied.

"Are you sure that is what Howard wants?" she asked, looking down her long nose at what she probably thought was nothing more than a little pissant standing before her.

I squeaked out, "Yes, ma'am."

Still looking hard at me, as if I needed to go away and not bother her, she finally picked up the phone and dialed someone. She talked to that person in such low tones that it was obvious she didn't want me to hear. Now very uncomfortable, I almost turned to leave. However, at that moment I heard a door shut and down the long hallway of the building came the familiar man with a limp.

"Good afternoon, Terry. I'm glad you could make it. Come along and I will introduce you to Andy."

With that and no more strange looks from the receptionist, I followed Howard down another long hallway of many strange smells. Howard walked into a room, and I followed closely, not having the slightest idea what to expect. In the bed lay a very old man who looked as if he were sleeping. He was gaunt and fairly tall from the size of the figure under the covers, and his skin was a sickly yellow. I almost split right then and there. Hell, this guy is dead! I thought. Howard reached over and touched the man's shoulder, and he was awake in an instant.

His flashing blue eyes looked wildly around as if to locate and grab someone. Boy, if I hadn't been frozen with fear, I would have zoomed out of the room, out the door of that hospital, and down the street in a heartbeat, never to return!

"Andy," said Howard, "I have someone here to see you."

"Who the hell is that young scamp?" a strong, gravelly voice asked as those faded blue eyes looked clear through me.

"His name is Terry Grosz, and he lives out near me. Terry has a real love for the history of the county and her people. Seeing as you didn't have anyone to visit with, I thought you and the boy might hit it off and help your healing-up time go faster."

The ancient scarecrow with the surprising energy examined me as if I were a piece of meat for sale in one of our local butcher shops. I didn't move and was not too sure my heart was working. But for some reason, I stood my ground. *I am glad to this day I did!* "Come closer, boy, so I can take a better gander," barked the strong voice from the frail-looking body. Howard stepped aside, and I slowly moved closer. Out from under the covers shot a withered old hand. I instinctively jumped back, only to be stopped by Howard's reassuring hand on my shoulder. "Glad to make your acquaintance, boy," Andy grumbled with his hand still outstretched for me to shake. As I said, it was a withered hand, but when I finally shook it, it had a surprisingly strong grip, kind of like one you would get from a hardworking man of about forty. "Grab a chair and sit down so we can palaver," he instructed, and strangely enough, I found myself obeying without a second thought.

"I have work to do and will leave you two alone so you can get better acquainted," said Howard.

"Thank you, Howard," uttered the old man, and you could tell the tone held real appreciation. With a grin, Howard left the room. "Tell me about yourself, boy, and don't leave anything out," Andy commanded. In the next moments, which turned into a magical hour, I found myself telling the old man all about myself, what I liked and disliked, my love for history, my classes at school, how good a cook my mom was, and everything else under the sun that a fifteen-year-old boy might share. He was especially interested in my roving, hunting, and fishing tales, if the eagerness in his face and the sparkle in his eyes was any measure. I found that discussion and others that followed to be fun, especially since Andy seemed to be hanging on each and every word. It soon became apparent that he was starved for any human kindness or contact. He listened intently, was full of good questions, and laughed easily at my fumbling or wrecks in life. He knew my Uncle Lanoie from having worked in the same company years earlier, he laughed at the story of my first bear hunt, roared until the tears rolled off his cheeks (partly from laughter and partly from the pain of his broken hip being jarred as he laughed) when I told him about washing the cows' hind ends instead of their udders, knew *exactly* where the old Chinese graveyard was that had been made into a garbage dump (that was sad news to him and pissed him off because one of his close friends, Hang Moon, had been buried there), and thought many of my other stories were just as great. What a great old man, and what a wonderful time I found myself having.

The next thing I knew, Howard was asking if I needed a lift home. It seemed as if I had been with Andy for just a few minutes, but I had been there for over two hours! Man, I had to get home (our house was three miles away), I thought as I jumped up. "Yes, I could use a ride home," I said.

"Come on, then," he replied.

"Mr. Swingle, can I come back sometime and visit with you some more?" I found myself asking.

"You bet, son. I would like that," he said with an intense smile. Out came that old bony hand from under the covers, and this time I grasped it eagerly. With that and a final wave, out the door and into Howard's old red bomb pickup I went.

"How did it go?" he asked.

"Great," I said. "May I come back again if I have the time?"

"Please do," said Howard, "because you are all he has." He let me off on the road leading to my home, and off I scooted to share the day's events with my mom.

For the next several weeks, my time with Andy was pure heaven to my way of thinking. That old man was full of tales, trails, and footprints from the early days in California. I remember our second meeting as if it were yesterday. When I arrived to visit, it seemed that Andy was bursting at the seams with something he wanted to tell me. Turning painfully in bed so he could look at me, he said, "Terry, remember where that old Chinese graveyard was located?"

"I sure do," I replied.

"Well, just down from there and to the east a little ways is another Chinese graveyard. That one was there before my arrival in Quincy. It is very old, and if my memory serves me, there were about fifty graves there as well. That used to be the main graveyard for the Chinese in the area. However, one night a bunch of drunken miners took a Chinese woman up there and had their way with her. She was so distraught and disgraced in the eyes of her community that she killed herself shortly thereafter. Of course, nothing happened to the white men responsible because they were messing with a 'Chinawoman,' and no one cared in those days. However, the Chinese community felt their graveyard had been desecrated by the event and created a new one farther up the hill. That must have been the one you discovered while quail hunting. In fact, a pile of Chinese killed while building the railroad through the Feather River Canyon years later were laid to rest there. One was my friend Gee Shoon, who used to be the Chinamen's 'head shed.' That meant he was responsible for finding them work on the ranches, railroads, or mines. Gee would contract out the Chinamen for work, especially later on for the railroads, for a slice of each man's daily pay. He was also buried in the graveyard up on the hill. He lived at the Silver Creek Chinatown near the town of Spanish Fork, but for some reason, instead of being buried there with his own, he chose the Quincy graveyard. Had more friends there, I suppose.

"Terry, for a long time the Chinamen didn't allow white men to participate in their events. Burial was one of them, so that is why I am not certain which graveyard my friend Gee was buried in. But you know, the bad acts didn't stop there on their graveyard. Several local miners needing bricks for a fireplace drove their wagon up there one day and took most of them headstones! I whipped the shit out of one of them for doing that. People really didn't like Chinamen in those days, and it was about three weeks afore any saloon in Quincy would let me in the front door. That was all right by me, though, because I didn't think that way. My mother, bless her soul, raised me to be tolerant of everyone because she used to say no one knows what God looks like."

For the longest time he just lay there and said nothing more. It was as if he was collecting his thoughts or memories. Then, jabbing a bony finger into the air, he said, "It felt real good to break that bastard's nose for what he did to them folks and their graveyard. Truth be told, it ended up like a curse on their very souls for what they did that day. About a week after taking them headstones, their cabin burned down with one of them all drunked up in it. Served his miserable carcass right! The other one, the one with the broken nose, went down the

Feather River and commenced working a claim on Rich Bar. He got killed several weeks later in a fight while working someone else's diggin's when that party went to Oroville for groceries. So I guess it all came out in the wash. But that isn't why I need to talk to you. At the bottom of Quincy Hill going toward East Quincy and off to the right near the crick was these fellows' cabin. Some say they buried their gold from their diggin's up the creek under the cabin floor. I don't know if that's true, but you need to go have a look-see. Look for the first small ravine or crick bed at the bottom of Quincy Hill. Follow it toward the first hill to the right until you come to another small crick bed. Their cabin was right there at the fork of them two cricks. About thirty yards above that easternmost fork, they had their garbage dump. If you don't find their gold, you should be able to find their garbage dump. And since you like to find old bottles, there sure as all get-out ought to be a passel of them out there."

I was all ears! First because of the history flowing from my bed-ridden friend, and second for the chance of digging up some buried treasure! Man, I could hardly wait for my afternoon to end that day. I can't even remember the rest of what Andy and I discussed. *But it wasn't anything like what was yet to come.*

The very next day after school, I sprinted home, changed my clothes, hopped on my bike, and was gone. First I went to the end of the ravine (now nothing more than a small intermittent stream) behind Twiddle's old taxidermy shop. Turning from there toward the small hill to the right, not far from the old National Guard armory, I tracked backward on my trail. Soon I came to another fork in the dried-up streambed. Laying my bike on its side, I began to look around. Just as Andy had said, there was a pile of flat floor stones (all overturned—someone had already looked for the buried gold), a few square nails, a few old burned utensils (which I still have), ash from the cabin fire, and a mess of river stones and crumpled red brick (the old Chinese grave stones) where the fireplace had once stood. Not finding much there, I walked up the stream bed as instructed, and there under a lot of fine gravel were pieces of old purple glass (high in lead), a few old rims from rusty cans, and some larger but rusted-out black powder tins, the contents of which had been used for blasting. Delighted, I began to dig with my hands and a digging stick. Before long I had unearthed about a dozen deep-purple "pumpkin seeds" (old whiskey flasks with rounded bottoms and flat sides so they could fit in a rear pocket). They came in all sizes, from those holding just a few ounces of whiskey to those probably holding a little more than a pint. Most were in excellent condition. Then the find of all finds! Out from the ground came a pottery spirits jug about sixteen inches tall and maybe three inches through. I had seen lots of these bottles at other dump sites, but none ever whole and unbroken! This one had a long crack on its side but was otherwise intact. Then came about a dozen old pottery beer bottles. Quickly biking to Boyd's Super Market (which burned to the ground over forty-five years ago), I got some paper bags, rode home and gathered up some old rags, then pedaled for all I was worth back to my treasure trove. Wrapping and bagging all my finds, I carefully carried the lot home on my bike. Placing my valuable pumpkin seeds in my sock drawer, I displayed my other finds on the shelves in my bedroom. Man, talk about excited! I had a real piece of Plumas County history, and all because of an old man's great memory. Today that gravel flat that held other old miners' cabins (as I was soon to discover) is covered with buildings containing Forest Service offices, a donut shop, a Chinese restaurant (how ironic!), a trash relay station, several other businesses, and a new graveyard. Somehow I preferred the land in its earlier form. ...

The very next day, I was back to meet with Andy, carrying some of the finds I had located as a result of his great memory. For the longest time Andy just ran his bony fingers over every item as if trying to read what the pottery and glass had to say. After feeling the bottles for many long, quiet moments, Andy started to discuss the history of my finds: what each had contained, how in those days they had drunk more warm beer than cold, how many miners drank a pocket mickey full of whiskey each day, how some of the miners injured their backsides when they fell on their back pockets holding and breaking the mickies, and on it went. I had ears the size of a mule listening to the history roll off that old man's lips! Then he slid into their eats. I discovered that the miners and I had a lot in common, especially in my earlier years, when it came to chow. Beans, lots of beans, were the mainstay. Bacon, many times rancid but eaten anyway because of the cost ($1 a pound on the diggin's), the occasional potato, rice, oysters, and onions (many of the wild variety dug from the county's soil). Cooked bread (as he called it) baked in the Dutch oven or cast-iron frying pan, cornbread (if the cornmeal could be afforded), and lots of scalding, strong coffee (grounds and all — he said it kept men regular). According to Andy, breakfast, lunch, and dinner were always followed by a hand-rolled smoke, cigar, or mouthful of strong chew from twists of good Virginia tobacco (if it could be found—it usually came in barrels). When I asked about wild game for their meals, Andy just got a wide grin. "Terry, in many parts of the country, especially near the towns or diggin's, the trees and game were all gone. Killed off when the miners first arrived. The trees for building homes, firewood, and mining timbers, and of course the game for food or barter. Times was tough in those days. We just couldn't go to any old supermarket, you know, and if we could, money was a little short," he said with an experienced twinkle in his eyes. "Besides, when men have the gold fever, they ain't interested in doing much other than mining the yellow metal. That is why a lot of other men got rich off one's diggin's by supplying wagons to haul stuff, lumber to build, and fresh meat to eat."

Over the days that followed, Andy seemed to be getting weaker. But each time he shook my hand, he still had a good, firm handshake. And his voice remained strong, as did his memory. Those alert blue eyes still shone like torches on the darkest of nights. I figured he was just getting tired of talking so much to a nosey kid, so I let it slide.

I still have a few of those things I discovered as a result of Andy's memory. They sit proudly in my current home as a reminder of the days of old and a relationship between a boy needing somewhere to go and a dying man needing to share his legacy before it turned to dust and soft breezes in the late afternoon. ... Unfortunately, all my pumpkin seed whiskey bottles were broken. It seemed that my sister had tired of always having to put away my clean socks, shorts, and T-shirts in my chest of drawers after Mom washed them. Finding my bottles in my sock drawer one day, she took them all out and broke them with a handful of rocks. ... To this day, I have yet to find another rare pumpkin seed whiskey bottle. Without Andy's help, I doubt I ever will.

Entering Andy's room one day, I noticed that he was sleeping. Quietly sitting there beside his bed, I listened. His breathing was deep when he inhaled and very quiet when he exhaled. He looked thinner and even more yellow, but he was still alive, and I guessed that was a good sign.

"Why didn't you wake me?" boomed Andy's voice. Jumping about ten feet in the air from the surprise, I about missed the chair on the way down. "We need to get going. Time's a-wastin'. When I drove a mud wagon for the California Stage Company to La Porte, Marysville, and back, it was wonderful. The air was always clear and cool but downright cold in the winter. That was until the deep snows stopped all passage except by skis [yes, they had skis in those days. Made from long, slender wooden slats with a single push pole for control and as a brake when coming downhill]. In good weather and with a stout three-span [six horses], I could make the seventy-mile trip in anywhere from twelve to eighteen hours. In bad weather a lot longer, if at all. I always had mud and rock slides to contend with, and more than oncet, everyone had to get out of the stage and help clear off the road. I used to make that run twicet a week in the good months. If it snowed, and it sure snowed in those days, maybe not at all. In fact, sometimes I would put snowshoes on the horses in La Porte to help them get on down the road. That was funny to watch. The snowshoes were nothing more than paddles that fastened onto each horse's foot. For the first mile or so until the horses got used to it, they walked funny. But oncet they got the hang of it, it seemed to help them with their footing.

"The old California Stage Company stop in Quincy is long gone, but I used to gather up my passengers—no more than nine, with three riding on top of the stage—and off we would go. About six miles east, I would stop at the Ramelli Ranch and let them out to pee. The ladies would go into the family's outhouse by the old carriage house and the men wherever it didn't offend the ladies. It seemed the rattling and jerking of the wagon would just sort of shake them dry. Then we would board up and head up to La Porte, or Rabbit Town, as it was sometimes called, passing Nelson Creek along the way. If someone wanted to hunt or fish, the stage line would charge them a dollar to fish and five dollars to hunt. I would let them out to fish one day and pick them up coming back two days later. They always had big bags of fat trout, many of them over eighteen inches long. I used to always get some, being the driver, and man, they were sure welcome over the usual fare I had at the stage stops [beans, coffee, biscuits]. If they wanted to hunt, I could drop them off or they could hunt right from the top of the stage. If they saw a big buck or bear, I would stop and they would just shoot it from where they sat. Then I would rest the horses or mules while the hunter cleaned his game and threw it onto the roof of the stage. Sometimes I would arrive with as many as four deer on the roof or in the boot [back part of the stage usually reserved for passenger baggage and covered with a leather covering]. The hunter would sell them to the miners just as fast as he could drag them off the stage once we got to La Porte. Meat, especially venison, was always in short supply in the gold camps and seemed to always be a welcome treat. Even into the

1920s that was the case until Fish and Game people got nasty about selling wild game. In those days the limit on trout was twenty-five, and you could kill two bear and six deer per day. There weren't any limit on 'fool's grouse' [blue grouse]. It didn't make much difference what the limits were in those days. Whatever you saw and could eat, you killed. Most of the run we was far enough away from much of the mining activity, and in them canyons, there always was a pile of game. I would stop about every ten miles to rest the teams and let my passengers out to stretch their feet and relax their hind ends. That also gave them time to 'go and see a man about a horse' if the need arose. I would use that time to check the traces on my team and get a little relief off the hard leather seat up on top as well. Then off we would go again. I can still remember seeing griz in them days, and sometimes a wolf or two. But they didn't bother the stage or teams none."

"Why was it called a mud wagon, Andy? Were you in mud all the time?" I asked.

"Naw. It was an ugly sort of thing, not like them graceful Wells Fargo Concords. It was built heavier, had more leather strapping for a cushioned ride and wider rims for all the rough roads we had to go on. Some even came with just canvas tops. But it was damn sturdy, and I never broke down where a little elbow grease and some wire couldn't fix the problem.

"My passengers were from all walks of life. They was preachers, gamblers, ladies of the night, a whale of a lot of miners, teamsters, and the like. All in a hurry to get to La Porte or other gold fields and all in a hurry to get back oncet they had been there, it seemed. Especially with winter coming on. Getting grub into the camps during the winters was real chancy. As a young man, I can remember a lot of winters when fifteen feet of snow on the level was normal. People just boarded up their windows and lived in the dark most of that time. Tunnels to and from your hay barns was common. Throwing snow that high when digging out just wasn't an option. Most of the independent miners got the hell out before the big snows came. Those working for the big mines, like the Plumas Eureka or Jamison mines, would stay through the winters. Being big like that, they would freight in what they needed during the summer to last them through the winter.

"The most people I ever carried were ten. See, I only drove a three-span, and to take any more people plus the freight was just too hard on the team. In fact, if I brought a load of gold down from the mines, I always had at least three men riding shotgun. If it was in the form of bullion, many times it would be placed inside the stage on the floor with the passengers. In fact, sometimes the mines would just melt down the gold for the month and make a heavy block out of it and send it down the mountain to Quincy that way. Then, if someone tried to rob the stage, they would get a faceful of shot from my 'shotguns' riding along. And if they did get the gold, how were they going to carry a two-hundred-pound block? From Quincy, Wells Fargo would take the bullion to San Francisco, where it would be minted into coins."

Andy had driven his last mud wagon stage to La Porte in 1926, and he had a seemingly endless supply of stories. On and on he droned, with a young lad sitting beside the bed with a case of the big eye, hanging on every word. I don't know how to explain it, but hearing these tales from someone who had been there when the West was woolly was nothing short of wonderful for a lad like me. Here I was, not only living in the mining country but now listening to a man and legend who had lived during that time and was willing to share his life with me. I cherish those moments to this day. I only wish I had known then what I know now because I would have so many more questions for him. ... I am especially saddened that I can't remember more of our conservation. He was full of living history, and unfortunately, I have only captured maybe a tenth of what he said to me that day so long ago. ... What a loss.

The next time I went to see Andy, the nurse wouldn't let me in. He had had a bad night with his hip, and it seemed it was best for me to leave him alone so he could get some rest. I was really disappointed. I had discovered some more bottles from our secret place and wanted to share them with him. But two days later I was back, and he was better, although weaker than normal and running a temperature.

As soon as he saw me enter the room, he beckoned me closer with a bony finger. Slapping my hind end down in the chair beside his bed, I handed him a small paper bag. In it were some of my mom's famous homemade pastries. Man, did his dimming old eyes light up! Reaching in, he took out a buttery pastry and wrapped what few teeth he still had around it. "*Ummmmm,*" he went with pleasure. It felt great to be able to do something for my friend who had so patiently shared his life and times with me. I sat there until he had finished all four pastries. Handing me the paper bag, he said, "Don't let them nurses see this bag. They will figure I am getting some feed on the side, and that will piss them off. Especially that one who is the size of a steam tractor!"

With that, he lay back as if he was going to sleep. But then he opened up with another story, and what a story it proved to be! "Terry, a long time ago I took one of those fancy Wells Fargo Concords from Quincy to Oroville. I didn't get to do that very often, only when the regular driver got laid up or the like. In this case the regular driver had a bad case of the trots from some food he had eaten earlier at a stage stop, and he couldn't continue driving and visiting every bush along the way. It didn't take me long to get ready, and soon we were on our way. We first went through Spanish Ranch and then on to the stage stop at the hotel in Buckeye. There I changed out a horse that was going lame, and from there we drove over Buck's Summit and down toward Oroville. What a grand trip that was! Through some of the most magnificent timber and countryside you ever did see. Some of them trees had to be at least three hundred feet tall and ten foot through. [I would log some of those trees as a young man several years later, and Andy was right. Many a Douglas fir or sugar pine log cut thirty-two feet in length would be *all* one logging truck could carry at a time! They almost looked like the mighty redwoods.] Game, especially black and grizzly bears, was everywhere. That caused some problem with the horses that day, but I just stopped and let the bears amble out of the way as my man riding shotgun kept them covered. There was lots of grouse, quail, and flocks of band-tailed pigeons that made such a clatter when they left the trees, it always made me look up. It was truly a grand sight to see.

"That particular day I was a-sitting behind a spirited three-span of stout horses that would have put a smile on any driver's face. Most of the trip, although long in hours, was the usual ups and downs through the mountains. However, there was one long grade to pull just this side of Oroville, and in order not to lather up my team, I let them walk the climb. About halfway up the draw, I had a kid on board who wanted to take his .22 and hunt some quail around the hill. That was fine with me, and I let him out to hunt and plink his way to the top, where the horses were usually spelled. I remember cautioning him not to dally because I had a schedule to keep. He assured me he would keep moving, and we parted company. We moved slowly up the long, steep grade, stopping frequently to let the horses blow. Up near the top, I approached a mass of boulders that the road wound through. Not paying much attention because the horses knew where they were going, I was surprised to see a man all of a sudden standing on the right side of the road with a double-barreled shotgun pointed right at Slim, my man riding shotgun, and me! It all happened so fast, I drew back hard on the reins, halting the horses and setting the wheel brakes. Slim had the shotgun stuck stock down in our front boot and didn't even have a chance to make a play for it.

"Sitting there, I got a closer look at our robber. He had on nice pants and fancy clean boots but had a white sack over his head, which laid partially down over his shoulders. There were three holes cut in the mask, two for the eyes and one for the mouth. I could see he had a mustache through the hole cut out for the mouth. He wore a white duster over the rest of his clothes. That and those two *big* barrels from the shotgun was all I could see. He hollered, 'Throw down the strongbox, you sonsabitches, or I will clear the both of you off the seat!' I was still holding the horses, so Slim grabbed the box from between our feet and slung it to the ground beside the coach. I don't know what was in it, but it was very heavy and really clunked when it landed. In fact, when it hit the ground, it partially smashed open from so much weight inside. *Pow* went the outlaw's pistol, and the lock flew open as many of the passengers, surprised by the shot, shouted out and moved around inside the stage in terror. The man with the hood walked back to the coach and demanded that everyone get out, and if anyone made a move for their iron, he would kill them where they stood! The folks in the stage came tumbling out, and except for a female passenger starting to cry, everyone did as they were told.

"Walking back to the strongbox and with an eye on Slim, he bent over to examine its contents. Just then *zip* went a bullet by the outlaw's head before he could take any of the strongbox's contents. Whirling, the masked man tried to locate the place where the bullet came from. *Zip* went another bullet, and this time, that was all it took. The outlaw jumped back into the thick manzanita brush and was gone in the blink of an eye. I heard the sound of a horse's hooves fleeing down the mountain. By now Slim had his shotgun out and hammers back for whoever was now shooting in our vicinity. Then out from the dense brush stepped the kid I had let off to do some hunting as we slowly climbed the hill. Boy, were we glad to see him! 'Did I get him?' he yelled.

"'No, he got away,' yelled Slim.

"'Damn,' said the kid, 'I had my bead right dead on him!'

"Slim got off the stage and, looking around, could see where the outlaw had waited in ambush by the boulders. He tracked the footprints of the running outlaw to where a horse had stood. Returning, the boy and Slim loaded the broken strongbox back into our boot for transport to the stage office in Oroville. Inside the broken box I could see gold coins, watches, paper money, and some Wells Fargo payroll sacks. Sure was easy to see why the robber picked this stage.

"Coming down off that grade into Oroville, I kept the horses moving at a pretty good clip, and Slim kept his shotgun in hand with the hammers back all the way in case we got another surprise. Boy, the attempted robbery really set Oroville abuzz as the sheriff took off with a posse to see if they could trail the outlaw. They never caught him, and many folks said the robber was a fellow named Black Bart. I have no idea, but I will tell you this: I never saw shotgun barrels look so big as they did that day up on the mountain. I heard later that Wells Fargo, out of gratitude, gave my young lad with the .22 rifle a fifty-dollar gold piece for putting the robber to flight."

I could tell Andy was exhausted as he fell back in bed and in moments was once again asleep. As I left quietly, my head was buzzing! To have heard such a story was wonderful. I was vaguely aware of the history of Black Bart, and boy, my head just danced with the information Andy had shared. But it left more questions unanswered than all get-out. Was it really Black Bart or some other outlaw? Why didn't the robber shoot back at the kid? When the kid was shooting, why didn't Slim go for his shotgun and put an end to the robber? I couldn't believe my friend had been a real stagecoach driver who had been held up! And he was telling his story to me, a nothing sort of kid. ... Man, I couldn't wait to get home and tell the story to my parents. What a disappointment that turned out to be. Dad listened and then just shrugged it off as if it was a fairy tale. When I approached Mom, instead of listening, she told me to wash up and comb my hair. Dinner was ready. So much for sharing my exciting day with Andy with two tired parents.

The next day I was back at the hospital for more. I had a hatful of questions and was hopeful that Andy would have some answers. When I walked into the office, the receptionist looked up and then reached for the phone. Waiting for her to get off so I could ask permission to see my friend, I was surprised to see Howard Larson coming down the hall toward me. "Terry, may I see you for a moment in my office?" he asked.

"Sure," I said, following him to his office down the hall.

Stepping inside, he asked me to sit down and then sat down heavily himself behind his desk. "Terry, I don't think there is any nice way to say this, but your friend Andy Swingle died in his sleep last night!"

Jesus, the words went through me like a cold knife! Tears welled up instantly in my eyes and soon flooded down the front of my shirt (as they are doing now as a result of those wonderful memories from long ago). I didn't know what to say and found it hard to breathe. Andy had been acting as if he were tired more and more each day, but his flashing eyes and the firm handshake I could still see and feel had said otherwise. Rising unsteadily to my feet, I brushed away my tears and thanked Howard. Then I left his office and walked down the hall and out the door, never again to see or talk with my friend Andy Swingle.

The following Christmas I was in the historical Quincy Court House to see Sheriff W. C. Abernathy. I wanted to order a .22 pistol through the mail for my dad as a Christmas present. I had worked my tail end off doing odd jobs and had finally amassed enough money to make my purchase. However, in those days you had to be eighteen to purchase a pistol through the mail. Pistols could be purchased over the counter at any age, just as long as you had the money, but all I had looked at locally were way out of my price range. However, I had found one that I could afford in a catalog—a nine-shot J. C. Higgins—and was bound and determined to get it and surprise my dad. Walking into the sheriff's office, I was soon admitted to the room where he was sitting. As was usual in those days, it seemed that he knew everybody in the county, including me. I laid out my story, and he supported my plan. The pistol would be ordered in his name, and when it arrived he would call me and I would come into town and get it. With that bit of business done and the money in his hands to purchase the handgun, off I went, but not before I noticed a tall glass-and-wood display case sitting in one of the blind portals of that old courthouse. Walking over to it, I was surprised to see all kinds of Indian arrows, pottery, grass and willow-bark baskets, old Civil War muskets, black powder handguns, old handcuffs from the jail, and other historical items. The case even held a German Luger and a Colt .38 pistol I had dug up on one of my many treasure hunts some years earlier. Most of the stuff was what history was made of, and as usual, I ate it up. Looking at all the items in the shelves, my eyes swept downward to the lowest shelf holding the heavy things such as cannon balls, balls and chains from jails and bad guys long past, stone Indian grinding tools, and *a Wells Fargo strongbox!* It was busted all to hell and the lock had been shot off, but it still dangled on the locking loop fastened to the wood. My memories instantly flooded back to my short time with a wonderful man named

Andy Swingle, Plumas County stagecoach driver! Beside the strong box was a faded note written by hand in old-time script. I don't remember all the words because of the tears welling up in my eyes, but I recall that some of them spoke of an attempted stage robbery just outside the town of Oroville, California, by Black Bart. I don't remember any of the names on that note certifying that little piece of history, but I did remember that the relief stage driver, on that fated stagecoach that fine day so long ago, *was identified as one Andy Swingle.*

8

To Cut a Tree,
to Grow a Man

NOT HAVING A DAD during a portion of my life forced me to get out at an early age and earn a living. The money I earned went to help my mom with the household expenses, with the remainder salted away for college. I grew up in a lumbering community high in the eastern Sierra Nevada Mountains in a small town called Quincy. It was a great place to be raised and live, but just about everyone depended on or worked in the lumbering industry, and by its very nature the work didn't come easy, with many men and women aging before their time. I worked in parts of that industry as a young man and realized that it was not for me. Not because I hated the work, couldn't do it, or felt it was beneath me but because, I felt life held something different for me, and I wanted to discover what it was.

My first serious work as a young man in the lumbering industry was in the local box factory at age fifteen. My mother worked there, and I got a job through her influence. That was fine except it was a violation of federal law because I was underage and working in a dangerous occupation. However, I needed to make a man's wages, and that was one of the few avenues available. Many times, to avoid a citation, I had to stay hidden when the safety inspectors came by to inspect the plant. More than once I remained hidden in the warehouse until George Dean, the plant manager, gave me the all-clear signal. I quickly decided that working in that extremely noisy plant was a one-way ticket to deafness and after one summer's work vowed to look elsewhere. Approaching my sixteenth summer, I needed to work somewhere where I could make even more money. College was a must to my way of thinking, and not having wealthy parents (my mom had recently remarried, and both worked in the box factory), I figured I needed to pay my own way. In those days, that was possible. If you could work, the outfit that employed you paid you a man's wages, and working in a man's profession allowed me to finance my way through six years of college. I am not sure that is possible in today's world, considering the laughable minimum wage, the high cost of living, and skyrocketing college expenses.

In order to earn higher wages, I had to turn to another facet of the lumbering industry: logging. Still under age, I was in a quandary. Logging legally took only men who were eighteen or older. However, I knew that was where I had to work if I was to accumulate enough money for college in my remaining two short years of high school.

Come the end of that school year, I gathered up my courage early one Sunday morning and headed out to Meadow Valley, where the woods boss for Meadow Valley Lumber Company lived. Even in those days, I was big for my age. Standing six foot four, I weighed around two hundred pounds. Having been raised to work hard all my life, I looked every bit the part of a strong and work-hardened young man. That was the easy part. To get by a gruff old woods boss who brooked no laziness or liars, I had to gird my loins. Work was hard in those days and very dangerous if you did not mind yourself when working in occupations such as logging, farming, or mining. Time was money to those outfits, and if you didn't work hard, you hit the road with your pink slip in hand! The woods boss, well, he was the law west of the Pecos, much like a ship's captain. He hired, fired, ran the logging show, and knocked you on your ass if need be! So you can see why I went to Meadow Valley that day with a whole lot of trepidation.

I approached the pleasant-looking home of the woods boss, gathered myself up to look my biggest and oldest, and knocked on the front door. For a few long moments nothing happened. Then I heard footsteps as someone approached the door. The door was jerked open, and standing there filling the frame was Cal Cole, woods boss for Meadow Valley Lumber Company. He was an older man but still imposing in size and bearing. "Yes," he boomed, "what can I do for you?"

Gathering up all my courage and standing as straight as I could, I said, "Mr. Cole, my name is Terry Grosz. I am six foot four, eighteen years old, weigh two hundred pounds, and am ready to go to work." Bold words from a pissant of a kid, but I needed the chance and was willing to lay everything on the line for the opportunity.

For the longest moment Cal just looked me up and down from head to toe, as if he was judging a side of beef. How I wished he would say something, I thought as I tried to hold my best "lumberjack" look. ... "How old did you say you were, boy?" boomed his voice once again, followed by a piercing look.

"Eighteen, sir," I replied, not daring to even wiggle.

"When were you born?" he boomed.

Damn, I was starting to lose heart with all this hollering, but hang tough, I told myself. "June 22, 1939," I replied. That was exactly two years before my real birth date. A white lie, I guess you could say. I had figured he might ask me that question, so on the seven-mile walk to his house I had rehearsed what I was going to say over and over again. That included the false birth date, so it sounded natural.

Cal glowered down at me, making sure of what he was seeing and hearing. "Be at our Meadow Valley shop Monday morning next, no later than eight o'clock," he replied. With that, he abruptly closed the door in my face.

Damn, I had the job! I just stood there in amazement for the longest time before I could get my wits about me. Then I got the hell out of there before he changed his mind.

The next three months, and several summers thereafter, were some of the best years of my life. I was given the job responsibilities of a real man, in many different functions. I would learn the field operations of a logging show for that time period (ways of doing business have changed considerably since those days). The work was dangerous but invigorating, challenging, and maturing in nature. It was a time during which I started to really grow up, mentally as well as physically.

Come the following Monday, I was Johnny on the spot, but not without some advance preparation. First I went into town and purchased a pair of high-topped White logging boots for the god-awful price of $100! But according to several neighbors who worked in the woods, they were the best boot for that type of work (they were right). Next I found a man in my neighborhood who worked on my new logging crew and arranged for a ride to work for $1 a day (my share of the gas money). Then, taking some more money I had saved, I went to Boyd's Super Market and purchased lunch fixings for the week ahead. I figured the work would be hard, and I would need some good grits that would stick to my sides. Boy, how true that prophecy turned out to be! Dad gave me a gallon water canteen and his old hard hat from the days when he had worked in the woods as a young man, and I was almost set. A trip to the local hardware store saw me purchasing a heavy-duty set of leather work gloves, and now the gleam in my eye told me I was ready.

Standing in the yard near the machine shops and company logging trucks at seven-thirty, I just watched and learned. There were about fifty men standing around smoking, chewing tobacco, and visiting. None paid a damn bit of attention to me, so I just stood in the middle of the group, waiting to be told what to do. Then five battered man-wagons, or "crummies" (like vans of today, only with no side windows), pulled up next to the jumble of men. Without being told, the men began loading into the vehicles. Out of nowhere came Cal Cole's voice. "Terry," he yelled, "you get in that last man-wagon. You are on the brush crew."

Grabbing my lunch bucket and water jug, I boarded the man-wagon. It was full of men, but they made way for me to sit on one of the bench seats lining the inside of the van. With that and the closing of the doors by the driver, we pulled out of the yard in a convoy. I introduced myself to the buzzing sound of the men in the dark, broken only by the lighting of a pipe or the glow from someone puffing on a cigarette. The men got pretty quiet in the lurching van, probably trying to sleep as we sped down numerous dirt roads to somewhere. Soon the van filled with clouds of road dust. Since we were last in the line of five man-wagons, we ate the most dust. As I would soon discover, the brush crew was at the bottom of the social heap when it came to the logging industry. But that was all right. I was finally making big money! A whole $2.02 per hour (my mom was making $1.25 an hour and I had made $1.05 an hour at the box factory)!

Finally arriving at the "landing" (a wide spot in the road built for the logging operation) after a forty-five minute ride into the mountains around Buck's Lake, we all bailed out. What a sight to behold! A *huge* Washington Track Loader (like a crane) stood in the middle of the landing. I could see that it was for lifting trailers off the logging trucks (logging trucks in those days always carried their trailers) and loading logs onto each logging truck. It was a massive piece of twin-boomed machinery (joined at the apex of the booms) with huge twin diesel engines to generate the power needed in lifting the heaviest logs. In front of the boom of the Track Loader on each side were two decks of logs all cut to length, limbed, and waiting to be loaded.

When operating, the trucks would back in between the two decks of logs. The Track Loader would hook onto the truck's trailer, lifting it straight up. The logging truck would zoom out from under the trailer, and then it would be lowered to the ground. The logging truck would hurriedly back up and hook up its trailer, and the driver would then hook up all the air hoses, making the truck ready for loading and travel.

The Track Loader had a main cable three inches in diameter. From the end of that, dangled two inch-and-a-half-thick cables, each holding a huge C-shaped steel hook. On the bottom of each hook was a sharp point, enabling it to be stuck into the end of a log. Two men (hookers) would select logs from each side of the deck and with those massive hooks would hook the ends of the same log. The Track Loader operator would then engage the loader, lifting that log high into the air and placing it on the logging truck. The hookers, with the aid of long ropes attached to the bottom of the C-shaped hooks, would guide the logs onto the truck so a tight stack could be created. Jerking the hooks from the log just laid in the truck, the hookers would run to the next log. That process was repeated until the truck was loaded. Once loaded, the driver would fasten a few cables and binders to secure the load. Then he would pull forward a short distance and strap the load down with the remainder of the cables and binders. In an instant another truck would back into the previous truck's place, and the process would begin again.

Sitting at the edge of the landing were fifteen D-8 bulldozers ("cats" in loggers' jargon) without their blades. Also lined up single file along the edge of the road leading to the landing was a string of empty logging trucks and their drivers, waiting to be loaded. Some of those trucks were owned by the company and some by independent truckers. In the early morning one could hear more on the way (we would load about sixty trucks per day). *Varoom* went the Track Loader's twin engines as men streamed from their man-wagons to their work assignments. Cat skinners headed to their assigned cats, riggers and choker setters followed their assigned cat skinners, the hookers went to the log decks in front of the Track Loader, and I along with the rest of the brush crew walked up the hillside above the landing. As I walked into the forest, I met my new crew boss. His name was McMaster, a man in his fifties. Our job was to chop the brush, slash (leavings from the process of logging), limbs, and the like into manageable sizes. Then we tamped or scattered those waste products over the bare soil where the cats had scarred the land as they dragged their logs down the hill to the landing. In so doing, we curtailed the soil erosion that would have followed during the next set of rains or snows. By reducing large piles of brush and slash, we also reduced the danger from raging forest fires. The work simply entailed the use and knowledge of double-bladed axes and chainsaws. Simply, I say ... well, to a country boy used to such tools since I was old enough to hold them, they were simple. *Simple but deadly!* You had to be a bit of a woodsman and know how to use the very sharp axes and extremely dangerous chainsaws. If not, down the mountain you went in a crummy, holding your foot where a missed ax swing had cut into your boot, tendons, meat, and bone. Or even worse, holding a severed limb cleanly removed by the whirling and deadly chainsaw! An injury that would keep you off the mountain for many a week, if not permanently. ... *And in those days the company was not responsible for you or your care.*

After about one day, the job on the brush crew got pretty boring, but I was working my way to college, and having to do this kind of work reinforced that drive. Plus, hiking all over those mountains kept me in excellent physical shape for football practice coming up in the fall. We had to work all over the areas where the cats had dragged (skidded) out the logs, and to say the least, what a mess. But after we came through, somewhat rearranging the lie of the land and its cover, it didn't look too bad. The company was only selectively cutting the timber (only certain trees marked by the Forest Service, leaving the rest), as opposed to clear-cutting (where every tree of value is removed). So for the next month I cut brush and helped take three guys down the mountain with severely cut feet from carelessly swung axes and one fellow with terrible gut pains. All went straight to the hospital, the three with cut feet never to return and the fellow with the gut pains to die. His intestines had rotted away from within. He had been injured in an earlier logging accident when a cat had rolled over on him, crushing him underneath as it tumbled down the mountain.

After working for two weeks in the woods, along came payday. When we arrived back at the shops and truck barns at the end of the day, the paymaster was yelling out names and handing out paychecks. When he finished, I did not have a check. Walking over to the paymaster, I asked if he had a check for Terry Grosz. "Nope," came his reply. "Your mom has your check, son."

"How come?" I asked, incensed.

"I don't know, but those were the orders from Cal Cole," he replied. With that he walked away, leaving me dumbfounded! I later discovered that Cal *knew* how old I really was! To protect himself and the company, he had my checks go to my mom (under her name), who worked for the same company but in the box factory division.

Still standing there in shock, I felt a hand on my shoulder. Turning, I looked into the pockmarked face of the company's union steward. "I need twenty dollars from you to put against Dale's pay [the man who had died from rotten guts] for his widow. The company will match whatever we raise, so twenty dollars is your share [over a day's wages for me]. Bring it tomorrow when you come back to work [I didn't mind helping the man's widow but just felt that was my option, not the damn union's]. Also, you need to bring your initiation and union dues for a full year tomorrow as well [Where had I heard that before?]."

"You know," I said, slowly getting madder by the moment, "I am only working for three months. Then I go back to school. Can't I just pay three months' worth of union dues?"

"Naw, kid, it is all or nothing. If you don't want to pay, that's all right. This isn't a closed shop, you know. *Just don't come to work tomorrow unless you bring me the money or pledge it in writing out of your next paycheck.* Your call!" With a leering, rotted, tobacco-stained mouthful of teeth and a "take that you punk" look, off walked my "helpful" union steward. ... There went another $60 out of my paycheck.

Arriving home, I hurried into the house and asked Mom for the money from my first paycheck. "Can't have it," she informed me. "That is your college money and not to be spent foolishly." With that, she went back to preparing dinner, and I knew that to argue further was a waste of my time.

"Would you please tell me how much I made at least?" I whined.

"A little over two hundred and twenty dollars take-home," she replied. Hot dog! I thought. I am rich! "Your dad will cash the check when he goes to the store tonight and will bring you the money for Dale's widow, your union initiation fees, and your dues for the year," she flatly stated. I could tell from the tone of her voice that she loved unions as much as I did. I started to boil once again and then, realizing the folly of such a reaction, walked into our washroom and got ready for dinner. Unions were only part of the issue. The lumber companies had a tendency to use you up in those days and then look for someone else to fill your shoes. Take my mom, for instance. She worked two weeks less than twenty years (the magic number to get a company pension) and then *was fired!* Her work was excellent, to say the least, for all those years, but to avoid paying out a full pension, the company fired her. And of course, the unions made sure that kind of thing didn't happen. *Yeah, right!* For working two weeks less than twenty years, Mom got a monthly union retirement check of just $80! That was less than $3 a day to live on, and that was *before* taxes.

"Grosz, step over here," commanded Cal Cole's voice. Turning away from my brush-crew buddies, I hurried back to the landing. "You are off the brush crew. This next month I want you working with Bert Jones as a powder monkey [handler of explosives]. Any problems?"

"No, sir," I replied, happy to be off the boring brush crew. "Where do I go from here, sir?" I asked.

"See that old red pickup over there?" he asked as he pointed. "Well, get your ass over there and give Bert a hand. His assistant blew his hand off yesterday, and now Bert needs some help. Try not to do anything foolish," Cal barked.

"Yes, sir," I said as I hustled over to the red truck. No one was there, so as I waited I looked it over. In the bed of the truck were about four hundred pounds of 20 percent dynamite in wooden boxes. There were all kinds of tools, plungers (used to send electricity down the lines to the electric blasting caps to set off the dynamite), rolls of heavy blasting wire, and a *small first aid kit!* Guess you didn't need much first aid if you blew your head or hands off. Inside on the front seat of the truck, smeared with dried blood from the day before, were about ten boxes of electric blasting caps.

"Hi, I'm Bert. What's your name?" asked a slightly built, unshaven man standing behind me who could have stood the use of a little bath water and soap.

"My name is Terry. I'm your new helper."

"Get in," he replied through tobacco-stained, rotting teeth, "and let's get going. We have a lot of ground to make up because I lost half a day yesterday bringing my partner out with just a stump of a hand. What a mess. He bawled all the way to the hospital, squirting blood every which way. ... On the way up, I will explain what you need to do. Then once we're there, I'll show you just once what to do. You better get it right the first time or down the hill you'll go too," he growled after spitting at least a gallon of tobacco juice on the floorboards of the pickup between our feet.

I just nodded as Bert drove around the Track Loader and into the forest on a single-blade-wide rough dirt road. The first big bump we hit, the boxes of electric blasting caps flew off the seat and scattered all over the floor! Bert never said a word, just kept bouncing along as I hurriedly but carefully picked up the boxes (from around the rivers of tobacco spit) and put them back on the seat. It doesn't take much to set off an electric blasting cap! The road was nothing but a badly plowed single track made by a D-9 bulldozer. We were now ahead of the logging show as we wound through the timber. Deeper and deeper we went until we were about one mile ahead of the rest of the crew. We met the D-9 operator coming back, making the road a little more passable, which eventually the rest of the logging crew would use as they worked their way through the geography of the timber sale. Stopping and getting out of the truck, I heard the angry roar of chainsaws and the thundering crash of Nature's giants falling to earth for the last time. Let me tell you, that experience was unforgettable! Here I was standing among ancient giant trees, many over two hundred feet high and measuring at least ten to twelve feet in diameter. Most were probably five hundred to maybe a thousand years old. This was virgin timber in its purest form, and I couldn't help but experience the beauty and joy of the moment in and among those noble giants. That was, until they fell to earth amid the crashing of limbs and the angry roar of chainsaws. I remembered what Andy Swingle had told me about his ride to Oroville on the stagecoach as its relief driver and the huge timbered forests he had driven through above Buck's Lake. Damn, it was just as Andy had said, I thought. And I wasn't far from roughly the same area where he had driven the stage!

"All right, kid. Get your ass over here so I can show you what to do," growled Bert. For the next hour I was instructed in what was expected. Then off went Bert, carrying a load of tools, loose blasting caps jammed in his shirt pockets, blasting wire, a case of dynamite, and his lunch. He was right: he only told me once what to do! In a few moments I was alone with all those giants of the forest looking down at me as they had at many a man over the past several hundred years ... only this time, they looked on in sorrow knowing what was coming.

Those cutting down the trees were known as fallers. Their job was considered the cream of the crop within the logging industry. In those days they got $1 a tree for every one they dropped to the earth, and usually they were on their way home by one in the afternoon. During that short period, every one of them made about $100! In the forest with the fallers were the company buckers (paid wages only). The buckers limbed the trees with their chainsaws and cut them into thirty-two-foot lengths until no more were left, then sixteen-foot lengths until no more were left, then eight-foot lengths. Before he moved on to the next tree, the faller, using a long-handled hammer with his special raised mark on the end, would hit the exposed end of the butt cut of the log to show who had dropped that tree (for payroll purposes). That strike would make an indelible mark in the wood. To keep things moving, each faller (depending on how good he was) had a company bucker or two assigned to him. Now, the faller, in order to keep his job (no women worked in the woods in those days), had to fell each tree in the same direction. If they fell the trees every which way, like the old game of pickup sticks, the bulldozers hauling out the logs could not do so without making one hell of a mess of the landscape. When the fallen trees lay in the same general direction, the 'dozers could drive along-side each log, hook them up with chokers, and haul them back to the landing with a minimum of fuss and land destruction. In those days, woe betide the man who made a mess of his timber falling or tore the countryside up with a 'dozer! Working among the fallers and buckers were the surveyors. They surveyed the roads to identify where they would do the least damage to the standing timber, reduced erosion through their line of direction, used the least number of culverts, and made sure slope and grade met Forest Service standards. They also laid out where the landings would be placed. Within the boundaries of those surveys were stumps from the freshly cut trees. Since most of those stumps would stop even the powerful D-9 (a monster in those days), that was where I came in as a powder monkey.

My job was to work between the survey lines, and any stumps therein (in the way of the road or landing) were to be primed for blow-ing. That entailed using what was affectionately called a "bull prick" (kind of looked like one), a heavy, pointed, solid piece of steel about four feet long. I would find two major roots at the base of the stump and drive that "bull prick" deep into the ground where they forked. Pulling out the tool, I would drill a hole in the end of a partial stick of dynamite with a sharpened wooden stick (no electrical charge in wood). Then I would place an electric cap into the hole on that stick of dyna-mite, making a wire loop around the end of the explosive with the blast-ing-cap wires so the cap wouldn't pull out of the stick. Then, with a long wooden dowel, I would shove the dynamite holding the blasting cap into the hole between the tree roots. That would be followed with another stick or two on top of the first, depending on the size of the stump. Running the ten-foot wire from the blasting cap off to one side, I would take a D-cell flashlight battery and, ducking my head, touch the two blasting-cap wires to the positive and negative ends of the battery. *Frump* would go the charge, blasting open a cavity underneath the stump. Dropping to my knees, I would clean out the hole with my hands, making a fair-sized opening underneath.

Later the head powder monkey would come along and, depending on the size of the stump, load into the hole anywhere from ten to twenty sticks of dynamite. He would then lay the two wires running from the electric cap on his sticks of explosive on top of the stump in clear view. Off he would go to the next stump I had primed and cleaned out for loading. After I had done a pile of stumps, I would double back to the truck and get several rolls of blasting wire. I would then return to my original starting point for the day and wire up the wires from the blasting caps lying over the tops of the stumps for blasting at the end of the day, wiring all the stumps together into a circuit for blowing. Usually I would pass the powder monkey coming back for the plunger and line testers. Finishing up back at the pickup, having hooked up all the stumps so that they were now a complete loop, the powder monkey would test the circuit with a small device that didn't use or give off any electricity. Once it was determined that we had a complete circuit, he would make ready to fire by hooking both ends of those wires to the hundred feet of wire leading to the plunger. We would wait until all the fallers, buckers, and surveyors cleared the woods (usually at the end of the day) and then check the lines once again with our device that read whether we had a closed circuit. This time, if we still had a closed circuit and everyone was out of the blasting area, the powder monkey would yell, *"Fire in the hole"* three times. If he heard no response, down would go the plunger and up would go the stumps (mostly just split in two. That way the D-9 could lift them out of the ground with just the front of his blade, thereby making the way clear for the road-building crew that was to follow). Once the stumps were blown, the road-building crew would come in and make the new road and landings as needed.

Sometimes it wouldn't blow! A deer or bear often would run through the lines or eat the dynamite (yes, bears like eating that stuff) after we had completed the circuit. Then we would have to walk the entire line looking for the break. Finding it, we would again have to hook the lines together, hoping there wasn't any static electricity in the line. Then back to the plunger to start the process all over again. Hooking those broken lines together always made for a hairy moment! If there was static electricity in the line and you hooked it back up, you might find yourself going the way of the stumps!

I did this kind of work for a whole month, and many times I would see Cal walking the logging show, checking on his men and firing those who needed it. I remember one time when we were running short of powder and caps. We had sent word down to town that we needed more and continued to work with what we had until they were delivered. Working above where the new road was coming through, I happened to look up, and not twenty feet away was the woods boss, quietly watching me while I worked. "Morning, boss," I said.

"Morning, Terry. I have been watching you, and you are doing me a real good job. Keep it up."

"Yes, sir," I replied. About then I heard a truck struggling up our rough access road. It was our powder and cap supplier, and he waved when he saw me. Waving back, I continued my conversation with Cal. He wanted to know if I was going to college and where. What my major would be and was I going to play football in college. How expensive college was and how long it would take. (Just routine questions, or so I thought. I would have a chance to revisit this conversation several years later in a surprising way on my last day of work for the company. ...) We spoke for another twenty minutes, which I found odd. Cal always wanted his men to be working their tail ends off. But he seemed to be taking an interest in me and what I was learning and wanted more information about me and my future. That was fine with me because he was the boss, but I still had a lot of work to do and didn't know how to break off the conversation so I could finish. Well, Clyde Barnes (no relation to my dad), the D-9 'dozer operator (the man I mentioned earlier who was cutting out our rough road), did it for us. Down through the woods he came, dragging a skid of logs. Waving to us, he continued crawling toward the road where a high bank stood. It was obvious what his intentions were, and when Cal and I saw what he was going to do, we started running toward him, yelling and waving our arms. He was heading right for the spot where the man from town had stacked twenty cases of dynamite on the new road—*right under*

*and out of sight of the high bank Clyde was heading for and couldn't
see because of the high profile of the cat!* That wasn't the worst part. The
idiot had left the electric blasting caps on top of the cases of dynamite!
Clyde, seeing the two of us waving to beat the band, just waved back.
Hell, he couldn't hear us hollering over the roaring exhaust stack immediately to his front, so he kept on coming.

Cal and I, knowing what was going to happen next, jumped behind
some stumps and buried our faces as Clyde drove right over that high
embankment, *right onto the cases of dynamite.* Still unaware of what he
was doing, Clyde dragged that skid of logs over the explosives with all
the smashed blasting caps scattered all over—but it didn't blow! Clyde,
seeing us duck, stopped the cat and just sat there waiting for us to re-
appear with a questioning look on his face. When we did, he was close
enough and had reduced the engine to an idle to hear what we had to
say. With that, Clyde looked down at the tracks on the cat to see crushed
and broken sticks of dynamite with the wires and blasting caps all intermixed. I don't think I ever saw a man go so white. For the next hour, Cal
and I crawled all around and under that idling cat, carefully removing
crushed sticks of dynamite and smashed blasting caps. Finally we felt we
had cleaned out all we could, and then Clyde carefully moved his cat
away from the danger area and unhooked his skid of logs. That was a
long day, and a real life experience! Clyde went on to live a full life and
is now buried near my mother's grave in the cemetery in East Quincy.
There is a picture of a bulldozer on his tombstone. Well, at least it isn't
shown flying through the air propelled by twenty cases of dynamite.
I think Clyde got a dose of my guardian angels that day. ...

The next morning at the landing, Cal walked over to me and said,
"You didn't have to help me clean off all those blasting caps and sticks
of dynamite yesterday."

I said, "Well, you did, so I just figured if it blew, we would be together wherever it sent us or our pieces."

"I thought you wanted to go to college," he said.

"I do, but I figured you knew what you were doing, so I followed."

Cal looked at me for a moment and then yelled at a man walking
nearby. "Nordt, come here, will you?"

A really old man turned and walked over to us. He was not a tall man
but was built like a brick outhouse. He had arms like the cartoon char-
acter Popeye and a barrel chest measuring sixty inches in girth if it was
an inch. His legs—well, they looked like matchsticks. Muscular match-

sticks, I might add. "Yeah, what do you need, boss?" came a deep-voiced reply.

"Nordt, this is your new choker setter. He works well and is young enough to stay up with even you, I would bet."

Nordt just looked me up and down and said, "I don't know, boss, he looks a mite puny."

"Well, you ran your last choker setter off, but I will bet a month's pay you don't run this young pup off," Cal replied with a slight grin.

"Glad to meet you, kid. You got a name?" Nordt asked as he extended his gnarled hand.

Taking it, I was surprised at the strength it held! It was a crushing handshake, and if I hadn't been as stout as I was, I would have lost a hand! "My name is Terry," I replied. "Glad to make your acquaintance, sir."

"Let's go, boy, time's a-wasting," he growled.

Running back to the powder monkey's truck, I gave an explanation to Bert as to where I was going, grabbed my lunch and canteen, and hustled over to Nordt as he headed for a cat.

A choker setter is the one who fastens a special cable to the lengths of logs to be removed from the forest. Each cable is thirty feet long and has a loop on one end and a hooking device on the other. When the cat comes by the log all hooked up with a choker, the loop from one end of the cable is hooked on the main towing hook on the rear of the 'dozer. Then you scramble out of the way, and the cat heads for the next log (remember, the fallers tried to fell the trees in parallel lines for ease in removal). On the other end of the choker cable is a pointed nubbin. That point facilitates shoving the cable under the downed log and out the other side. Then you reach or scramble over the log, grab the nubbin, and hook it into the sliding bell. The sliding bell is nothing more than a heavy rectangular block of steel with a hole on both ends. The cable runs through one of the holes, allowing the bell to slide up and down the cable, depending on the size of the log. The other hole has a shallow groove leading into it, a hollowed-out portion so the cable can lie flush with the block of steel. The choker setter runs the nubbin under the log, bringing it up and around the log. Then he pushes the nubbin through the hole on the sliding bell. When he grabs the cable above the bell and pulls it tight, a steel lasso is in essence made out of the choker. Then the loop (the part attached to the cat) is laid on top of the log, and the choker setter moves on to the next log to be set.

In those days a crew consisted of a cat skinner, a choker setter, and a rigger. Each crew was assigned a portion of the forest with downed trees. The cat would head up the mountain, dragging anywhere from six to a dozen chokers weighing about thirty pounds each. At a certain point, the rigger would unhook the chokers, leaving them out of the way of the cat. Then the rigger would guide the cat into position to hook up and remove logs previously set, in the process keeping the cat from being high-centered on boulders or stumps. At the same time the choker setter would be hooking up the chokers onto logs from the pile of chokers recently left on the trail behind the cat. Once the cat had all the logs it could drag or skid, it would head back down the mountain to the landing. In its absence, the choker setter and rigger would set the next skid of logs. Then the rigger would go to the bottom of the skid and guide the returning cat in for another pickup. Releasing the empty chokers, the rigger would head into the next batch of logs to be removed while the choker setter took the just-returned chokers up the mountain to set on a batch of new logs. And on it went throughout the day. On Nordt's crew there were *two* choker setters. I found that odd as I boarded the cat, finding a place to sit and hold on for dear life.

Across the landing we steamed in third gear until we got to the mountain's edge. Shifting down into second, up, up, up we went. It was thrilling and terrifying. It was all I could do to hang on as the powerful twenty-five-ton cat clawed its way up the mountain, sometimes at such a steep pitch that water sputtered out from under the radiator cap and the front ends of the tracks were popping backward, wanting to come off the ground and flip the 'dozer over! Enjoying my new duties and excited by the new challenge, I looked over the cat and new crew more closely. Nordt had done this a million times before, judging from his looks. He had to be at least seventy! I thought. A fellow named Rick was the other choker setter. He was a lean, tall drink of water with a knife scar running the full width of one side of his face and across the nose. He was a heavy drinker (as I later discovered, catching him drinking on the job many times) who spoke little, appeared sullen, and preferred to be left alone. I had no problem with that. ... Paul, the cat skinner, had only one eye, and in the socket where the eye had been was an open, red, running, and constantly oozing hole! It was ugly to look at, but you couldn't help yourself. At least, I couldn't! I had never seen such a thing. He sometimes would push a marblelike false eye into the hole, and it was so ugly I would find myself staring once again. It seemed that our cat skinner had been a tank driver in General Patton's army. In a fight with a German Tiger tank, his tank had been hit and he had taken a piece of shrapnel in the eye. However, he was a master at the helm when it came to making that cat do things I would not have thought possible. The only bad thing about this chap being blind in one eye was that it made him dangerous on that side with the cat. He wouldn't use his good eye to look around and cover his blind spot. That was your job, and when he chose to go, you had better not be in the way!

Stopping the cat on top of a ridge, the three of us bailed out. Putting our lunches and water on a stump where they would be seen and not run over, we commenced our work. Nordt guided in Paul to a bunch of logs that had been set the night before. Rick and I grabbed about twenty chokers between us and trudged up the hill, dragging them farther into our area of responsibility. "You set there," Rick yelled as he pointed to a tangle of logs (the new faller who had created such a mess, I learned, had been fired the same day), "and I will set further up." With a nod, I headed for the mess of logs laying every which way and commenced setting my mess of chokers. Getting that done, I headed up to give Rick a hand and, seeing he was set as well, crawled up on a stump and sat there. Boy, I thought, this choker setting is a pretty cushy job. Plus, I was making twenty-three cents more per hour! Talk about tall cotton. Then below, I could hear our cat coming back. In fact, it sounded like two cats ... sure as hell, here came two cats! One was driven by our skinner and the other was driven by a new man who was learning the ropes. Nordt guided the first one into my area, rigged the chokers, and took off to guide the other one farther up the hill. In the meantime, "my" cat dropped off ten more chokers. Now I had to hustle my ass to set those ten chokers before he returned. Rick was facing the same problem, and it was then that I realized what was happening. Nordt was so tough, *he rigged for two cats!* That meant his choker setters had to hustle or get their asses chewed by Nordt and the cat skinner. Man, I kicked my speed up to hustle, and that I did for the next four hours!

Come lunchtime, I was more than ready to eat. In fact, my normal-sized lunch proved to be less than I needed, and from then on I made and ate twice as much food per day! For the first two weeks of this newest detail, I ran my hind end off, losing twenty pounds in the process! That was a real trick, seeing that I had been pretty lean and hard before that. Plain and simply, that old man kept both of his choker setters going at a dead run, especially if we were close to the landing (meaning the cat made shorter trips). But I had made up my mind not to let that old man outperform me, and he didn't (only because I was more than fifty years younger than he, though). I later discovered that Nordt was seventy-three at the time! That made me even more determined not to be outdone. But, what a great old man he was. As good a soul and worker as I would ever have the pleasure to work with.

One afternoon as we gathered for lunch, Nordt, Paul, and I (Rick had quit in disgust at having to work so hard) laid our lunches out on the stump serving as a table and began to yak as friends will between bites of food. Paul told many tales of what happened to him in Patton's army, and we laughed heartily together at each other's stories. Then Paul did something unbelievable. We still had fifteen minutes left on our lunch hour, so he took out his used-up chew from his lower lip (half a tin of Copenhagen—a damn stout chewing tobacco) and laid it on a dirty handkerchief on top of the stump to dry. Then he took out the remaining half of a can of "Cope," stuffing the powdery, "all-man's" tobacco between his lower lip and teeth. His lower lip stuck out as if someone had hit him. In a few minutes his old Cope on the handkerchief was dry and he carefully dumped those leavings into another Cope can pulled from his other shirt pocket. I noticed it was almost full of leavings from previous chews. What the hell is he going to do with that? I thought. But back to work we went, and after a few moments of hard work I didn't give it any further thought. Choker setting for two cats, now that Rick had quit, caused me to move at a dead run or get eaten alive. It was damn hard work, but man, would I be in great shape come football season.

Dragging my carcass into the man-wagon that afternoon, I gladly slid in alongside my cat skinner and laid my tired back against the wall of the vehicle to relax. I no longer rode in the brush-crew crummy but in the one used by my cat skinner and rigger. Paul took his pipe from a pocket and commenced to load it. Taking out that old Cope can, he dumped the leavings into the bowl of the pipe, tamped the used chewing tobacco with his finger, and lit up! Damn, that mess smelled like he was burning human hair and rubber bands! And that wasn't the worst part!

When finished stinking up the crummy, Paul took out a small penknife and scraped out the inside of the bowl of his pipe. Instead of knocking out the ash on the floor of the crummy with all the other spit, cigarette butts, and the like (now you know why they called it a crummy), he carefully put the rubbery scrapings from his pipe into a new can of Copenhagen! With the tip of his penknife, he carefully mixed the sludge from the scrapings of the pipe into the fresh Cope! Brother, you talk about tough! He literally ate the entire can of Cope! From then on, I gave Paul my utmost respect just because he was so damn tough. I bet when he died, there wasn't one coyote in the forest tough enough to eat him. ...

The next day I was going to show everyone on the job just how tough I was. It seemed as if everyone chewed, smoked, or did both on the job. No smoking in the forest, mind you, because of the fire danger, but in the crummy or on the dirt of the landing. Smoking in the crummy was a real treat. ... The inside air was nothing but a blue haze of pipe and cigarette smoke and flying tobacco spit. On the way home the previous evening, I had figured, "when in Rome, do as the Romans do." Stopping off at Boyd's Super Market, I bought a pouch of Red Man chewing tobacco. Now, to you unwashed, that brand is like chewing gum! It is for wimps, but it was a start in what I thought was a *real* man's world. ... The next day found me proudly taking a big mouthful of the sweet-tasting and great-smelling chewing tobacco. Almost instantly, because of the sweetness, my mouth filled with tobacco juice. Being "Mr. Big Stuff," I kept my mouth full of the juice as I headed over to a log to set a choker, figuring I would set the choker and then spit (no use working in one's own spit). I slid the nubbin of the choker under the log, and *whooom*, up flew a cloud of angry, and I do mean *angry*, yellow jackets! These little stinging bastards live in a nest in the ground and are about the size of a honeybee. On a gentle day, they are meaner than a car-hit owl, and it goes downhill from there. ... You won't even know you have discovered their nest until they have swarmed all over you, causing all kinds of trouble. They can sting their targets numerous times with a reusable stinger! I had a faceful of those little bastards, and the rest went down the front of my shirt, up my pant legs, and all over my neck and arms before I could say "boo"! Down that mountain I came like a jet rocket! Slapping them off my face and body, I ran until they got tired of stinging the hell out of me and went back to defend their nest. I was a mess. I must have had several hundred stings all over my body, which in minutes made me feel sick as hell. However, not as sick as when I discovered that my mouthful of chewing tobacco and spit was nowhere to be found. I soon discovered where that mess had gone, if my guts were any indicator. ... I had swallowed the whole damn thing! Man, you talk about broadcast puking. You had a world champion in me if you measured the distance of the spew! I was one of the sickest chaps you ever saw. God, I wanted to die. Then I heard a cat returning from the landing, and that meant get my butt back to work! I don't have good memories about the rest of that afternoon. Nordt, Paul, and the other new cat skinner just laughed their tail ends off at the green, big stud of a football player. Come quitting time, I wasn't much better, but I knew I would live. I don't remember how far I flung the rest of that pouch of Red Man chewing tobacco, but it went at least a mile into the canyon below. I hoped the deer enjoyed eating it.

Finishing the summer, I quit my job in the woods just a few days before school started. I had made a pile of money, I had toughened up my body to rock hard, and I had met some damn nice folks, not to mention worked in a location as close to heaven as one can get on earth. Suffice it to say, I grew a lot that summer, both physically and mentally.

The following summer I approached Cal Cole and asked for my old job back. Giving me a hearty handshake, he told me to be at the shop next Monday. When I showed up for work I was assigned a new job as a rigger with my own cat and crew. As I soon discovered, I had a first-time choker setter and cat skinner, so I stayed busy breaking both of them in as well as getting our allotment of logs skidded down the mountain. One thing I remember that summer is the general size of the logs we hauled out. More than once I would hook up two chokers on one thirty-two-foot log and have to use one D-8 pulling and one D-8 pushing to get it out of the woods. And the giant Track Loader had all it could do to lift logs that size onto a logging truck. In fact, many times the Track Loader would lift one end onto the logging truck and then lift the other end. Many a logging truck went out of the forest that summer with just a one-log load! I remember one thirty-two foot section of a Douglas fir having 11,247 board feet of lumber in it! Just like a redwood log. I think those days with timber that size (other than redwoods) are long gone. ...

Over the next several summers, I eventually worked my way up to a cat skinner. The summer after my sophomore year in college was my last in the woods. From that time on, as a wildlife management student, I worked for various federal agencies during the summers to gain additional practical experience. That last summer in the woods as a logger, I was skinning cat and loving it. There is nothing quite like pushing twenty-five tons of power wherever you want to go. But all good things must come to an end, and Cal Cole and I had a long talk on my last day of work. He thanked me for my long and good service to him and the company. However, he told me never to come back because if I did, there would be no work there for me. Hurt at that revelation, I asked, "Why?" I knew I had done a good job and earned my keep.

Seeing the hurt, Cal said, "Look around you, Terry. All you see are men with a dead-end job. They work when they can and then gather in their 'rocking-chair' payments when there is no work because of the winter snows. They will die here, many never realizing their full potential. That is not for you, son, so leave while you have all your fingers and bones intact and don't look back." With that, he handed me a plain envelope with instructions not to open it until I got home, shook my hand, turned, and walked away. There were tears in that old man's eyes, and that was the last time I saw him alive. There were tears in my eyes that day too. Another memory and milestone. ...

Still feeling a little dejected, I hitched up with my ride home and left the logging industry forever. I was dating Donna in those days, so I raced home, showered, and made ready to go out with her. Mom was starting to wash my clothes and ran across a crumpled plain envelope in my shirt pocket. "What is this, son?" she asked.

"I don't know, Mom. Cal Cole gave it to me and told me not to open it until I got home."

Mom handed me the envelope, and I opened it. To my surprise, there were three crisp $100 bills in it and a note that read, "Go far, son, and do us proud." It dawned on me that Cal had taken me under his wing in order to help me make the most out of my years in the business. That finally became clear in conversations we had had months and years before, and the job changes almost every month so I could learn and earn more money for college. A man with little or no education helping a kid who wanted to help himself ... a kid who would have made one hell of a logger, except that he was destined for different things.

I did go far, and if Cal were still living, I know I would have made him proud!

9

Forest Fires I Have Known

The Mosquito Creek Fire

TOOT-TOOT-TOOT went the whistle on the Washington Track Loader at the landing. What the hell? I thought. Members of the woods crew had been taught that three toots on the Track Loader whistle meant we were to head for the landing posthaste. *Toot-toot-toot* went the whistle again, and this time I didn't need an invite to get moving. Down the hill I trotted, falling in behind my rigger, whose stubby legs were just a-churnin', kicking up little dust clouds as he went. As we passed our skid cats coming up the hill, my rigger stopped and gave them the news regarding the emergency whistle since the cat skinners couldn't possible hear anything over the roaring sounds of their 'dozers. Both cat skinners immediately turned their machines around, slipped them into higher gears, and hauled ass, banging and clanging down the mountainside. *Toot-toot-toot* went the whistle again. Careful to watch where I put my feet so I didn't roll an ankle or fall and break something, I hammered downhill like a man possessed, vaulting logs, brush piles, and large boulders along the way. This was the first time I had heard the emergency whistle, and I figured they didn't blow it unless they had a damn good reason.

Approaching the landing, I could see a crowd of men gathered next to our man-wagons. Cal Cole was in the middle of the crew, obviously giving instructions. Not wanting to miss anything, I really turned on the burners and promptly ran an unseen and partially buried limb up my pants leg. At the speed I was going, that was all it took. I rolled ass over teakettle for the last few steps onto the landing, spilling me in a huge dust cloud in front of God and everybody! Much hooting and laughter was my reward. About then two Forest Service trucks towing lowboys (trailers used to haul heavy equipment such as bulldozers) rolled up onto the landing. Behind them came six of our company's trucks, also pulling lowboys. Man, something big was happening, I thought as I joined the crowd gathered around the boss. Another lowboy approached the landing carrying a mess of 'dozer blades that appeared to be for our skid cats. The Track Loader operator took off at a trot for his monster machine and fired it up. Swinging the massive boom around, he dropped its main line to the ground so the hookers could remove the log-loading apparatus from the end of the cable. They hooked up another attachment for heavy lifting of a different sort; then the boom was swung over to the lowboy carrying the dozer blades. Hurriedly a skid cat rolled into view, moving under the booms of the Track Loader. The two hookers hooked the cable onto a blade on the lowboy, hoisted it off its trailer, and carefully placed it next to the front of the skid cat. Several mechanics started hooking up the blade while several more cats slid over to the lowboy carrying the blades and formed a line. It was obvious they had been here before. Just as fast as one cat could be hooked up with a blade, turning it into a bulldozer instead of a bladeless skid cat, it moved off and the process was repeated. The cats with blades moved over to a company fuel and grease truck parked at the edge of the landing, where they were refueled, quickly greased, and loaded onto a waiting lowboy.

As a new group arrived at the landing, Cal called for our attention. "We have a major forest fire in the Mosquito Creek area, and the Forest Service has called up this entire logging crew and a number of our cats to help fight it. Load up into the man-wagons and we will soon be en route to the fire. When we get there the Forest Service will sign us in, issue our firefighting gear, and deploy us on the fire lines. Any questions?" Hearing none, Cal said, "Load up. This fire may take a few days or weeks before it is under control, so be prepared for the long haul." With that, we loaded into the man-wagons and waited for a Forest Service escort to lead us to the Mosquito Creek fire camp. The cats and our grease monkeys (men who serviced the equipment) would follow just as soon as they got everything squared away, loaded, and chained down.

You may be aware from watching news coverage during the 2001 and 2002 fire seasons out West that there are professional state, tribal, and federal fire crews who fight forest fires, usually not loggers. However, in the 1950s when timber fires occurred, loggers, lumbermen (people working in the lumber mills), and people off the streets were about the only readily available pools of manpower the Forest Service had (women were not allowed on the fire lines in those days, unlike today's fire crews). If the fire got really serious, the state would sometimes send in convicts and the National Guard to help as well. However, it was usually the woods crews who hit the fire lines first because those men were usually woods wise and physically hardened for the rigors associated with working on a fire line. I don't remember many professional firefighters in those days other than a few Zuni Indian crews brought in from the reservations and some Forest Service firefighters attached to their fire trucks. In fact, until too many people died of heart attacks, the Forest Service would often stop all highway traffic in the immediate vicinity of the fire, and if you were a healthy male (just about anybody with a heartbeat) and someone else could drive the car home, you were impressed into firefighting service. You might be wearing dress clothes and low-slung shoes—it didn't make any difference! The Forest Service would issue you the clothing you needed from the commissary in the fire camp.

Hot dog! I thought. I am going to fight a timber fire! This would be my first, and boy, was I excited! You worked many long hours on the fire lines and could earn pay at the rate of time and a half. Then I noticed a calm that had settled over the older men. They did not seem very excited, time-and-a-half pay or not. In fact, they almost seemed saddened. I couldn't figure out why, but I was smart enough to keep my mouth shut, watch, and learn. I would soon learn the reasons for the somber mood among the more experienced men.

After several hot hours in the lurching man-wagons, we finally arrived at the fire camp. Glad to be out of the stiflingly hot, strong-smelling man-wagon, I jumped out to have a look at the camp. What a zoo! Hundreds of men were hurriedly moving every which way. Long lines were standing in front of a tent to sign in. Other long lines stood in front of supply tents waiting to receive firefighting tools, canteens, hard hats, gloves, and, for those impressed right off the highways, the appropriate clothing. In another part of camp were vehicles of every sort: trucks, pickups, bulldozers streaming out of camp toward the fire lines, fire trucks, tankers carrying water to refill the fire trucks, company water trucks to wet down dusty roads, fuel trucks, hardware trucks carrying every firefighting tool from their stores in town, grocery trucks loaded with every type of food imaginable, ambulances, helicopters buzzing low overhead, biplanes (N3N Stearmans), firebombers roaring overhead carrying borate to the fire, and everything else from the devil's kitchen to add to the mayhem. Chainsaws roared as they were tested. In another part of camp were the outdoor kitchens: huge portable propane stoves with plate-steel cooking surfaces capable of cooking fifty steaks or twenty dozen eggs at a time, lined up under nearby trees. Mounds of bread, cakes, and pastries; boxes of candy bars; sack lunches by the small mountain; barrels of iced soda pop; cartons of milk (didn't have bottled water in those days); watermelons; and canned fruit juices surrounded the cooking area in organized profusion. In another part of camp a bulldozer was hurriedly clearing out a flat from the brush and old woods debris for the men to sleep on when they came off shift (in those days that meant sleeping in the dirt in disposable paper sleeping bags).

"Terry, get your ass over here," came my rigger's voice through the fog of my interest in the fire camp. Looking around, I found Nordt standing in line waiting to be signed in by Forest Service administrator types and assigned a job on the fire lines. Hustling over, I took my place behind my friend. While waiting, I had a chance to continue looking over the area. We were deep in a coniferous forest composed of many stately virgin ponderosa pine, sugar pine, Douglas fir, and incense cedars, huge trees spaced as thick as the hair on a dog's back and taller than the clouds. The landscape was almost straight up and down, typical of the geography around the Feather River Canyon country. It seemed as if the Forest Service had taken over the few pieces of flat ground. Off to the west, my eyes spied the culprit causing all the stir: an enormous plume of white-and-black smoke angrily soared up to fifty thousand feet before leveling off like a giant anvil. The size and height of the plume spoke to the danger and power that lay underneath! The fire camp was several miles away, yet the scope and degree of what we faced had a humbling effect on anyone looking skyward.

Moving through the check-in line, I was assigned a shovel as my weapon of choice. Next we were sent to the supply tent and issued metal, already filled gallon canteens of water, heavy leather gloves, files (to sharpen our axes, shovels, and McClouds—a hoe-rake combination firefighting tool), and small first aid kits. With that and a warning to be careful around the area's many rattlesnakes, off we went to the outdoor chow hall. Standing in line (we did a lot of that in those days), I got a close-up look at what was considered standard firefighting grub. Mine consisted of one platter full of fried spuds, one platter stacked high with five steaks, one with a dozen eggs (sunny side up), a quart of buttermilk (thick with butterfat in those days), and a watermelon right off a semi (I could *really* eat in those days!). Heading for the base of a pine tree, I sat down and polished it all off with little difficulty! Not knowing what lay ahead of me in the grits department, I wanted to make sure I could last through whatever the Forest Service threw at me.

"Meadow Valley logging crew over here!" yelled a voice. Grabbing a sack lunch (made in those days by local groups to earn money—consisting of two bologna sandwiches, a piece of fruit, a candy bar, and several cookies) and my shovel, I hustled over to the spot now crowded with other company loggers. "This is Jim Johnson, your Forest Service crew boss," announced a spit of a man wearing a Forest Service uniform. "He will lead you on the fire line and will be responsible for how the fire is fought in his sector. His word is law! Any questions?" Hearing none he said, "All right, you men board up on those National Guard trucks over there." He pointed to four huge National Guard 6 × 6's. Those things can climb a tree if necessary! It was ironic that the one I rode in that day was driven by my future brother-in-law, Dee Barbea. The men and I ambled over to the trucks and loaded up with a lot of good-natured but nervous chatter and clanking of tools. In no time the trucks wound through the forest on a hastily made dirt road toward the plume of smoke still boiling skyward from the canyons far below. As we got closer to our destination, the men grew silent as the air temperature started creeping higher. Soon, over the straining truck engines, we could hear the roar and crackling made by a very hot timber fire. A timber fire is, plain and simply, hell on earth! My first glimpse was of a blazing orange monster wall of flame coming our way from the canyons below! Preceding the wall of flame were dozens of trees exploding with a loud *whoosh* before the fire even got close to them.

The trucks lurched to a stop with such haste that all of us standing up in the back were thrown forward in a heap. Quickly untangling ourselves, we bailed out to the commands of our forest ranger directing us to hurry up and gather around! The heat was becoming intense as it swept up the canyon below our position. The smoke was choking thick, and the burning embers swept along by the blast furnace below were flying through the air like so many angry bees. When one of those embers landed on your skin, you instantly got burned; if it landed on your shirt, an instantly burned hole was your reward. It didn't take long before everyone was swatting themselves. Our trucks hurriedly fled the scene, leaving a vacant feeling in every one of us. "Form a line across this area," our ranger yelled over the roar of the fire as he gestured directions with his hand. Quickly forming a line about one hundred yards long and off to one side of the roaring monster (one doesn't get in front of the fire but to the sides to pinch it off), our shovels, Pulaskis (a combination ax on one side and flat pick on the other), and McClouds fairly flew as we tried to build a twenty-yard-wide firebreak down to the mineral soil to stop the advance of the hungry fire. That was accomplished in short order as we dug in conjunction with three powerful D-8 bulldozers working side by side like combines in a wheat field, pushing up a roll of soil from the forest floor. The roar was louder now, accompanied by a scorching hot, skin-drying, eye-stinging wind. Hot embers constantly filled the air like millions of tiny stinging bees as streams of frightened animals began to move by us with no other thought than escape. Two mule deer fleeing the wall of flames and seeing the line of men and 'dozers frantically working above them froze for a moment, then turned and ran back into the wall of fire, exploding into flames as they did! I had never seen burning deer before.

By now the heat and smoke was so intense that we lowered our heads into its flow, letting our hard hats take the brunt of the superheated gases and ash passing by. God, this is really getting hot, I thought, noticing that the legs of my jeans were beginning to smoke! Soon little fires broke out behind us, and many of the men broke from the main fire line in vain attempts to put them out so we wouldn't be surrounded by two walls of flame. The roar heard as we arrived had now turned into the sound of a thousand freight trains all howling to be the loudest! Glancing over at our Forest Service supervisor, I couldn't help but see anxiety written all over his face as more and more little fires started behind our hastily drawn fire line.

"*Fall back!*" he yelled, and our battle line hurriedly dissolved. Men hurried to the rear of our first line, as did the clanking bulldozers. But no one broke in mass panic, just a hasty retreat and reorganization! To panic during moments like that would only result in one bursting into flame like the mule deer. Forming a second line on a ridge running at angles to the edge of the fire, the 'dozers and men frantically tried to build another fire line and remain hooked to two other fire crews on our right and left.

Whoosh! Several trees behind our new lines blew up into roaring white-hot torches! The trees next to them did the same, and soon we had fire on two sides plus one in the treetops, and damn hot ones at that. *"Run!"* shouted several men, including our fire boss. The words "crown fire" raced up and down our fire line, and in an instant everyone was running for their lives, me included. Damn, I thought as I hurdled a log, I wish I hadn't eaten that whole watermelon for dinner! Moving across the ground like a striped-assed ape, I hauled my tail end farther to one side and out of that inferno. My clothes were smoking, my eyes were so dry from the intense heat that I could hardly blink, and my hair was starting to curl and smoke under my hard hat. Following that mob of men, I managed to keep my shovel but lost my canteen. I never did figure out what happened to my sack lunch. Running until I got to a place out of the line of the fire, I stopped and gulped in great mouthfuls of air. Air that was cooler so I would not choke every time I tried to breathe because it was so damn hot! Other men gathered on our hillside and once again, without any direction from our fire boss, began building a fire line down to the mineral soil. Shoveling as hard as I could, I began to realize that this firefighting shit was pretty serious business. Now I knew why the older men who had fought forest fires before had been so quiet in the man-wagons when they found that we were going onto the fire line. Two of our 'dozers (the third had been forced over to another crew when the fire breached our lines) joined us, and we made the dirt and forest-floor duff really fly! The fire, having sent us on our way earlier like a bunch of fleeing African meerkats, tired of that game and went off in another direction, consuming everything in its path. In so doing, it split our three fire crews, and the groups did not get back together for another fifty-eight hours! Yep, that was how long I worked on my first fire before we were relieved by a fresh crew. Fifty-eight hours with no food and only a gallon of water (taken from a man injured on the line who was hauled off for treatment). I guess you could say things got a little crazy. ... After that stint I was kind of glad I had eaten a ton of Forest Service grub back in the fire camp.

The Mosquito Creek fire consumed another thirteen thousand acres of virgin timber before it tired of destroying such a fine forest and lay down. It finally died out after several heavy afternoon thunderstorms aided our puny efforts to slow and then stop the consuming monster. I made a ton of money on that fire and earned every damn dime of it! I also grew up a bunch when I realized that firefighting was a very dangerous and sad business. Dangerous, well, that speaks for itself. Sad because there is very little that is positive about the loss of timber, brush, wildlife, soil fertility, and the other havoc wreaked by such fires. Throw in the costs of fighting an out-of-control giant; follow that with the lost revenues in surrounding lumber communities because of destroyed timber, erosion, and reduced economy; add the recreational losses; and you are starting to get a partial picture of a forest fire's destruction. In small comparison to the other losses, my arms afterward were full of little water blisters from the heat and flying embers. I lost my eyebrows, eyelashes, and arm hair, and my shirt finally fell off in rags after getting so damn hot. Last but not least, I looked like the old-time blackface actor Al Jolsen and smelled like what horses leave on the highway after a Fourth of July parade. I spent five days on that fire before being relieved by a fresh crew of loggers and sent home to clean up. I remember I was so dirty that my mom made me take a bath out on the lawn with the garden hose *before* I came in the house and took another one in the tub! She threw my clothes away. The only thing I saved were my $100 pair of White boots! Oh well, my clothes probably wouldn't have fit anyway considering how much I grew during that first firefighting experience. ...

The Lites Creek Fire

IT WAS A HOT, dry July Saturday afternoon, and I was getting ready to go to the movies with my old school chum Ran Slaten. *Wheeeeeee* went our local mill firehouse siren, and I looked all around to see if I could spot any smoke. *Holy crap!* Many miles down the Feather River Canyon toward Oroville was a plume of smoke boiling thousands of feet into the air. A forest fire and a big one, I thought as tingles of excitement and nervousness ran through me. Later I learned that the fire had been set by sparks from the Union Pacific locomotives locked in dual tandems (four engines) as they struggled up the Feather River Canyon pulling a one-hundred-car train. I hurriedly called Ran and canceled our afternoon plans. Slipping into my work clothes and grabbing extra socks and shorts, I slipped on my hard hat and sprinted out the door. My dad was doing the same, and the two of us jumped into his Jeep pickup and headed down to the local mill. This was a common practice in small mountain-town lumbering communities. The forests in Plumas County were not only the sources of our livelihood but also the places in which we lived and recreated. Able-bodied men didn't have to be told to get it in gear to protect their homeland.

As we drove into the mill yard, I could see other lumbermen streaming in from all points of the compass. In the middle of the yard was the mill boss standing beside a Forest Service representative. It was obvious the Forest Service had a huge fire on its hands and, once again, was turning to the local lumbermen and loggers for firefighting manpower. About then several large green Forest Service buses drove up, and without being told the men began loading up for what was sure to be another "hurrah" with a forest fire. And from the size and height of the smoke plume, I thought, this one is a real monster!

Down the Feather River Canyon on state Highway 70 we went and into a fire camp just off the highway below the Quincy-Greenville turnoff. This time, instead of signing up as a common laborer, I signed up as a timber faller (one who cuts down trees). I had brought my dad's big Homelite chainsaw and figured I was going to make some real money without killing myself! *It is amazing just how dumb youth can be. ...* "Faller with personal chainsaw," I announced to the timekeeper when it came my time to report in.

"That will be $5 an hour for the saw and $4.97 an hour for you," he announced without looking up and seeing a pretty green kid standing before him.

Hot dog, I quietly yelled inside. That was the kind of money I needed to make if I was going to pay my way through college!

"Wait outside by the supply tent for your swampers" (helpers), the timekeeper mumbled, sounding already bored with his work and probably mad about his lost weekend. When I stepped outside, several of my logging buddies, seeing me with a chainsaw and knowing I was nothing more than a kid who was long on guts and short on brains, winked knowingly. My grin returned those sly winks. I figured I had cut a blizzard of wood for my dad at an early age with a chainsaw, so timber-falling in a forest fire couldn't be all that bad. ... However, I was soon to discover that falling timber was a *real man's work*, and I was only halfway there!

"Mister, we are your swampers," chirped a meek voice from behind me. Turning, I recognized several high school buddies from a mill town down in the canyon who were doing the same thing I was: lying about our ages so we could earn some real money. We had just enough knowledge about falling timber on a forest fire and swamping to be dangerous! "Hey, guys," I said as we recognized and warmly greeted each other. "Ready to do some cutting and gutting and show some of these older men what it is all about?" I asked with a big-assed grin.

"Let her rip," said Jimmy as Ronald smiled and nodded.

"Let's get the rest of our gear and get on the line, then," I said. We went to the supply tent and drew a mess of chains for the saw, chain-saw files, axes, fuel cans with premixed fuels (oil and gasoline), wedges (used to jack a tree off a bound-up chainsaw), first aid kit, and canteens.

Soon the three of us were lurching along in a National Guard 6 × 6 truck with a mixed load of firefighters from other area logging crews. Cross-country we went, climbing hills through the forest (no roads) that were so steep, I began to get concerned about flipping over backward and being crushed! But the military drivers knew their rigs, and we eventually got to a ridge far enough away but still overlooking one hell of a roaring monster in the canyons and on the hillsides below. "Ground crews form up with the cats, and you fallers over here," yelled the Forest Service fire boss. Staggering under the weight of my saw and a load of other equipment, I walked uphill to where the fire boss stood. "You three, follow that cat and its crew. I want every tree next to their line on the fire side dropped back onto the oncoming fire. I don't want any trees becoming torches right next to the fire line aiding the spread of the fire behind us. Got that?" he yelled, raising his voice partly out of the thrill of firefighting and partly out of fear. "There will also be another falling crew with you, so try to keep the trees from falling on each other," he added.

Off we went. Falling in behind a D-8 bulldozer as it cleared a fire-break, I let the other faller tackle the first big tree needing to be dropped over the ridgeline into the oncoming fire. Walking along the firebreak, I took the next tree, which just happened to be a huge and very old sugar pine. Looking up quickly to see if it held any "widow makers" (limbs hung up in other limbs above my head that could fall and injure or kill me), I began my undercut, designed to help topple the tree over the ridge away from the men on the fire line. Then I began my back cut. The sawdust literally flew as the sharp chain cut through several hundred years' worth of growth to the time the tree was a sapling and out the other side. Soon one of my swampers yelled, "Down the hill," as the gap between the tree and stump slowly widened, the trunk cracked, and the tree rolled off into history. Hustling over to the next tree needing to be dropped over the ridge, I repeated the process, dropping a towering ponderosa pine into the draw below. What a loss of good saw timber, I thought as I trotted over to the next tree to be dropped into the oncoming, all-consuming fire. Soon the sweat began to roll off me as tree after tree along the firebreak was dropped over the ridgeline into the onrushing fire far below in the canyon.

After fifty minutes of such hard labor, my saw ran out of fuel, sputtered, and stopped just as I threw the kill switch. Sitting down to rest, I let my two swampers put a file to the chain, refuel the saw, grease the bar sprocket, and refill the automatic oiler. The break felt good as I let the sweat evaporate off me and stretched my tiring and cramping back (we didn't have anything like Gatorade in those days, only salt pills). This hard work in a bent-over position had its drawbacks, I thought. Then my mind went to the almost $10 an hour I was making ($8 an hour more than I made as a logger), and I felt better. ... Soon Jim and Ron had my saw serviced, and back to work I went, dropping tree after tree as I worked my way down the ridge toward a high point on the far hillside some hundred yards away. By now the air was getting hotter and filling with burning embers. However, I had my hands full safely dropping the towering trees and paid little attention to the flying sparks. Stopping the spot fires on the other side of our fire line was the worry of the fifty Zuni Indians on our fire crew and the cat skinners, I thought as I kept the chain whirling through the wood.

The fire was getting closer, and along with the burning embers came another problem. The upslope winds from the fire were starting to pick up and howl as they swept up and over our positions. They whipped the towering trees around more and more, making them dangerous to cut down. You had to be careful in timing your cutting or the saw would get pinched on the stump when the weight of the tree shifted with the violently changing winds, stopping the chain. If that happened, you could have a dangerous tree just barely hanging on the stump and were helpless to cut any further. In the worst-case scenario, your tree might fall back onto the fire crew, who were not paying attention to what you were doing! So as the winds began to howl, my swampers would shout out instructions to me on when to saw and when to pull the saw out of the tree. *Damn,* I thought, *this falling business is getting a little more complex than I figured. Certainly not like cutting wood with Dad!* But I continued using all my skills (plus the new ones I was rapidly gaining), and the trees continued safely falling into the canyon below. However, the smoke was getting extremely thick and the air hotter than all get-out. That combination forced the other falling team and us out along the ridgeline to stay in air where we could see and breathe yet still do our jobs. Soon we lost sight of our ground crew and the bulldozer due to the heavy smoke pouring over the saddle in the middle of our ridge! Unbeknownst to us, our supporting fire crew had been turned back by the very same fierce heat, smoke, and winds.

Then below us on the fire side of the canyon, I heard the familiar *whoosh* of a fire starting to crown (racing across the treetops, sometimes as fast as forty miles per hour)! The other faller and his swamper heard it also. Standing there for a split second, the five of us stared at the horror developing below us. *A wall of fire was now racing our way!* We started to run back toward our old fire line and some sort of safety but soon found ourselves cut off by sixty-foot-high sheets of flame! Running back again, we all dropped our gear as we sprinted toward the safety of a small rocky point overlooking the Feather River far below. That is, all except me. I didn't drop my dad's saw. He had worked hard to save enough money to buy the damned thing, and I just couldn't leave it there on the hillside to blow up when the fire hit it (I didn't know that the Forest Service would replace it if it was lost). So I ran with my cumbersome saw, following the others to the small point of rocks at the end of the ridge. We finally reached it only to find ourselves surrounded on all sides by the fire! Some flames were at a greater distance than others, but all were coming our way! It was pretty obvious that it was just a matter of time before we were burned to death! We slid over to the far side of the point, where the fire still had a ways to come from below to get us. At least here, for a short while anyway, we could still breathe air that wasn't filled with smoke and burning cinders. We tried to dig holes in the rocky ground to lie in and perhaps survive the flames, but to no avail. The rocky point was just that. And with nothing but our bare hands, any digging in the rocky soil was futile.

Then salvation came in the form of a small Bell helicopter passing by. It was a Forest Service contractor who had been flying injured firefighters off the line and scouting out the fire's perimeter. Seeing the five of us perched out on that point of rocks waving our shirts like crazy with the fires burning below brought him humming right over. "Get in, quick," yelled the pilot as he hovered near where we stood! "I will take the two smallest first. One in the seat and one in the rescue basket. Hurry! I am low on fuel." Jim and Ron needed no further prodding in light of our circumstances and jumped in. As Jim fastened his seatbelt, Ron lay down in the rescue basket and the chopper lifted off in one smooth, flowing motion. Drifting over the edge of the Feather River Canyon from our rocky point, it dropped at a dizzying speed to Highway 70 far below. Soon I could hear it coming back, and none too soon to my way of thinking. Smoke was beginning to roll over our ridge in such clouds that it was getting hard to see and breathe. Zipping up out of the canyon and over our point of rocks, the pilot swung his chopper in a wide circle and came back over us. "Hurry, get in!" he yelled as he struggled to hover in the smoke and violent updrafts coming out of the canyon below. Being the largest of the three remaining men on the mountain, I told the other two to get in, and they didn't have to be told a second time. *Zoom*, off the rocky point the chopper dropped with one man in the seat and the other lying in the rescue basket (that had to be a ride in and of itself!). Soon I lost sight of them in the increasing smoke. For the longest time I heard nothing, and I began to worry as I recalled the pilot's words about being low on fuel. The flying burning embers, intense smoke, and heat were becoming a serious problem. Taking out my handkerchief, I urinated on it to get it wet and placed it over my nose and mouth, hoping it would help me breathe. Soon even that measure had run its course as the handkerchief dried out. I began to cough and my clothes began to emit little wisps of smoke! This is not a nice place to be, I remember thinking; yeah, this being a faller is sure easy stuff!

Then I heard it—or did I? *Yes,* it was the sound a chopper makes when struggling to gain altitude flying straight up out from a canyon floor several hundred yards below. By now there was so much smoke and updraft that I wondered if the pilot would see me, much less be able to hover. But to his credit, he bored right through the dense smoke. I remember that he made the nicest curls in the smoke with the tips of his rotors. Then, narrowly missing a pine tree because of the tremendous updrafts and crossdrafts, he swung back around and came straight at me. "Get in, I am almost out of fuel," he yelled (I found out later his spare tank had malfunctioned and would not pass its fuel to the pump)! As he swung by, I reached for his skid to pull him down and steady the craft, only to have a violent updraft rip it out of my hand. The chopper disappeared over the other side of the ridge almost on its side, and I fully expected to hear it crash. But the good Lord was still watching over me, and all of a sudden out of the smoke back that brave pilot came! This time when he drifted by I didn't drag my hind end. ... Tossing my dad's saw into the rescue basket, I lunged in alongside. Come hell or high water, I was going this time. ... The chopper dropped slightly with the addition of my weight, then lifted off and fell over the edge of the canyon plunging pell-mell for the highway below.

"Get in," he yelled as I tried to struggle from the heaving rescue basket into the front seat. However, we were heaving and pitching so much that I was afraid to risk a jump from the basket and have the chopper disappear from under me. Standing in the basket, I reached in, grabbed the seat, and hung on for dear life. At that moment the chopper's engine sputtered and ran out of fuel! Down we plunged in a shallow glide as the pilot fought the controls trying to set up an autorotation. Closer and closer we zoomed toward the highway below with its cars blocked on two ends, allowing us a small emergency landing strip in the middle. Down, down, down we plunged, and if I had been strapped into the seat, the ride might not have been so bad. But here I was just hanging on, half in and half out of the chopper, and I knew damn good and well what would happen when we hit! Saying a quick prayer, I dug my fingers into the seat and hung on for all I was worth! At the last second, the pilot pulled the chopper back up into the air, and then we fell maybe ten feet to the highway. *Kaboom* went the skids as we hit the road. One skid folded slightly, tossing us a little sideways. The chainsaw and I sailed out of the chopper and onto the highway. I landed on my feet, then bounced and thumped to the ground backward, taking the hide off one elbow and banging up my hind end. *Pow* went the saw as it landed right beside my head, bending its bar and busting the chain in the process. Other than that, it and I were both all right! Pretty soon the fallers and swampers from our rocky point were excitedly talking all at once about our recent experiences. Man, it was good to be off that part of the mountain, I thought as I looked upward. The point was now engulfed in flames, and I could hear the quiet *pop-pop* of the fuel cans and chainsaw fuel tank left up on that mountain exploding in the burning hell.

The Forest Service eventually came to pick us up, taking us back up on the mountain to continue our work. A trip to the supply tent at the fire camp replaced the bar on my chainsaw, and back to falling I went. Jim and Ronald had had enough with the close call and wild chopper ride and chose not to return to the fire. The chopper was eventually refueled on the highway and flew back to the Quincy airport for minor repairs to its skid, but not before I got that pilot's name and address so I could send him a bottle of the best whiskey I could afford (and have my dad purchase with my money, since I was still under age).

My adventures didn't end there. Later that evening I was still falling timber back into the path of the fire. The tree I was cutting was a big

old Douglas fir that was already partially on fire! Cutting like a banshee while my two swampers watched for falling debris from the tree's
canopy, I kept feeling what I thought were hot embers landing on the
back of my neck. For a long time I just ignored the stinging in favor of
paying attention to what I was doing. The tree had a rotten core (making it even more dangerous to fall), and I had to be really careful as to
which way it fell. Finally after about the tenth stinging "ember," I
reached up to rub my neck and pulled my hand away *filled with honey-
bees!* Taking off at a dead run, I hurdled about a four-foot-high log,
tearing out the crotch of my black jeans! Finally outrunning my stinging adversaries, I stopped and surveyed the damage. I had a slightly
swollen neck and a mass of busted pride considering my hind end was
hanging out for the whole world to see. Letting the fire in the tree go
as far as I dared, I hurried back and cut like a son of a gun. Again the
bees, hearing a chainsaw going at the bottom of their tree, started circling around and down to get to their adversary. This time I got it done
before too many bees had discovered me, and down the tree went, bees,
honey, and all, into the fire. But not before I had been nailed several
more times by the survivors. Before I finished my shift I came to grief
twice more because of not having a crotch in my pants, both times
when I stepped into a yellow jackets' nest (they nest in the ground).
Let's just say it was not a pleasant experience, especially in the dark
when I couldn't see them until it was too late. ...

Coming off the fire line the next morning, I saw to the care of my
saw and swampers. Then off to the supply tent I went. As luck would
have it, they did not have any pants in stock that were my size. My next
stop was the first aid tent, where I was treated for numerous stings on
my unmentionables. Not to be outdone by a bunch of bugs, I got one
hell of an idea that was to later bear the bitterest kind of fruit. Taking
my pants off in the first aid tent, I took a lot of large safety pins and
pinned the crotch of my pants back together (they didn't have any
pants my size in the supply tent). Then, *not being a dummy,* I took a
roll of heavy tape and taped over the area held together by the safety
pins, inside and out. Now my pants were fastened together and covered
heavily with tape to prevent further mishaps.

Going back on the fire line that evening, I again found myself in the
middle of a hot zone falling timber back into the fire. Tree after tree fell
as the sweat just rolled off me from my exertions and the heat of the fire.
Cutting one sugar pine with a snaggy top, I set about reducing it to fuel

for the oncoming fire and a stump. Both swampers kept watch for falling limbs and other burning materials as I cut away at the base of the tree. *Wham-wham-wham*, in quick succession I got hit in the ear, neck, and cheek by bald-faced hornets! They lived in a nest high in the tree and were already pissed at having a fire next door. Then when someone started cutting down their home, that did it! Down the tree they came, and the first three zeroed in on me as nicely as you please. Hitting the kill switch on the saw, I took off running for my life. Being hit by a bald-faced hornet is almost as bad as being hit by Sonny Liston! Approaching a small but deep ravine, I made an Olympic-sized jump, clearing it nicely. However, upon landing, I discovered that I had a major problem: my wide-legged jump had stretched my jeans to their limit. *All the safety pins had opened up and upon landing were waiting for me, letting me know they could sting just as fiercely as the hornets!* Let me tell you, I was not sure what was the worst: the hornets on the head or the fire in my crotch now that the pins had come undone! Suffice it to say that for the next several days I walked a lot like the old-time movie actor Walter Brennan. ...

The really nice experience about that fire was that when it was all over, I cleared over $1,800! That was the equivalent sum of five months' logging! As on every fire I fought, *I had earned every damned nickel of it!* That was the last time I ever used Dad's chainsaw on a forest fire.

The Bonta Ranch Fire

A RANCHER NOT USING his gray matter accounted for my next fire-fighting adventure. It seemed he was doing some blasting and in order to drive the blast downward had covered his explosive charge with an old mattress instead of mud or dirt. His blasting went off well, as did a million flaming parts of the mattress flung to the four corners of the dry forest. That bit of stupidity set off a forest fire near present-day Grizzly Creek and got the errant rancher a firefighting bill for over $1 million.

There used to be an old dairy ranch just east of Grizzly Creek off state Highway 70 where the Forest Service set up its fire camp for what was then called the Bonta Ranch fire. That fire camp sat pretty much where the new state rest stop now sits. The Meadow Valley logging crew, along with other Sierra Valley logging crews, was tapped to fight that fire. This time the terrain lent itself to heavy use of bulldozers and the Forest Service's new aerial battle plan. Instead of using the ancient N3N Stearman biplanes with their reduced loads of borate, it was now using World War II TBMs and TBFs carrying bentonite. Those aircraft could haul many more gallons of fire retardant than the old biplanes and, with their more powerful radial engines, could safely barrel into and out of almost any situation. Plus, bentonite proved to be a much better fire retardant than borate. These planes were being serviced at the Beckworth Airport, just a several-mile hop and jump from the fire. All those factors added up to a smaller forest fire of about ten thousand acres by the time all was said and done.

When our logging crew first arrived, we were assigned to the hot spots of the fire and worked about five days in and out of the rolling canyons in that capacity. Then the Forest Service brought us off that line and put us on mop-up for another three days. My first evening on mop-up, I was back in the fire camp to eat, refill my canteen, and return to the fire line with the rest of the logging crew. About that time, in drove three buses, modified with bars over all the windows, full of convict firefighting crews. Curious, I walked closer to get a better look. From one of the buses an inmate yelled, "Hey, look. We are on a farm. I wonder if the farmer has any daughters!"

Seeing an opportunity to set that lad straight, I said, "Yeah, he has several daughters. But you get to fooling around with them and you will get shot at."

There was a pause from the bus, and then that same voice said, "That won't be the first time we have been shot at, sonny."

With that shot across my bow, I retreated from being a smart-ass and returned to my logging crew. However, a new adventure was to meet me the next day.

Mop-up is fairly easy but dirty work. Basically, you work along the edge of the old fire line long after the fire has burned out to find any remaining hot spots and put them out. That way, if the winds come up, the fire can't restart from an old hot spot and spread to other parts of the forest. On that particular day, I saw our section boss approaching, leading twelve men. "Terry," he yelled, "got a minute?"

Stopping my activity of putting out a smoldering stump, I walked toward the Forest Service chap. "What's up?" I asked.

"I have a convict crew for you to supervise," he replied.

Now, just imagine that ... here I was, a snot-nosed kid, too young to work in the woods, vote, or buy booze, yet being placed in charge of twelve grown men, and convicts at that! "Are you sure you want me to do that?" I asked.

"You bet," he responded. "We are short men for a few days, and all of you loggers are going to have to pitch in so we can get this mess cleaned up. We have several more large timber fires starting up, and we need to get this one out so we can move you guys on to the next ones after a short break. In fact, there is a big one just starting up in the Tahoe-Truckee area, and we need to move you guys over there before it gets any bigger. So the quicker we get this one out the better." (The Tahoe-Truckee fire would eventually burn about thirty thousand acres.)

"Okay," I replied. "What do I have to do?"

"Just keep them working, and if they don't or you have any problems with any of them, let me know and they all will go back to their buses and back to the big house. They aren't supposed to have anything other than what they are carrying, and none of them can smoke or have smokes on the line. It seems cigarettes are a big exchange item with them in prison, so don't let them have any. [Cigarettes were a standard-issue item on the fire lines because almost everyone smoked in those days. They could be procured at the fire camp from the commissary tent.] You will be responsible for the next mile of line, and try to have it out by nightfall if possible."

"Yes, sir," I replied as he walked off with no more guidance than that. Looking over at my charges, I must have presented quite a picture. A green kid, dirty as all get-out from five days of firefighting, with a look of wonderment on my charcoal-covered face and a tightly latched hind end. There was an old guy (I later learned he was called "Pops" and was a respected ringleader of the bunch) at the head of the line, and the rest looked like hard cases to me. Most were built like brick outhouses (weight-lifting went on in prisons even in those days), many had scowls on their faces, and about half the crew were big, burly, angry-looking black men. That was a first for me. We had only about three black kids in the high school I attended, and they were all great guys. This bunch, however, looked like they could eat sawdust and crap out two-by-fours! Realizing the best defense was a good offense, I said, "All right, guys, let's spread out along this old fire line and put everything that is smoldering back into the burn for about twenty yards."

All the men looked at the old guy on the crew, and he gave them a nod. In minutes my crew was busy doing what I had asked. I positioned myself in the middle of the group, and soon all of us were sweating in the hot summer sun. Then Pops came over to me and asked if he could speak. "Sure, go ahead," I replied.

"Do you think there is a chance the men can have some canned fruit juice?" he asked.

Since everything was moving right along, I said, "Sure. Let me see if I can get someone going back to camp to bring us several cans." Shortly thereafter Jimmy Olds, one of my logger buddies, was going back to fire camp to get a wound dressed, and I asked him to procure some fruit juice for me. Soon we got into several stubborn hot spots, and I walked over to a small Oliver tractor sitting on the fire line, fired it up, and gave my crew the advantage of a piece of machinery to dig out the burning stumps. They all thought it was pretty slick that such a young kid could run a 'dozer, especially since it made their work easier!

About that time Jimmy came by carrying four large cans of various fruit juices. Handing them up to me on the cat, he turned and ambled up the hill back to his crew. I could see the convicts eyeing the ice-cold cans of juice and told them, "Finish this hot spot and we will open them up." Boy, you talk about incentive—the hot spot in the stumps was all but obliterated. Then Pops came up and asked if he could distribute the juice, and, not seeing any harm in it, I let him. It was pretty obvious that he was the real leader of this crew as he passed out cups of the juice to the thirsty men. It was also readily apparent that fruit juice was high on their list of desirables and, from the level of work I got out of them afterward (with one exception), was well worth the investment. From then on I saw to it that my crew had lots of canned fruit and fruit juice to consume.

I had one rather large problem—a *big* man with more muscles than any man ought to have who pretty much refused to work. I tried every trick in the book to get some work out of him (I think they were paid fifty cents per day), all to no avail. Finally out of exasperation, I told him that if he didn't work, I would have to report him to the guard and the entire crew would have to come off the line and return to prison. Rearing back with his shovel, he threatened to knock my head off if I didn't leave him alone. Not wanting to take on any man with his build weighing at least three hundred pounds, I wisely retreated and left him alone. But it pissed me off. Heading down the mountain to get one of the prison guards and Forest Service supervisors, I was intercepted by Pops. "Where are you going, Terry?" he quietly asked.

"Going to report Robert for not working," I replied.

"Can I handle it for you?" he asked, still speaking softly.

Realizing the quiet power this man held over the others, I said, "All right, but if he doesn't get with it and get to work, the whole crew is off this mountain."

"Terry, we could use some more fruit juice. Do you suppose that would be possible?" he asked.

Not realizing what was happening, I said I could do that, and off the mountain I trotted. Returning twenty minutes later with armloads of juice, I saw Robert really tearing up the hot spots! Great, I thought. Maybe Pops was able to reach the man in a way that I couldn't. When I walked over to Robert to compliment him on his work, I was shocked out of my boots! *His entire face was one bloody pulp!* "What the hell happened to you?" I asked in disbelief.

"I fell into that log after stumbling over a root," he replied through thickened and badly split lips.

I just stared! The man was a mess.

"Can I help?" a quiet voice from behind me asked.

Turning, I saw Pops standing there. "Have you seen Robert?" I asked.

"Yes, I have. He stumbled and fell into that log over there. But he is all right now and will work as you ask." There was a twinkle in his eyes that spoke to knowing more about the "accident" than met the eye. ... Realizing there must have been some frontier justice meted out while I was gone, I said nothing as I handed Pops the canned fruit juices. He again disbursed the juice, and I noticed that Robert got none.

"Terry, we need a favor. All of us have been working very hard for you, haven't we?"

"Yes, you have," I replied.

"I know it is wrong to ask because of prison regulations, but the men sure could use a smoke. If they had some, they would be very careful and not advertise it," said Pops.

I knew exactly what was going on: it was an attempt to get me to break the rules and be blackmailed from then on! I had read the book *Escape from Alcatraz* and was no dummy regarding what came next. Do one nice thing for them and then they have you, I thought. Next you are bringing them more and more to keep your skirts from being exposed. Just as I had read in *Stalag 17,* once they had you, *they had you!* I began to rear back and chew his ass out, but then I stopped as I quietly realized they were human beings, just as I was. They had normal human needs just like anyone else. They had been convicted for their crimes, but they were still human beings, and what was wrong with getting them a few smokes other than violating a prison regulation? Without saying a word, I walked away from the conversation. An hour later I returned with four cartons of cigarettes wrapped up in a blanket. Walking over to where Pops sat watching his men work, I laid them on a log and walked off. I had no further trouble with my crew and never even saw them or even smelled them smoking those cigarettes.

That evening it was darker than the inside of a dead cow when a convict four crews down the line from us stepped off a large rock and was promptly snapped in the hind end by a "rattlesnake"! There was instant terror in the ranks, especially by the man struck in the last part over the fence. Before a supervisor could get to the injured man, several convicts took their axes, sharpened the blades, and cut the man across the ass several times, and deeply! I guess they figured that was needed to stem the flow of the poison into the rest of the body. ... When the first aid crew finally reached the man, he was bleeding badly from the ax cuts, so much so that the aid people couldn't even see where the snakebite was because of the tissue damage. A helicopter was called to airlift the injured man to a hospital before he bled to death. The chopper was guided onto an open spot on the mountain, and the man was loaded onto a stretcher. The chopper wound up and, taking off downhill in the dark, struck the top of a tree and damaged the rotor. *Ka-boom* went the chopper as it hit the ground, and now we had double trouble. After a frantic hour, a National Guard 6 × 6 truck worked its way to the injured man (no more the worse for the rough landing by the chopper after hitting a tree top) and was carried off the mountain. Finally, after bouncing all over the mountain without any roads, the National Guard got the man to an ambulance waiting in fire camp. From there he was rushed to the hospital in Portola. Bottom line (no pun intended), the man had stepped off a rock, had bent over a large blackberry vine, and when he lifted his foot off the plant had been struck in the hind end by a large blackberry thorn! He was not used to the wild and, remembering the training about the rattlesnakes, instantly believed he had been bitten. It took over forty stitches to close up the wounds caused by the subsequent well-meaning ax cuts. The chopper was trucked out several days later with a bent rotor. I guess all's well that ends well. ...

On the third day of mop-up I was released by the Forest Service and told to go home, get cleaned up, and report two days later to their office in Quincy for reassignment on the Tahoe-Truckee fire, which by now was a roaring monster. Walking down to the fire camp, I picked up a paper sleeping bag and, filling it with six cartons of cigarettes, walked back to the fire line. Shaking hands with the convicts, whom I had come to like over the three days we had worked together, I said good-bye. Walking over to Pops, I thanked him for all the help and told him to use the paper sleeping bag if it got cold. Laying it at his feet, I started off the line. "Terry, is that your green Jeep pickup parked next to the dairy barn?" Pops asked.

Turning, I replied, "Sure is."

"How do you like it? I have been in prison so long, I never got familiar with one of those newfangled four-wheel-drive vehicles."

"Yeah, Dad and I really like it," I answered.

He just smiled, especially when he looked in the sleeping bag.

As I walked down the mountain, a guard was coming up to take my convicts off the line for chow. Funny how Pops knew about that being the family Jeep, I thought. But I was done for the time and quickly forgot about the oddball question in favor of thinking about a long bath in scalding water once I got home—and one of Mom's great home-cooked meals.

After I checked off the fire line with a bunch of my logging buddies, we turned in our fire equipment and went to chow. It was nice to relax, and most of us spent about an hour over dinner discussing the fire and the next fire's possibilities. Finished and realizing how great it would be to get home and clean up, I walked over to Dad's Jeep. He had arrived on the fire two days before and had asked me to take the Jeep home; he would get a ride home from one of his buddies. I noticed the truck bed was full and covered with a tarp. Figuring Dad had loaded it with something for whatever reason, I got in and started it up. The next few miles home with the cool wind flowing over my tired body felt great. Life was good, I thought, especially with the vision of another large firefighting check soon to come.

Arriving home, I parked the Jeep in the back yard and let Mom know I was home. After hosing off in the back yard, I walked inside and took a long, hot bath. I was getting dressed when I heard Mom calling to me. "Terry, come here," she said.

Stepping outside, I saw her standing by the side of the Jeep. I walked over and gave her a hug. "What's up?"

"What is all this?" she asked, pointing to the bed of the pickup.

Looking over her shoulder, I was amazed to discover that the entire bed of the truck was filled with cases of food, including canned fruit and juice! Not believing what I was seeing, I walked around Mom for a closer look. I couldn't believe my eyes. ... "Where the hell did it all come from?" I asked myself out loud.

Then I spotted a note fastened to a case of canned hams. It read, "Thank you for being such a great person to all of us when you didn't have to. All of us appreciated being treated like men once again. Pops."

I just stood there. ... There had to be many hundreds of dollars' worth of food in the back of that Jeep, all somehow stolen from the Forest Service by a bunch of convicts hell-bent on returning a favor to a snot-nosed kid who had treated them like human beings.

Mom and I spent the rest of that afternoon delivering those food-stuffs to poor families within our community. We did keep the government tarp that had been used to cover all that contraband, though.

I fought many forest fires over the following years while logging. In fact, I fought the monster Tahoe-Truckee fire just a few days later and almost got burned up on that one with a bunch of my buddies due to being positioned poorly too close to the fire's leading edge. If it hadn't been for a nearby creek and a brave borate pilot flying an N3N, we would have burned to death. Sounds like a story for next time! In every instance, I made good money, and my mom saw to it that every penny went into my college fund. I didn't run out of those hard-earned dollars until my second year as a master's student.

After the Mosquito Creek fire and others, I too sat quietly in the man-wagons as we went to our next fire. There was no more excitement on my part, just the realization of the great loss of part of our national heritage through that thing called fire.

10

To Bomb a Beaver Lodge

GROWING UP as a boy in the small mountain town of Quincy, nestled in the eastern Sierra Nevada Mountains of Plumas County, I had many friends. One who has remained a dear friend to this day is Ran Slaten, who lived in my neighborhood for many years. Over those years, through thick and thin, we became the best of friends. We hunted deer, jump-shot mallard ducks, fished for the elusive rainbow trout and black bass, target-shot California ground squirrels with our .22 rifles, rode our bicycles for miles throughout the countryside during the summer months, explored old gold mines, attended church, were in DeMolay and Scouts together, and ... *flew.* That's right ... *flew!* Ran's dad, Bill Slaten, a good man and great dad (to me as well when I didn't have one), owned several airplanes. One was a J-3 Cub made from canvas, string, spit, a song and a prayer, and an underpowered 65-horsepower engine with a gravity-feed tank. Slow was the word of the day for that little two-passenger aircraft, but man, we could go everywhere with it when the urge to explore struck our fancy. Bill also owned a Cessna 172, a great and forgiving high-wing airplane that also allowed us to explore the geography in which we lived, but at a somewhat faster pace than the lumbering J-3 Cub. Both Bill and Ran learned to fly, and it was only natural that the friendship between us kids would extend into this new world of the air. Once Ran got his pilot's license and could take passengers with him, guess who mashed his ass in the seat either behind him in the J-3 Cub or alongside in the Cessna 172.

At first the flying was nothing out of the ordinary: from point to point or back and forth as Ran gained hours of flying time and increased his confidence as a pilot. In fact, Ran was a natural-born pilot. He had a sense and soul for flying that showed right from the get-go. After about six months of "standard bomber turn" flying, we began to get a little bored with this routine thing. When that happens with a couple of dumb-as-a-box-of-rocks teenagers, *watch out!* Soon Ran and I were flying at low altitude through the rugged canyons and over the high mountain lakes for the excitement that questionable activity offered. That was soon followed by our "wildlife times," when we flew at low altitude looking for all kinds of wildlife throughout the county—and in those days it was everywhere! Big mule deer bucks, the occasional black bear, the even rarer mountain lion, flocks of band-tailed pigeons (we had to be careful to avoid hitting them), ducks on the beaver ponds, Canada geese on Snake Lake, and golden eagles east of the Sierras in the black-tailed-jackrabbit-filled sagebrush valleys of Sierra Valley. Now, there was a challenge—the eagles, I mean. Ran used to fly the J-3 Cub right alongside those graceful birds as they soared, then reduce the power until we were just drifting along in the sky together. When the eagle tired of that game, it would drop one wing and soar under the plane and out of sight. That maneuver would always leave the two of us breathless and with big smiles on our faces. There really is something about the majesty of eagles, especially from twenty feet away in an open-sided airplane! But soon even those adventures became tame. Now, you readers with any imagination can see a wreck coming when two teenagers with only an ounce of horse sense between them are turned loose with a piece of equipment like an airplane.

In those days Ran and I were World War II buffs. We were into just about every aspect of the rules of combat, equipment, and strategies, but we preferred the air-war portion of that "hurrah" hands down. So naturally, having several airplanes at our disposal, we began practicing, or acting out if you will, some of the roles in "air power." At first that included short takeoffs and landings under full power, touch-and-goes on the runway, and eventually making "emergency" landings on small rural dirt roads. Then we got into *really* low-level flying, buzzing bridges and railroad tunnels (and the old steam engines), and anything else that offered a challenge. Soon we graduated to "bombing": dropping things out of the airplane to see if we could hit something. Any kind of a target offered a challenge: bridges, old abandoned cars, lakes, trains (not the engines). At first we used only water balloons. "Only," I say! If one of those one-pound water balloons had hit a person on the head—or any other living thing from those heights or at those speeds— it would have been all over. But what the hell. We hadn't graduated to anything living at that stage of the game.

The J-3 had a set of doors on the right side that could be opened up on one part, down on the other, and latched. With the whole side of the plane open, it was easy for the bombardier (me sitting in the back of the plane) to launch out the water balloons upon Ol' Ran's command of "Bombs away." God, we had a ball! Nothing was safe, and after a while we got so we could drop a water balloon into a pickle barrel from twenty thousand feet. *Well, not quite!* But we were pretty good nonetheless. ... Tiring of water balloons (they got expensive, plus several times they broke in the airplane at inopportune times, like when we hid strong downdrafts), we graduated to rocks. Yep, that's right! Rocks make one hell of a puff of dirt when they hit the ground or a splash when hitting the water, and that was more like a bomb to our way of thinking.

Ran and I would load the Cessna 172 up with about one hundred pounds of rocks, and I mean *big* rocks, and away we would go. Again, Ol' Ran was the pilot of our "B-17" (a fabled World War II heavy bomber) and yours truly was the "bombardier" sitting in the back seat. At first we selected easy targets such as isolated high-country lakes. When the rocks hit the water going hundreds of miles per hour, a tremendous splash would be the result. We always tried to pick abandoned things to bomb. It was then, and is today, illegal to throw objects from an airplane, for obvious reasons, so Ran and I always made sure we worked our magic in remote, out-of-the-way areas. Well, more or less ...

When "bombing" with rocks, especially the big ones, we noticed that when first released, the rocks would fall straight down as Ran circled the plane so we could watch. Then, usually just before they hit, the rocks would look as if they were running horizontal to the ground. That made it even more exciting as we had to really lead a target from the Cessna 172 because of its greater airspeed. That meant dropping our projectile way in advance of the target. That took some real doing and a whole lot of Kentucky windage, but we had not just fallen off a turnip truck. ... Ran would open the side window and I would hang my arms out the window holding a big rock. Ran would make his approach, and when he felt it was time to release the "bomb," he would shout over the rushing wind, "Bombs away!" I would carefully release the rock so it missed the wing strut and fell below the tail of the aircraft. That way we had a clean bomb run and an undamaged airplane. *Aaaiiee,* what idiots we were. ... Down would plunge the projectile as Ran stood the plane on its wing and circled. Down, down, down it would hurtle until it got closer to the ground. Then it would start its horizontal run, and the tensions would run even higher in the plane as we anticipated a "hit." *Ka-booom* would go the rock with the appropriate splash (over water) or puff of dirt (over land). The two of us would cackle like a couple of Rhode Island Red roosters at our cleverness and accuracy.

Well, soon the two of us tired of "bombing" inanimate objects. Flying out to Sierra Valley thirty air miles to the east, we tried our bombing prowess on the California blacktailed jackrabbits living on the sagebrush flats. Here we would fly low and slow, looking for a running rabbit. Soon it would stop and hide under some sagebrush. We would swing wide so as not to alarm it and then make a fast run back to where it remained hidden. No matter how hard we tried, the rabbits turned out to be a bitch to hit. It seemed that just as soon as we released our rock on a sitting jackrabbit, off it would go like a striped-assed ape. We later discovered that when we dropped the rocks, they made one hell of a sound hurtling through the air. No wonder the rabbits got the hell out of Dodge! I would too if something came through the air for me and obviously howling mad from all the noise it made. Well, after an hour of wide misses we tired of our sport and headed back to the airport in Quincy. Passing over an area called the Loop (where train tracks made a wide loop to climb in elevation), I spotted a beaver house.

"Ran," I yelled, "swing back over that beaver house we just passed. I think I can hit it."

Standing the plane on its wing tip, we spun around and headed back. Picking out a nice large rock, I made ready. Ran made a picture-perfect run and at one thousand feet elevation over the house, I let my projectile go. Down it went, gathering speed until it had to be going at least a million miles per hour. Over several beaver dams it sped and then started its horizontal run. Hot dog! It was right on the money as it sailed toward the beaver house, spooking several dozen mallards off the ponds in the process. *Ka—blamm* went the rock—*right* on the beaver house! Great mounds of mud, dirt, and sticks flew high into the air! Man, you talk about impressive ... but not as impressive as about six beaver fleeing their home after the impact and swimming across the pond asking each other if Bucky Beaver was having "gas" problems again. What a hell of a hit! It couldn't have been better placed if we had used a Norden bomb sight from the big war. There was a great hole in the side of the beaver house, indicating what an impact a twenty-pound rock made hitting something from that altitude. Man, you talk about a high: we now had discovered our calling. Tough targets in isolated places—what an opportunity awaited!

For the next several days, just about every beaver house we could reach felt the wrath of our "B-17" and its "bomb" runs. We got so good, it was uncanny. You can guess what is coming next ... *bam*, we kicked it up a notch! There is a lake in Plumas County near Quincy called Snake Lake. In those days it was a great lake for bluegill, black bass, and brown bullhead fishing. It was also home to a large contingent of nesting Canada geese. Out in the middle of that lake sat a *huge* beaver house. Without using our heads, as usual, off we went with a load of large rocks. As our "B-17" gained altitude, I looked for other targets of opportunity. Finding none, I turned my attention back to Snake Lake as it approached through the whirling propeller. Making a high pass, Ran lined out our course. Down we plummeted, losing altitude until we were only one thousand feet over the far end of the lake as we began our run. Grabbing a thirty-pound spherical rock, I made ready as I hung it out the window. Ran and I were so intent on making a one-hit bomb run that we failed to observe the fishermen fishing along the shore some distance from the beaver lodge.

"Bombs away," shouted Ran, and I let her go. Within seconds of our drop, we could see the antlike figures of fishermen running for their cars and rapidly driving away! We remembered the horrible wailing sound the rocks made flying through the air. Ran, realizing that someone could get the number off the plane and report us, poured the power to the engine to effect our getaway. *Ka-boom* went the rock into the lake adjacent to the beaver lodge, throwing up a huge spew of water. Any fishermen left, with the howl of the falling rock and monstrous splash, chose to flee the scene posthaste.

Ran and I were laughing like a couple of knotheads as we cleared the far end of the lake over a stand of timber. *Downdraft!* Ran fought the controls of the plane as it started to settle into the tops of the towering pines. ... As the landing gears whanged across the treetops, we held our breath. Fortunately, the row of trees at the end of the lake was only a narrow band, followed by a several-hundred-foot dropoff into a canyon below. Into that canyon the plane hurtled, finally catching itself with the engine running at full power. As he pulled the plane out of our shallow dive at 220 miles per hour, I could tell Ran was breathing a whole lot easier. Now I could restart my own breathing as well. ...

Heading back toward the airport with the danger long past, we began to cackle again. We had almost hit the beaver house, scared the hell out of a lot of fishermen, put several dozen Canada geese into flight, and beaten the "hangman" when we hit the downdraft. I guess we had a lot to cackle over. "Ran," I said, "there is a big beaver house on the Ramelli Ranch alongside state Highway 70. Before we put her down for the day, let's hit that one." Ran turned around and grinned as he headed the Cessna east in the direction of the Ramelli Ranch. State Highway 70 makes a half-mile-long, east-to-west straight run into the eastern side of East Quincy. Lying on the south side of that stretch of highway for about three-eighths of a mile was a large flooded pasture with a small beaver house on the extreme eastern end. The beaver house was sitting about thirty yards from the edge of the berm on the highway, making it a sweet and easy "bombing run" using the highway as a guide. At the very end of the straight stretch of highway just before entering East Quincy was a large road cut that was so deep it left steep red-earth hillsides at each side of the highway. This was going to be a peach of a shot, to our way of thinking. However, with the scared-fishermen scenario from Snake Lake still fresh in our minds, Ran flew out both sides of the highway to make sure no one was coming down the road. It was all clear for at least several miles on either side of the beaver house. With that, Ran dropped to about one thousand feet and began his run, flying from east to west. Selecting about a thirty-five-pound rock from the floorboard of the plane, I hung it out the open window, waiting for the order to drop. We hammered right along without any sideslipping, and the run was going to be perfect, I thought. Approaching the beaver house, Ran finally said, "Bombs away." I let the huge rock slip from my hands, and it disappeared from sight. That will teach some damn beaver to build his house in a pasture I would soon be haying, I grinned. Down, down, down went the rock in a line just off the edge of the highway and right for the beaver house.

Holy crap! From the east came an old red pickup heading down the highway, going toward East Quincy! Where the hell did he come from? I thought in panic as I watched the rock continue falling toward our target. Keep in mind, there wasn't a whole lot of margin for error between the highway and the beaver house! Ran and I just hung there as the rock and the pickup headed for the same stretch of highway near the beaver house. The rock started its horizontal run, indicating that it was almost on the ground. Only it was heading more along the highway than toward the beaver house! The driver of the pickup, oblivious to the danger from above, kept driving unawares down the highway as the huge stone fell toward the bed of his pickup. We had misjudged the distance to the beaver house and had dropped our rock too far past the initial point of release. Now we had to just sit there in terror as the rock hurtled directly toward the unsuspecting driver. Ran and I found ourselves "blowing" through pouched lips as if we could push the rock to one side of the pickup, but to no avail. By now the rock had run horizontal for what seemed ages and had to hit at any moment.

The truck passed the hay field and started up the hill going through the road cut, *and then it happened!* The rock sailed right over the top of the pickup and slammed into the hillside not twenty feet from the right front fender! *Ka-bloom* went the rock as it slammed into the hillside, throwing a huge mantle of red dirt over the pickup and erasing it from view. Our hearts were up in our throats for the longest moment. Then out the other side of the dirt cloud came the pickup, driving all over the road as if the driver had just had the crap scared out of him. Oh my, you talk about relieved! Then the pickup skidded to a stop, leaving a cloud of blue tire smoke in the air, to see what the hell had happened. Ran realized we'd better get the heck out of there before we were recognized and darted for the oak forest near the Ramelli ranch house. Once there, we beat a hasty retreat for the Quincy airport and safety.

When we landed, there was the local game warden waiting for us. He waved us over, and again out hearts went up in our throats. "Ran," shouted Paul Kerr, "I need a ride to Snake Lake. I just got a call that someone up there is dropping bombs on the geese, and I need to go and have a look-see." With that, Paul got in and Ran took off once again. Of course, we kept our mouths shut. ... As I said earlier, we hadn't just come off that turnip wagon! Flying over the lake, Paul determined that whoever it was had long gone and directed us to return to the airport. Holding my breath the whole time, I hoped he wouldn't look on the rear floor of the plane where I sat, for there on the floor were still some unused "bombs."

Letting Paul off by his patrol car back at the airport, Ran taxied the plane over to the hangar and killed the engine, and the two of us got out. Swearing never to divulge what had happened that day, we removed the remaining rocks from the plane and tossed them into the weeds beside the hangar. Later that evening I drove to where that rock had hit the side of the bank on state Highway 70 by the red pickup.

There was a hole at least three feet deep and about six feet wide where that huge rock had hit the bank. There was also a set of skid marks just past that point. ... Had I hit that pickup, I am positive it would have killed the driver.

Ran and I never dropped anything out of his airplanes after that, and this story has never seen the light of day until now, some forty-eight years after the event. I hope that guy we almost hit in the pickup isn't still around, or he may come back and bust both of our chops!

11

"No Safe Takeoff"

IN THE EARLY SUMMER of 1959, I graduated from high school. After a summer's work in the woods as a logger, I went to Santa Barbara City College in the fall. My major was declared as prepharmacy, but after discovering that I was dumb as a box of rocks in classes such as advanced math, foreign language, and chemistry, I changed to a general studies major. The next two years at the city college proved tougher than I had originally thought college would be. Goofing around academically in high school so I could play sports, hunt, and fish had done nothing to help me at the college level. I found myself working my hind end off and by the end of my second year had finally achieved a C+ average and was ready to move on. Visiting the school's library near the end of my sophomore year, I began examining course catalogs from other colleges. One was from Humboldt State College in Arcata, California. Quickly glancing through with no preference in mind, I spied a listing for a major field of study titled "Wildlife Management." That's it! I thought. I want to be a wildlife manager. Setting out the rest of my life was just that simple. Typically, I didn't know what it meant, what courses had to be taken, what the field entailed, if there were any jobs in that arena, or even who hired such a beast. But that was beside the point. My guardian angels had spoken, and I knew what I wanted to be. The rest is history. I finally graduated in 1964 with a bachelor of science degree in wildlife management and in 1966 with a master of science degree in wildlife management. I spent the next thirty-two years in wildlife law enforcement, working at the state and federal levels, loved it, and never looked back.

Was Humboldt easier than my old city college? Not by a damn sight! The studies were extensive and difficult, and the competition for decent grades was unreal. The job market in that field was extremely limited, but again, with the help of my guardian angels, I succeeded. However, like a knothead, I am getting ahead of the story.

One day just before the end of my second year at the city college, I got a letter from my old elementary and high school buddy Ran Slaten. The gist was that he had never flown in Southern California and wondered if he could fly down to Santa Barbara when I finished my second year, pick me up, and fly the two of us back home in his private aircraft. Hell, yes! I thought. What a wonderful idea! Back went my reply, and over the next few weeks we solidified our plans for what turned out to be one hell of an adventure.

Come the day for me to leave Santa Barbara, I was more than ready! I had had a gutful of Southern California and was seriously homesick for my beloved Sierra Nevada Mountains. It was hell being from the mountains and having to live in an area where all I heard were the sounds of automobiles and where I never saw the stars because of the city's lights, stood in line to go to the bathroom, and breathed smog all day long. Not having a car made all that even more grim. After all, to a Northern Californian, anything south of Frisco is Mexico. ... So yeah, I was more than ready to come home.

My friend Bill drove me and my accumulation of junk from two years of college out to the Santa Barbara Municipal Airport. Good Ol' Ran. There he sat off to one side of the runway by a group of airplane hangars in his Cessna 172. I exploded from the car and gave him a warm embrace. Ran just grinned and said, "Let's load up. We have a long way to go and a short time to get there before dark." Not needing any further prompting, the three of us began loading the Cessna with my boxes of schoolbooks, bags of dirty laundry, sacks of oranges, grapefruit, and lemons, potted plants (my mom loved flowers of any kind), and many pounds of other accumulated stuff. Tightly packing it all into the back seat and storage area of the aircraft, we soon discovered that we had a problem. There was so much weight loaded in the back of the plane, not including Ran and me, that the Cessna wanted to sit on its tail! We had Bill lift the tail up while Ran and I got in and fastened the seatbelts. Ran started the engine, the pull of the propeller lifted the tail, and we were set. Waving good-bye to Bill, we taxied off toward the airstrip. Receiving clearance from the tower, Ran ran the engine up and checked the magnetos. The engine ran fine on each one, and we were prepared for takeoff. "Hold on," said Ran as he applied power to the engine. After a long run, we lifted off and swung out over the ocean to gather some altitude and airspeed before tackling the coast range of mountains immediately adjacent to the airport. Adjusting the trim tabs and cranking up the RPMs, Ran turned toward the towering mountains and we were on our way. As usual, like anytime I flew with Ran, it soon became an adventure.

Ran's plan was to cross the Coast Range and land at the Bakersfield, California, airport. There we would take on fuel (he had only half a tank at present) and then fly home to Quincy in one fell swoop. Great plan, but we had a small problem ... the plane was so heavily loaded that it couldn't climb up and over the Coast Range straightaway as one would normally do! Instead, Ran had to climb the mountains in increments, flying back and forth along the range to slowly gain altitude. Finally we made it over the top but in so doing had another problem—*because of the excess weight and having to fly back and forth numerous times to gain altitude, we were almost out of fuel!* And the Bakersfield airport was still miles away. Dropping over to the east side of the Coast Range, Ran put the plane in a fuel-saving shallow glide as we hammered on toward our fueling destination. He handed me a road map and, as I gave him what had to be a blank stare, told me to look for any old military or county airports. *He didn't think we had enough fuel to reach the Bakersfield airport!* Let me tell you, I looked those maps over with a fine-tooth comb. Every time I located a safe haven in line with our route of travel, I would let him know and we would fly toward that with an emergency landing in mind. Reaching that haven and still with fuel, we would head for the next emergency landing field, and so it went. Finally the Bakersfield Airport loomed into view. Boy, was I happy to see that piece of real estate! That was, until I looked over at our fuel gauge. It read, "NO SAFE TAKEOFF"! We were so damned low on fuel, we didn't have any. ... And a look at Ran did nothing for my confidence! We both held our breaths (as if that would help) and didn't even wiggle in our seats. I guess we felt that to do so would break the spell and the whirling of the propeller. On and on that little plane hammered, and finally our wheels safely touched down and the two of us looked at each other as if to say, "No big deal." ... No wonder my guardian angels were so feather-thin by the time I retired.

Taxiing over to the fuel barn, Ran commenced refueling. As the fuel tanks filled, the tail gradually sat back down on the runway. Overloaded—yes, I think so! Ran continued fueling until the plane's tanks were topped off. Then, as casually as if it were the safest thing in the world, he had the man at the fuel pumps lift the tail back up so we would be level. Ran started up the engines, and again the pull of the prop kept the tail off the ground. Sitting there, Ran logged the hours flown and amount of fuel taken on board. Shaking his head, he looked over at me and said, "We had about one and a half gallons left in the tank when we landed!" I never said anything. I didn't have to. ... As we taxied to the end of the runway, I remember how hot the air was. We had both windows open, but the sweat was just pouring off us in what had to be at least 100-degree heat. Any readers who are pilots will likely be cringing at this part, knowing what that does to the lift of an airplane. ... Then Ran did something I had never seen him do before. He taxied *clear to the end* of the long commercial-aircraft runway, even to the point of resting the tail over the end of the runway. Revving up the engine, he checked the magnetos and said, "Hang on. It is so hot out and we are so overloaded that I might have to use the entire length of the runway to get airborne." As he firewalled the throttle, the little Cessna staggered down the runway like a gooney bird. Slowly, ever so slowly, the air-speed indicator crept upward. I knew our takeoff speed was seventy-two miles per hour, and damn, we were a far piece from that. Slowly the runway began to dissolve under our wheels, and again, the two knotheads mashing their lead asses in the seats held their breaths. But we were fast running out of runway! Soon the end was in sight, and the little Cessna could only make seventy-one miles per hour! Ran was leaning forward in the seat like that might give us an extra ounce of energy, and I found myself doing the same. "Hang on," he shouted as the last of the commercial airstrip disappeared under our wheels. With that, he pulled the yoke back into his stomach. The little Cessna lurched into the air, *then started back down!* Ran kept the yoke pulled back, flaps down, and the engine at full throttle as the plane struggled to stay in the air. The beeping of the stall-warning horn sure was distracting, I thought. ...

The combination of intense heat and aircraft overload sure offset the long runway. For many miles the plane and Ran struggled for more air speed and altitude until we realized we had another problem! The struggling engine was now overheating. ... Soon the engine temperature was in the 200-degree range and climbing. Still flying in that damn hot air and at low altitude, we had to make a decision ... and fast!

"Ran," I said, "we need to lighten this plane and fast so we can climb into a cooler atmosphere. If we don't, the engine will overheat and we will crash."

Ran nodded as he continued to closely watch the gauges and dials while struggling with the yoke.

"I don't dare open up the door. Since we are only going seventy-five miles per hour, that may slow us down enough to cause a stall. But I can open the window."

Ran gave me a quick quizzical look as if to say what the hell are you talking about, then hurriedly turned back to his instruments as I opened my window. It was still hotter than a pistol outside, maybe hotter than 100 degrees. Reaching into the packed rear seat, I grabbed a box of my college books and manhandled them over and into the front seat. Grabbing them by the handful, I started throwing them out the window. When the box was emptied, out it went as well. "Two hundred and ten degrees," Ran's worried voice proclaimed (I think 220 was the magic boil-over for the engine). Hurrying, I grabbed another box of books, and they rained down from the plane as lost history. Three more boxes followed, and I figured we had lightened our load by at least one hundred pounds. Hastily looking over at the gauges, I could see that we had gained a few feet in altitude and another couple miles per hour. However, the engine temperature stubbornly hovered around the 210-degree mark. Reaching into the backseat, I grabbed a hundred-pound sack of oranges, and soon they rained down on whatever lay below. Damn, I thought, there goes Mom and Dad's chance to savor some fresh-off-the-tree fruit. Grabbing a similar-sized bag of fresh grapefruit, I sent them out the window like yellow cannon shot as well.

"It's working!" proclaimed Ran. "The heat is backing off just a bit, and I'm gaining altitude and a little more air speed. But still not enough to safely start climbing for the mountain ranges ahead of us." I really hated to lose all my things, many of which were for my family, but survival teaches a strong lesson quickly. Out went my sack of lemons and another box of books. The life-giving gauges held steady except for the air speed, which was now around eighty miles per hour, and we seemed to have gained a little altitude.

"Ran. Do we have enough air speed for me to open the door?" I yelled.

"Try it and see," he yelled back over the noise of the air roaring through my open window. Slowly I opened the door, aware of the drag it would create. Sure as hell, the plane slewed to the right and our air speed dropped like a rock. On went the stall buzzer again as I hurriedly dumped out the last two boxes of heavy books and six heavy potted plants. All that remained in the rear of the plane were two sacks of dirty laundry, and I was bound and determined to hang on to those since I had little to wear once back home. Quickly closing the door to reduce the drag, I looked over at the gauges. The air speed shot up to almost ninety and the engine temperature started down! *Hot dog!* We had done it!

With most of the weight gone, the plane returned to what we considered normal. Our air speed continued to climb until Ran trimmed back the throttle. The engine temperature dropped into the normal range as we increased our altitude and climbed into cooler air. Well, the two crazies of Ran and Terry had done it again (with a liberal sprinkling of help from my two guardian angels). We would survive another adventure, but then another problem arose. Ran did not know how to navigate in the area we were in, so we used a road map. This worked fine until it started getting dark and we couldn't see the landmarks. This created a little bit of a problem until Ran figured out our course while I flew the plane (no, I didn't have a pilot's license). Soon the familiar Sierra Nevada Mountains appeared on the horizon, and we breathed a little easier. Now we were over familiar territory. Just as the sun was setting, we touched down at the Quincy airport. A perfect three-point landing, I might add, without the aid of the runway lights.

Ran taxied over to the tie-downs and killed the engine. I opened my door and was instantly aware of the cool, clean-smelling mountain air. I was home! After I helped Ran tie down the plane, we loaded my remaining gear into his "Old Red Rat" (an early-model Ford two-door, painted bright red) and headed for our homes. We both lived on the same street in East Quincy and traveled the miles between the airport and our homes in a few moments. Grabbing my two duffel bags of dirty clothes, I thanked my friend and gave him my last $20 bill to help pay for the gas. Then I walked up the street to my house and a good home-cooked dinner. Somehow, as I look back on that episode and all the problems we had, I think I owe Ran more than just a $20 bill for gasoline! Maybe fifty years of friendship, and the years I hope are still to come, will help pay the bill in full. ...

A week later Ran brought me one of my books that had fallen out on the floor of the plane and had not been tossed with all the rest. I don't recall the author, but it was titled *Safe Flight and the Power of Navigation.*

12

Alaska

IN THE FALL of 1961 I decided it was time that I worked in Alaska for the experience it had to offer me as a careerist in the field of wildlife management. That fall my fiancée, Donna Larson (now my wife of forty-three years and counting), typed over one hundred job applications for just about every type of state or federal summer wildlife resource work occurring in that far-flung state. Soon the responses came flooding back. One potential job that held some interest for me was working out of the cannery town of King Salmon, netting and tagging sockeye salmon. Initially I was a little disappointed because I was a wildlife major who would be working on a fisheries project (wildlife-related summer jobs for college students were practically nonexistent). But I soon realized that it was one of the best job experiences I could have. I got to see some of the most spectacular country in Alaska while working with a species unique to my academic training and experience. As it turned out, a series of pretty amazing experiences came from that summer's adventures. In later years as a conservation officer, I would protect several species of salmon from poachers using gill nets, dynamite, spears on the spawning grounds, rifles, and snagging implements to kill them during their migration. In so doing, the ring of experience and respect for a unique species came full circle for me.

The Adventure Begins
AT THE END of May my official employment papers arrived. I was going to be working for the U.S. Department of the Interior, Bureau of Commercial Fisheries, as an IASS-3 (that bureau no longer exists). I was hired to work on a sockeye-tagging crew of thirteen college students. Our first duty station would be at a camp twenty miles upstream from King Salmon on the Naknek River. Our job was to net, tag, and

release as many sockeye as we could before the run ended (eventually over thirty-four thousand fish). I discovered later that I was hired because they needed someone big and strong to pull a thousand feet of lead line to shore once the net was released. The top of a basic drift net is lined with floats, and the bottom portion is strung with a leaded line, that is, a cotton or nylon line with small lead weights every foot or so. The lead line holds the bottom of the net fully extended so trapped fish can't swim under the net and escape. When the salmon run on the lower portion of the river subsided, we were to close camp and travel into the upper reaches of the Naknek River system, counting the salmon on the spawning streams, retrieving our tags, taking scale and blood samples, and then releasing the fish so they could fulfil their destiny.

Alaska in those days had a haphazard method for taking salmon during the fishing season. They would open the season for a few hours, then close it for another small amount of time. This procedure would be repeated numerous times around the clock throughout the summer as long as the salmon ran. The thinking was that enough fish would somehow escape during the down times to guarantee healthy runs for the succeeding years. However, no matter how you looked at it, especially from the fisheries biologists' point of view, that system stunk! My boss, Dick Stratey, concerned about that system's potential for destruction of the salmon fishery, had developed a sockeye salmon migration-spawning theory that, if proven, could be used to better the system of harvest. Salmon return to their natal place of origin to spawn, and they migrate through chemistry. Basically, every stream has its own specific chemical composition, or "smell." That smell is imprinted on the salmon from birth, and to them it is simply a matter of following your nose. Well, it is a bit more complex than that, but that explanation will have to do. Dick's theory was that every day a new group of salmon destined for a specific stream or beach spawning area (an area of lake or river bottom fed by small underground springs) would commence its migration upriver from the ocean. The next day, another group would begin its run from the ocean, heading upriver to another stream in which to spawn. My boss postulated that some streams would be overrun with thousands of salmon, making the habitats unable to safely tolerate the spawning activity of such hordes. In these instances many "redd sites" (spawning nests in the streambeds built by fish using a rapidly digging motion of their bodies and tails) would be destroyed by spawning fish as previously laid eggs would be buried or loosened from their gravel nests to float downstream and be eaten by rainbow trout, Dolly Varden, stickle-back, or sculpin. On the other hand, some streams could support more salmon, but not enough would make it back to properly utilize the available spawning territory. He theorized that instead of opening and closing the salmon season haphazardly for a few hours at a time, the state could determine which runs needing harvesting (because of large spawning populations) and which didn't (because of low numbers on the spawning grounds). The summer research he was about to initiate involved tagging each group of salmon trapped daily with different-colored back tags, then going to each stream in the headwaters where spawning occurred to check the tags. If stream A held red-green-tagged fish and was loaded to the gills (no pun intended) with spawners, it would be wise to look back on the date when those migrating fish had been tagged downstream and to open the season during that period the following year. However if few spawners returned to stream B, one could again check the downstream tagging records and close fishing during that particular time of the run the following year so the underutilized stream escapement would be higher. It was a fairly simple hypothesis soon to be explored through good science. However, as with all wildlife when you think you have it figured out, *it didn't work.* Today the state of Alaska still runs its fishing programs with simple hourly openings and closures, leaving much to be desired biologically in the eyes of many fisheries biologists. And where commercial net boats jam into small areas to compete for the salmon, *it is a zoo!* The boats crash into each other, fights erupt, boats deliberately run over each other's nets, and on it goes. ... And the salmon, well ...

Included in my orders were airplane tickets from San Francisco to King Salmon via Seattle and Anchorage. Gathering up the needed gear for the summer, I rechecked my supplies. Hip boots, jeans, shirts, sheath knife (in case I fell in with my hip boots on and had to cut myself free), several belts in case one broke, sleeping bag, fishing gear, the usual supply of socks, undergarments, and the like. Also included on that list: *a heavy-caliber rifle!* It seemed that bears could be a problem where I was going, and I was instructed that a rifle would be required on site. The government would supply a bolt-action, 30-06 rifle left over from World War I, or I could bring a heavier-caliber, better-quality gun. So come the day of departure, I kissed my fiancée good-bye and loaded up onto a Greyhound Bus to San Francisco, carrying a rifle on board in front of God and everybody. In San Francisco, I took another bus out to the airport with my .348 lever-action Winchester rifle clearly in hand. I checked in and was assigned a seat on an F-27, twin-engine turboprop from San Francisco to Seattle. There I boarded a Boeing 727, again with my Winchester in hand, to Anchorage (the rifle was stored in the overhead bin). In Anchorage I boarded a Super G Constellation (a large four-engine propeller-driven aircraft) with Winchester in hand (no gun locks or any of that other silly crap that accomplishes nothing in the way of crime prevention) for my trip to King Salmon. I flew home the same way, with Winchester and ammunition in hand and at arm's length. Life was sure simpler in those days, and so were people.

Flying from San Francisco to Seattle was no problem. Flying from Seattle to Anchorage, *beautiful!* There is nothing like the view in Alaska when the sun is shining. Flying from Anchorage to King Salmon, *unreal.* The fog was so thick that from where I sat, I could only make out the inboard engine on the wing of our four-engine aircraft! And that engine was belching out oil by the gallon if the wide, dark streak streaming off the wing behind the motor was any indicator. ... Still, we made a perfect three-point landing, for which I was grateful.

About a mile from the airport was my home for the summer: nothing more than rather shabby old World War II military barracks with bunks on which to rest our sleeping bags. Sand on the floor was a constant reminder of the soil type around us, and just about everything I saw, even if new, looked as if it had been used hard and put away wet. For the next two weeks our tagging crew unloaded oceangoing barges arriving daily from the lower forty-eight and stacked those goods in several large warehouses. Just about everything known to man and needed in the Arctic came on those barges, having been sent months earlier from ports such as Seattle. However, there was a noticeable lack of fresh fruit, vegetables, and milk. Those items were either canned, boxed, bagged, or mostly not there at all. If fresh items came into the area, it was by air, which was very expensive. Hence, no fresh fruits, vegetables, or milk went to the field camps. Exceptions were made for fresh eggs and spuds, which came in by air. By the end of summer I had such a hunger for milk and fresh vegetables that it was unreal. The purpose of our chain-gang labor on the docks was simple. There were several hundred other summer crews in the field already scattered throughout Alaska who were supplied out of the King Salmon office. They had to be supported; hence the offloading and storage of a summer's supplies for about 250 men. Women were not allowed in the field in those days. The work was backbreaking, the sites remote, and the degree of danger great. Such were the social mores of the day (today women work everywhere). As materials were needed in the far-flung camps, the Fish and Wildlife Service with its many types of aircraft (mostly sea- or floatplanes) and vessels would load and ferry supplies to their final destinations.

Our eating facility was a real hoot. It consisted of a long, narrow room, big enough to seat over one hundred men at a sitting. At one end of our dining room sat the heart of the kitchen: a huge iron cook stove with a griddle large enough for twenty steaks, four dozen eggs, a ton of bacon, or ten pounds of hash browns at a time. That stove had reportedly been brought to King Salmon a hundred years before by sailing vessel and dog sleds. Our cook was a tall black man with arms like logs and an upper torso matching the girth of his stove. His name was George Washington Jefferson, and man, could that fellow cook and sing! Pies, cakes, cookies, grits, soups, and stews—everything that came from his kitchen was pure heaven, especially to those hungry, hardworking hounds unloading barges fourteen hours per day! Of course, if he hadn't been that kind of cook, he would have been on the next plane back to the lower forty-eight by the end of the first day. There is nothing worse in camp than a lousy cook. Many history books are replete with tales of bad cooks who were forced to walk across the desert without their boots, shot on sight by hungry crews, or wrapped in a green cowhide and left out in the sun to be slowly crushed as the hide dried and constricted. ...

My First Salmon

ONE EVENING a new friend named Doug Sherve and I took out one of the many boats from our landing and went fishing on the Naknek River. To me, a hill kid from the mountains of California, the Naknek was the mother of all rivers. In places it was over a mile wide, and it ran for hundreds of miles into the hinterland. The water was clear as German crystal, and you could easily see to the bottom of the river in twenty feet of swift-moving water. If you looked carefully, you could actually see the fish migrating upstream! Upriver we went for a few miles before anchoring on a partially submerged tree stuck midriver. From there we cast our fishing lures out into the river. Keep in mind, I was nothing but a small-town country boy. I had fished all my life, but only for small trout species. Attaching a large gold spinner to my eight-pound test line, I cast into the slow-moving river. *Bang,* I had a strike and a few moments later had a nice seven-pound rainbow trout at the edge of the boat. I released the fish, out went the lure once again, and much the same followed for the next hour. What fishing!

I was having a ball when all of a sudden during a retrieve, I hung my lure up on the bottom. No matter what I did, I just couldn't get it off the rock or log on which it was stuck. Not wanting to lose my precious lure (remember, in Alaska everything is about ten times more expensive than in the lower forty-eight), we released our boat and drifted downstream to where I was snagged. Pulling hard on my line, I tried to get the lure to tear free. All my efforts were to no avail. Doug kept moving the boat back and forth as I worked on unsticking the precious lure. Finally realizing it was a lost cause, I began to jerk really hard on the line to break off the lure. All of a sudden, out of the water not twenty feet from the boat leapt a *huge* fish with my gold lure firmly affixed to its lower jaw! That was what I had been "snagged" on! The damn fish, realizing he was hooked and being so big and strong, had just lain on the bottom like a log. I was so surprised that I fell down into the bottom of the boat, nearly breaking my left arm in the process. Doug almost fell right out of the boat (he was from a small town in eastern Montana, where they barely had enough water to drink, much less fish)! I had never seen a fish so large, which by now was ripping off line from my Mitchell 300 spinning reel like there was no tomorrow.

"Doug," I yelled, "follow that fish before it strips off all my line!"

Whipping the boat around, Doug idled closer to the fish as I continued my fight. Not knowing what to do with such a large fish, I just kept the line tight as down the Naknek River the salmon and we two knot-heads slowly drifted. About four miles downstream from where the fish had originally been hooked, Doug anchored the boat on a sandbar. Stepping out, I began to fight the tiring fish. After about thirty minutes, my prize lay gasping its last on the edge of the sandbar. It was a male (hooked lower jaw) king salmon that was *at least four feet long!* It weighed so much it was almost all I could do to get it into the boat. At that point my eyes were almost as big as that fish!

Sitting in the boat as we raced back to King Salmon to show off my catch, I could hardly believe my eyes. Lying next to my feet was the biggest fish I had ever caught in my young life! When we arrived back at the dock, I hauled the monster up to our walk-in cooler near the kitchen and carefully laid it out of the way on the floor. Running to my room as

Doug headed off to get a beer, I grabbed my camera. *Damn!* I was out of film. Racing out the front door of the barracks, I grabbed a truck and headed into the town of King Salmon to buy some film. Finally locating some fitting my camera, I purchased it and raced back to our facility. Man, I thought, wait until my dad sees the size of this one! Loading my camera, I raced back to the walk-in cooler. Flinging open the door, I charged into the cool box *only to find that my giant fish was gone!* There was blood and a few scales on the floor, but nothing more! Following a spew of fresh blood drops across the floor, I spotted my fish, or what was left of it. Hanging from a metal meat hook in the rear of the cooler was a huge tail and the lower half of my fish. *Jesus!* I raced around inside the cooler to find the other half, but it was nowhere to be found.

Running into the dining hall to ask the cook if he knew where my fish had gone, I slammed to a stop, totally stunned! There in his massive arms were about ten two-inch-thick salmon steaks. Another ten salmon steaks were already happily cooking on the griddle! Holy crap, did I ever yell. ... I about scared him to death with my war whoop, causing him to drop about half the steaks from his massive arms onto the floor. It turned out he had gone to the cooler and, seeing the huge fish on the floor, had figured it was there to eat, and since there was plenty for dinner had simply gone ahead. He had gutted the fish and thrown the guts and head out to the ever-present, always starved gulls. Then he had washed out and cut off the front half, cut a number of steaks, and commenced to cook dinner for the crew, not realizing it was the catch of a lifetime for a country boy. Crushed, I got him to pull the steaks off the griddle and weighed the cut pieces with the remaining half of the fish on a set of commercial-grade floor scales. That king salmon weighed in at seventy-six pounds, six ounces! And that was without the head and guts that the gulls had polished off in fine style! *I was heartbroken and still am to this day!* Suffice it to say, I didn't get a picture of the catch of my life, and that evening I ate several turkey sandwiches instead of a salmon steak dinner. ... To this day, I can still see that fish when he first jumped out of the water trying to throw the hook.

The Tagging Operation

AFTER SEVERAL WEEKS in base camp, the sockeye salmon began running and our crew was ready to go to work tagging our target species. We were assigned three twenty-foot Cordova skiffs. That was a unique type of boat, twenty feet long with a five-foot beam (width). They were

high bowed and possessed a stout stern capable of holding two Evinrude 40-horsepower outboard engines. The hull was composed of
three-quarter-inch oak planking, which was heavily fiberglassed, inside
and out. Covering the three directional skids under the boat were sheets
of three-eighth-inch-thick steel plating for all the unforeseen rocks in
the waters where they would be operated. In short, they were as stout
as a German Tiger tank and stable as an old British ship of the line. Into
those boats went our personal gear, a twenty-foot piece of railroad rail,
a thousand-foot-long by ten-foot-deep net of the finest Japanese manu-
facture, food, cooking gear, rifles, numerous wooden crates holding
two five-gallon tins of Blazo stove and lantern fuel, jerry cans of gasoline, cases of outboard motor oil, toilet paper (can't forget that!), cases
of mosquito spray (military brand with 76 percent DEET—try and find
that concentration today), sleeping bags, cases of Black Flag insecticide,
and thirteen champing-at-the-bit college kids hell-bent for their next
set of adventures! Cranking up our twin-40-horse-engine craft, up the
Naknek River we literally flew! Twenty miles later the outboard engines were still gaining speed with not more than a fourth of the boat's
bottom surface in the water when up on step. Yes, they were damn fine
boats and would be responsible for bringing every one of us home
come the end of summer—*except one!*

Finally our home for the next month or so hove into view on the
south bank far upstream. Not a castle by a long shot, but home. It was
a twelve-by-twenty foot wooden shack on the bank of the river. It had
a few windows on one side and a tin roof but other than that looked
used hard and put away wet like just about everything else I had seen
in Alaska. Tumbling out of the boats at the river's edge, we grabbed our
gear and formed a human chain to the cabin. From the boats to the
cabin our gear flew up the bank, and soon we were moved in to our
new living quarters. It wasn't much, but it did help keep the biting
clouds of mosquitoes, no-see-ums, deer flies, white-socks, and moose
flies somewhat at bay. After unloading our gear and securing the boats,
two of us were designated as the craphouse builders, several as cooks,
and the rest to tidy up the area, store the gear, and get the place ready
for the next day's ventures.

Try building a craphouse out on the tundra. ... First of all we had to
dig down through the permafrost (permanent year-round dirty ice)
while literally being covered with biting insects who haven't had a
blood meal since winter. Then we built a canvas-and-wood-frame

structure over the hole, rigged a canvas door, and had all the comforts of home. Well, not really. It took the biting bugs just about two minutes to discover a tender, exposed hind end sitting unguarded on a two-holer made from a Blazo fuel box, so prior to entry you had to spray DDT inside the crapper in dense white clouds to kill everything flying. You waited a few moments for the desired effect, then darted in to get your business accomplished. You did so in a flurry of a hurry because within minutes a whole new crop of Mother Nature's A-10 warthog critters would arrive, storming the Bastille looking for that tender backside and their next meal of "tenderloin." ...

As for our home, we did the same. Prior to entry, we sprayed a cloud of insecticide inside and waited for a few minutes, all the while walking at a fast clip around the tundra to keep the bugs off their feed. Then we would scramble inside, shutting the door posthaste. Once inside, we stayed put. Outside, the air literally hummed with the sounds of hungry creatures, and outside our few windows we could see black clouds of biting bugs patiently waiting for one of us to err and venture forth.

When getting ready for work during the day, a ritual was developed for each and every one of us. First of all, on went our clothing. Over that went hip boots and a three-quarter-length heavy rubber rain parka. Over our heads went the hood from the rain jacket, which was screwed down tightly over our faces. Onto our exposed faces went a gallon of bug dope, usually a brand called OFF. In fact, we used so much that the skin on our faces and hands often cracked and bled from the volume of chemicals used. With that, out into our surreal world we went, breathing in gobs of the aforementioned insects. It didn't end there! Come evening, we would strip down for bed only to discover that we all had bleeding, welt-covered ankles. The white-socks, a small flylike insect with white markings on the ends of their feet, would have crawled up the outsides of our hip waders, down the insides, up our pant legs, down inside our socks, and bitten small holes into our flesh around the ankles (points of blood constriction). We never felt the bites; those critters injected some sort of painkiller prior to biting. Then they would cut out a small circle of flesh and gorge themselves on the fluids released by the bite. Filled, they would repeat their travels in reverse and escape, leaving a welt that soon itched like the dickens! No wonder the Russians sold Alaska for a mere pittance! It took some getting used to, but soon we were down to a pattern of activity as everyone worked through these little inconveniences. I often wonder how much DDT my system absorbed during that month in the cabin and crapper of the tagging camp.

The first day of work found four of us in a boat anchored twenty-five yards offshore in front of our camp. Two burly men wrestled and held the long piece of railroad rail steady with one end resting on the river bottom, and the other two used a pile driver to drive it deep into the river bottom. About six feet of the rail stuck out from the water when finished, and to it was attached a heavy chain with a large ring on one end. Another group of men took the thousand-foot seine net, anchoring one end to the shore across from the railroad steel so it couldn't pull free. Then the net was loaded into the bow of a Cordova skiff and slowly unwound out to the piece of railroad steel anchored in the river. A short piece of rope was then fastened to the top net line when it was even with the railroad steel, with a hook on the end. That hook was then fastened into the ring chained to the railroad steel. Fastened to the hook holding the net to the ring was another length of rope that ran back to the bank. Once the length of rope on the bank needed to be pulled because of a net full of salmon, the hook would pull free from the ring and the net with its floats would drift downstream with the current. Continuing, the boat holding the remaining net was allowed to drift downstream, slowly playing out the remaining thousand feet of seine. Once at the end of the seine, that boat pulled to shore. Fastened to the end of the top net float rope and the lower lead line was a ten-foot-long two-by-four timber. That was to keep the end of the net from collapsing shut when pulled to shore. A rope was run from the top to the bottom of the two by four and tied off, and another rope was tied in the middle of that rope and trailed to shore. Attached to the bottom of the two-by-four holding the net open was a gunny-sack full of gravel to keep the net in place once anchored twenty-five yards from shore. So what we had was a net anchored at the upstream side from the bank out to a piece of railroad steel in the river. The net now trailing downstream with its lead line was essentially "anchored" to the river bottom. The top line of the net had floats every two feet that kept the net extended from top to bottom.

We used this trapping configuration because when sockeye salmon migrate upstream, they stay just a few yards off shore. They are a small-sized salmon, and the water currents that close to shore are moving more slowly, making it easier to swim upstream. So as the fish migrated upstream, they would pass between the riverbank and the inside of our net. Once at the front of the trap, they would run into the net running from the shore to the hook-and-ring combination on the railroad steel. They would bump the net, causing the floats to jiggle and dance in the water, letting the man at that end know there were fish in the trap. He would pull the rope holding the hook and the front of the net would release. The net would start drifting downstream, and the man at the head of the net would yell to the men at the far end because the salmon, realizing they were in a trap, would race along the inside of the net as they headed back downstream to escape. The man pulling the lead line (me) would give the rope he was holding a slow, steady pull (pulling slowly keeps the bottom of the net on the river floor, preventing escape from underneath). Once the end of the net was ashore, the fish were entirely within its confines. Then we slowly pulled the lead and float lines to shore from the bottom side until the fish were constricted into a small confine. There they were met by men moving a floating trap toward a point where the fish could be dip-netted out of the net's confines and placed inside. The floating trap was nothing more than an enclosed large net (sides and bottom) with rubber tubing around a two-by-four-framed top so the fish could not jump out. Once the fish were in the floating trap, we were ready to begin the tagging and other scientific work.

A floating platform made up of plywood decking laid over sealed and lashed fifty-gallon drums made up our riverside work station. Alongside the platform would be the live well, or fish holding pen. Next to that would be a large washtub full of water and MS-222 that sat on our floating dock. That chemical was used to anesthetize the fish so they could be safely handled (a salmon of any species is terribly strong and almost impossible to hold for the work to be accomplished unless it is drugged). Also on the work platform was a three-foot-high framed contraption holding a wooden trough shaped like a large V. It was sealed at both ends, and when a fish was calm enough to hold, it was taken out of the tub of anesthetic and placed belly-down in the trough. One man held the fish steady by the head and tail while another sexed and measured it. Then a stainless-steel pin holding a colored tag on one end was run through the flesh of the fish above the backbone but below the dorsal fin. Once out the other side, the sharp end of the pin was inserted into a center-cut hole on another colored tag. Then a twist was placed on the end of the pin with a set of needle-nosed pliers, holding the tag in place.

A scale sample was then taken from below the lateral line and to the rear of the fish. Then it was dumped over the side of the floating raft back into the Naknek River to recover and continue its migration. Once the fish were drugged, the entire tagging process took less than two minutes per critter, with the fish returned to the river none the worse for wear. Another man recorded the data as they were being taken, including the tag color combinations and the number from each tag. He also put the wet fish scale on a sticky-backed card for later evaluation. Later those scales could be read under a microscope and aged (one counted the rings on the scale just like the rings on a tree to determine the fish's age class). This process continued until all the fish were removed from the floating holding trap. Then the net was reset and the whole process began again. We worked at this endeavor during daylight hours (sixteen to twenty hours per day) until the sockeye salmon run ceased.

Problems
FROM THE VERY FIRST DAY of the salmon-tagging operation, we ran into a major problem. The Japanese net purchased from the lowest bidder (typical government process) was of such poor quality that when a fish hit the squares of the net HARD, the knots slipped, allowing the fish to run its head and gills into the net square but no farther. That was just enough to slam shut their gills plates, and if we didn't remove them quickly, they suffocated. We did everything under the sun to get the fish out of the net as fast as we could, but to no avail. With up to several hundred fish in the net at a time, we found ourselves killing about fifty beautiful sockeye salmon *every day* because of the lousy net! These are the fish a shopper in the supermarket today pays at least $6 for 303-sized cans of meat! Now, those fish ran from five to seven pounds each. Even big eaters like us couldn't eat 250-plus pounds of fish per day! Reporting our problem to our leaders in King Salmon was of no use. First, they had no money to buy another net, and even if they had, one could not be purchased and placed in use before the salmon run was over because of time-related purchasing requirements. Typical government horse apples!

But we had a saving grace. A mile directly across the river was an air force recreation camp, a place where noncommissioned officers could take some R&R from their regular jobs at their isolation duty stations and do some relaxing and fishing. After the first day we took our fish over to that air force station, and they gladly cleaned and froze our dead salmon. Then when each noncommissioned officer went back to his base after his R&R, he was given several very fine-tasting fish from the fast-filling freezers. As a result, none went to waste. There was another silver lining as well: the sergeant in charge of the camp would let us raggedy-assed kids shower and wash our clothes at their laundry facility because we were government employees as well. That was pure heaven because it was that or bathe in the 39-degree water of the Naknek River. I am here to tell you, when you bathe in water that cold, your heart really does pause for a moment when you first get in. And other external parts disappear up into the body. ... It almost was better to smell like an old bear than to bathe! That silver lining turned to gold when the sergeant allowed us to also eat in the mess hall when we brought them some fish. *That included eating all the fresh vegetables we could eat and drinking all the fresh milk we could guzzle!* Talk about a little bit of heaven. There were times when we could hardly roll into or out of our boats by the time we got back from such feasts. However, the ever-present swarms of biting bugs saw to it that we moved our carcasses speedily, bloated by the good food or not, from the boat to the protection of our cabin.

Grumpy and Stumpy

ONE FINE DAY, as Doug and I sat at the end of the net waiting for the call to close it, we heard someone yelling for help. Looking out over the river, we saw a boat about three-eighths of a mile away. It was drifting downstream, and two fishermen were standing up in it waving their arms. Realizing they needed help, I grabbed one of our boats and motored out to see what their problem was. Both were older men, and I thought they looked familiar, but the problem at hand and some fast-approaching rough water pushed that thought out of my mind. They had drifted down from the air force officer camp (six miles above our net site), fishing all the way. However, when they tried to start their outboard motor, it refused. Throwing them a rope, I towed them back to our tagging site, where we could work on their motor (you learn fast how to repair boat motors in Alaska if you spend any time at all in the bush). Doug and I pulled the cowling off their outboard motor and began trouble-shooting. We eventually discovered that they had used gas with water and rust in it, which had fouled their spark plugs and clogged their fuel lines. We started cleaning up their problem as the dark-haired man broke out a cigar and used its smoke to clear off the mosquitoes and other biters clouded over us. Soon we had the problem fixed except for their tank of dirty fuel. Taking one of our extra fuel tanks and lines, we exchanged it for the one in their system. I asked the stumpy one if they would bring our fuel tank back the next day, and he said they would. They also talked about how they were going to "kill" the officer in charge of the boat motor pool, or at least ship him to some faraway place, for not doing a better job in the care of equipment.

About then, Steve yelled, "Fish in the trap!" Doug and I sprang into action, forgetting the two men and their problems as we started slowly pulling the lead line. Without being asked, the two strangers jumped right in and asked what they could do. Soon the four of us were working the net and moving the fish into its upper reaches for tagging. Both men got excited at what we were doing and began asking a lot of questions. We gladly supplied them with answers and soon had them tagging salmon like professionals. This went on for a couple of hours, and we had a great time with the two bearded and grubby men. It soon came time for them to leave, but before they did, we loaded up their boat with fresh net-killed salmon. They were pleased as punch, and the brush-faced one even gave me a black, strong-smelling cigar that I smoked with relish later in the day. Off they went, and back to work we went as more fish moved into our trap.

The next day they returned with our gas tank and fuel line. They also brought us a fresh baked ham, a case of canned whole milk (oh God, manna from heaven), some fresh vegetables, and a box of the foul-smelling but damn good cigars. We all parted happy as clams, and we sent them away with another fresh boatload of the tremendously good-eating sockeye salmon recently killed by our crappy net.

The next day found us working in a heavy rainstorm as we hauled in tons of salmon. We worked our tail ends to the bone and at the end of the day were beat and dragging. We also had another mess of dead salmon courtesy of the cheap net. ... Over to the air force recreation camp we went to get rid of our fish and maybe get invited in for a nice hot meal as well. The sergeant met us at the dock and was happy to get the fish since he had another hundred men coming in for R&R the next day. We all pitched in and an hour later had the fish cleaned and into their freezers for preservation. "Come on, guys. Tonight is steak night, and you fellows are sure more than welcome to join us," said the sergeant. Man, that was music to our ears, since we never got steak and were soaked, tired, filthy, and all. Washing up as best as we could, into the dining hall we trooped, covered with fish slime, scales, blood, and such. Long hair and beards rounded out our routine! Realizing we looked and smelled like a troop of great apes, we got our food and sat off to one side of the dining hall so as not to embarrass our friend for his hospitality. We had no more than started eating our food (five steaks on my plate alone) when from another corner of the crowded dining hall boomed a voice: "Sergeant! Who the hell are those grubby hippie puke sons of bitches? How the hell did they get into this facility and by whose orders?"

Looking across the room about six tables away, I saw a tall, thin man heading for our table with a look of a mission written all over his face. Our sergeant rose from his meal, snapped to attention, and said, "Colonel, they are government employees and are here by my request. They bring us fresh salmon and have always conducted themselves in the most professional manner, sir."

By now the tall colonel had strode up to our table and, scanning our miserable carcasses with obvious disdain, continued his ranting. "I don't care who the hell these smelly pieces of crap are, where they came from, or who they work for. They are goddamned hippies, and I won't stand for them being on government property!"

"Colonel, as I said, they are here at my request. They are government employees and can legally be here. My directives clearly allow the air force to extend such courtesies to those in such a position. Sir, with all due respect, I would remind the colonel, he is at an air force noncommissioned officers' recreation camp, a place reserved for noncoms so they can relax away from the military command and structure," replied our sergeant friend as he held his ground.

"Sergeant, may I remind *you* that you are addressing a superior officer. To continue along the lines you have chosen will get you a general court-martial, mister!"

"Yes, sir," replied our friend.

"Now, get these pieces of shit out of here, and that is an order!"

By now we all felt like crap for getting our friend in trouble and were starting to get up and leave. Then, from out of the blue, another man yelled, "Colonel, you son of a bitch!" It had gotten quiet when the colonel jumped us, but when this second voice bellowed out from the crowded dining room it got so quiet you could have heard a mouse pissing on a ball of cotton. Even the air force cooks and servers in the kitchen and those along the serving line were frozen in place as they

watched this new drama unfolding. Across the room came the grubby
man we had pulled off the river several days earlier. He was still just as
grubby and apparently had been quietly dining with the noncoms
when our altercation started. Our colonel who had been doing all the
yelling was white as a sheet and was standing ramrod straight at full
attention!

"Colonel, you son of a bitch. How dare you come to this camp and
raise hell like you own it? You have thirty minutes to return to the officers' camp and pack your bags. *I hope Karachi is to your liking, mister,
because that is where your next duty station is going to be!*"

The colonel mumbled something and was out of there as if he had
been shot from a gun. All of us watched him literally fleeing the dining
hall and then turned to face the grubby man. He faced us and said,
"Gentlemen, on behalf of the United States Air Force, I apologize.
Sergeant, I apologize to you as well. It is entirely within your right to
run this camp within our policies and procedures, and it's obvious you
have done so." Turning to the hundred or so men sitting quietly in the
dining hall, the grubby one said in a tone everyone clearly understood,
"Gentlemen, on behalf of the General Staff, I apologize for the behavior
of one of my fellow officers this evening. It will not happen again.
Now, please return to your excellent meals before they get cold."

With that, the dining hall literally buzzed with discussions of what
had just occurred. The grubby fellow apologized once more, shook all
our hands, and told the sergeant to carry on. With that, he disappeared
back to his table, sitting down with his stumpy cohort to finish their
meals. We finished our meals that evening and throughout the remaining part of the month continued to bring over fresh fish "gilled" by our
lousy damn net. I never saw the grubby one or his stumpy sidekick in
Alaska again. Never saw that damn yelling colonel again either, now
that I think about it. ...

By the way, we later discovered from the sergeant that the grubby
one was none other than General Curtis Le May of the Air Force, and
the stumpy one was a man who had spent thirty seconds over Tokyo
during a dark period of time in the history of our nation. That's right;
he was none other than *the* General Jimmy Doolittle. ... A man I
chanced to meet and visit with in his later years at his office at 1612 K
Street in Washington, D.C., when I found myself stationed in that
same building with the Division of Law Enforcement some seventeen
years later.

A Monster from the Deep

ONCE THE SOCKEYE SALMON run petered out, our tagging camp was closed and we were sent back down to King Salmon to refit. After caring for our equipment, we prepared for our next assignment. From King Salmon we flew eighty air miles inland by float plane to an outback camp where we began the business of checking spawning streams and beach spawning sites for the fish we had tagged a month or so earlier. Our home for this stint included a ten-by-twelve-foot plywood cook cabin and a nine-by-twelve-foot wood-framed canvas tent. Our outhouse consisted of a wooden Blazo fuel-can box stuck on a point behind our living quarters where you could sit and gaze out across the beautiful landscape. We were situated on the south end of Grosvenor Lake at the headwaters of the Grosvenor River. Being immediately adjacent to that quietly flowing river all day and night, we could constantly hear the soft *plop* music of salmon jumping out of the water as they migrated to their natal streams. There were a lot fewer bugs there than on the tundra, and life started to get downright bearable. A crew of six was left there for the next assignment and the rest were flown to Coville Lake some twenty miles away to undertake similar duties.

Our assignment was to take two trusty Cordova skiffs and put one thousand feet of seine in the bows of the vessels (five hundred feet in each boat). That way, if we spotted any fish spawning along the beach or shallow lake bottom, we would make our approach in reverse from the deep-water side. Once close to our spawners, the boats would split up (still held together by the net) as we quietly backed toward the fish, slowly playing out the net from the bows of the boats and forming an escape-proof horseshoe of net around the fish as we eventually pinned them against the shore. Jumping out, we would slowly pull in the net until it was at the edge of the beach. From there we would remove and record the tags, get blood and scale samples, though it was harder now to get scales now because the fish were starting to absorb their scales for the protein source of energy. Keep in mind that once the Pacific salmon leave the ocean, they eat no more. In essence, they absorb themselves for the energy needed to migrate upriver and spawn. Once they spawn, they linger for a while, then die. It might seem like a waste, but it isn't really. Once dead, they rot, expelling their remaining energy into the salmon streams—so much so that it can be hard to stand the stink in those areas from thousands of rotting fish! However, those released nutrients provide a food source for the microscopic plant life in the stream. That provides for a bloom of such life, which in turn is eaten by the tiny salmon emerging from their eggs. So in essence, the adults continue caring for their young long after they are gone.

When we finished our scientific processing of that bunch, the two boats still "tied" together, with equal lengths of net back in the bows, would slowly cruise the shoreline looking for more of what were then called beach spawners. Day after day, mile after slow mile, this was our regimen. In one of the boats was a ten-foot aluminum tower structured so one of us could scramble up to sit in the top. This plus a set of polarized eyeglasses (for glare reduction) allowed the person in the tower to scan farther ahead of the boats and to spot the spawning salmon long before we alarmed them with the noise of our outboard motors. The unique glasses allowed us to see into the water better and, with the height advantage the tower offered, gave the observer a wonderful distance and depth-penetration viewing advantage.

The lakebed geography over which we worked was unique. A shallow-water shelf ran out maybe one hundred yards from the beach, with the water running from ten to fifteen feet deep. Then the shelf abruptly ended and the lake bottom dropped off steeply into black water, kind of like dropping into a deep canyon. It was a little ghostly being up in that tower looking down into the water at the edge of the shelf and then seeing it drop off maybe hundreds of feet into the deep black waters. Up from the depths of those waters at the edge of the shelf rose long, skeletonlike fingers of limbs from trees long dead, reaching out from the black waters almost as if asking for help or seeking to ensnare our boats.

One bright and beautiful day, it was my turn in the tower. Scrambling up into its heights, I took my position as observer as the two boats quietly motored along together. With those special glasses, I could see through the glare off the water for several hundred feet ahead of the boats and began looking for beach spawners, especially those wearing our tags, which were so brightly colored that they could be seen from many yards away in the clear water. *Jesus, what the hell is that?* About fifty yards ahead of the boats, right at the shelf-break line into the deep, was a long, dark object! It appeared to be about twenty feet long and was slowly moving away from our boats. It obviously was alive and appeared to be some sort of giant fish! Slowly it moved into the deep water until I could hardly see it. Taking off my glasses in surprise to look, I could see nothing but the glare off the water. Quickly putting them back on, I caught the last glimpse of the creature as it disappeared. I stood in that tower in utter disbelief! I had never seen such a large ... whatever it was. ... Turning to the guys below, I started to say something and then realized the critter was gone, and they couldn't see it without the special glasses anyway. Thinking better of saying something and appearing to be a little crazy, I kept my mouth shut and brain working in overtime. What the hell could it have been? A giant arctic char of some sort, or a massive white sturgeon? I had no idea and spent the rest of my shift looking in vain for another glimpse of the thing from the deep. Over the next few days, every time I took my spot in the tower I looked for it. No luck, and no one else ever said they had seen such an apparition. I finally convinced myself that it must have been my imagination.

I was in the tower on another fine day several days later, getting a nice suntan as I looked for beach spawners, when destiny hit again ... *there the something was!* Off the port bow about ten o'clock ... again, right at the deep-water line and slowly moving away from the noise of the boat into the deep, black waters. God, I could hardly believe my eyes and took my time making observations. This thing was at least twenty feet long, if not longer. It was definitely fishlike, and I could see its tail slowly moving back and forth as it propelled itself downward. Again with no show of speed or concern, it moved into the deep and out of sight. Hastily looking down from the tower, I could see from their activity that nobody else had seen anything. They were all smoking, shooting the bull, or lying against the bulkheads half asleep. Damn! I wanted to say something, but I just knew no one would believe a word without some sort of proof. Shaking my head, I got back to the duties at hand and let the latest revelation rest in the back of my brain. I had seen something, but what the hell was it? Was it dangerous? Was it a new species? How thought after thought tore through my budding scientific mind. I wanted so badly to share my discovery with my crewmates but quickly realized they also had scientific backgrounds—and I had better have proof of something of this magnitude or keep my mouth shut to avoid looking like a damned fool!

The work went on for another ten days, and then another shift in the work plan was in the offing. We moved our base camp to the south end of Coville Lake, where we offloaded our nets and other gear. Our crew was being split once again into smaller groups so we could cover more spawning streams now that the bulk of the fish had arrived in the area. While waiting for the plane carrying some of our supplies for our new camp, we had a chance to mingle with the rest of the crew we had been separated from weeks earlier. That also gave us the opportunity to eat some good food and, after the arrival of the plane, drink some beer. Our big boss, Dr. Charlie De Costanzo back in King Salmon, was about to pay off a wager: he had bet a case of beer for every thousand sockeye we tagged. It seemed that the sockeye-tagging crew from the year before had tagged only a little over 2,400 fish. Realizing he needed greater numbers to give the study the scientific weight it needed, Charlie had offered a case of beer per thousand of tagged fish as an incentive to our tagging crew. Since we had tagged over 34,000 fish, guess what the Grumman Goose (seaplane) was carrying?

When crews get back together, the bad news is shared with the good. One of our original thirteen lads had been killed. Two boat crews working in Lake Iliamna had had a strong blow come up while they were eating lunch on the shore. It was so abrupt and violent that both of their boats broke free from their moorings and drifted out into the lake. A tall, thin kid stripped off his hip boots, threw on a life preserver, and jumped into the water to swim to the boats before they got too far out into the vastness of the lake. The rest of the crew, standing on the shore and knowing better, yelled for him to come back, but he kept swimming toward the boats. The bottom line was that if any crew missed radio call twice, King Salmon would send an aircraft to locate them. Seeing that the radios were on the boat, I guess the kid felt they needed them for that contact, and away he went. *He never made it!* The water, fed by glacier melt from upstream, was a deadly cold 35 degrees; he developed hypothermia after swimming about thirty-five yards and succumbed before anyone could help. They found his body two days later and miles from shore, still floating in his life preserver.

One thing I remember clearly to this day is the sheer beauty of Alaska. It is beyond compare or description. But so is the danger lying just below the surface of that land. *It is everywhere and all the time.* Make one little mistake, and more than likely it will be your last. It is the only place I have been, in all my worldly travels, where I watched my *every* step. The danger always at arm's length was palpable, to me at least. It was almost as if the land was trying to kill you—and it often succeeded! Death was lurking at every corner, and there are lots of corners in that vast land.

Finally the Grumman arrived, and the first case of beer hitting the beach lasted but seconds. As did the second, third, fourth, and into the fifth (twelve thirsty men plus the pilot can do that). By then everyone was feeling little pain, and a lot of laughter rang out from the camp that day. That was, until I opened my drunken mouth and spilled the beans about the monster I had seen several times while working from the tower. ... The howling talk and laughter instantly died, and silence was thick in the air. All my buddies on the boat netting crew just looked at me as if I were a ghost. Man, I didn't know what to say. Then it happened! Everyone was trying to talk at once. *The whole crew had seen that or a similar monster of the deep along the break line!* All had tales to tell but, like me, had said nothing, believing that no one would swallow the story. For the next hour the talk was about nothing but the huge thing all of us from the two boat crews had seen numerous times. The guys from the other crews just listened in awe. They knew that all of us had not lost our marbles, so we must have really seen what we thought we saw. There were no answers but a damn lot of heated and questioning talk was in the air. When the limnology crew (graduate fisheries students) got back to camp that evening, we set upon them like ants on a piece of cake at a picnic. They looked at us as if we were nothing but a bunch of drunken goofballs. Finally we got through to them with our story, and they did nothing but shake their heads in wonder. They knew of nothing of the sort nor had seen anything that big inhabiting those waters. To this day, I have no idea what I saw. All I know is, I did see something that was huge, real, and alive. Thank God the others saw it as well!

Hardscrabble Creek and the Fish Weir

I WAS ASSIGNED the next day, along with another chap, to go up a nearby creek that emptied into one end of Grosvenor Lake in Katmai National Monument. It was named Hardscrabble Creek, and the name said it all: a small creek just barely navigable with a small, lightweight boat. Being the heaviest, I would get in the bow with all our gear while Larry would run the outboard. We would get the boat up on step in the deeper, lower reaches of the creek. Flying upstream as the water shallowed out, we would hope and pray that our being on step (level with only a small section of the stern of the boat in the water) would carry us to our campsite. Most of the time that strategy worked. However, as the season progressed and the water level dropped, we would always ground out a few hundred yards from camp. Then we had to drag the boat and its supplies over the shallow water and riffles.

Our campsite was nothing more than a level place right beside the creek. It was covered with three-foot-tall grasses intersected by numerous bear trails. Those trails in the tall grasses are the easiest way to get around Alaska's creeks, but those same trails have often been used for centuries, and many times in traveling them one is surprised by a very large bear coming the other way on his way to a salmon dinner at the creekside! That always makes for a memory of a lifetime. ...

"Flying" up the creek in the boat for the first time was a wonder in itself. Salmon raced from under the boat as we sped upstream. There were beaver scattered throughout, a wolverine or two, several gray wolves, and Alaskan brown bear *everywhere!* When I say everywhere, I mean at every turn in the stream. They didn't seem bothered by our presence, so we quickly calmed down. Arriving at our campsite in a light rain (an ever-present climatological aspect of that part of Alaska), we quickly set up our nine-by-twelve canvas tent and got our gear inside before it got too wet. Larry assembled the cots and, taking our sleeping bags out of the duffel bags, laid them out. I hopped too and soon had the Coleman lantern happily blazing away, providing some warmth and drying features to our tent. Then I whipped up supper from the many cans of supplies we had brought along. Soon the air was filled with good smells. As the creek noisily flowed by our tent, accompanied by the occasional tail-slapping sound of the migrating salmon, we had a repast fit for a king. After chow and cleanup (washing the tin plates in the creek sand like trappers of old), the two of us sat outside our tent in the light rain, wearing our raingear and watching the world go by. The creek was jug-full of salmon along with numerous bear loading up on the fish grits so necessary for their survival during the coming hibernation. Interspersed with the bear was the occasional wolverine or pack of wolves, who relished the fish as well. However, their fishing differed from that of the bears. They would wait on the creek banks until a bear caught a salmon, then take the fish from the bear by many means and ruses. It was a real treat to watch.

Having built our tent next to a major bear trail running through the tall stream-bank grasses, we were surprised several times by the presence of a five-hundred- to thousand-pound bear just feet away. However, they paid little attention to us with what riches awaited them in the creek. Finally it got dark, and, realizing we had one hell of a job ahead of us over the next several days, we hit the hay. I don't think I slept much that night. The air was full of the sounds a stream makes flowing over a rocky bottom. That noise was punctuated with the sounds of salmon racing to and fro, up and down the stream. Those songs were capped off by the sounds of numerous large bear, many times only feet away, splashing after their salmon dinners or making loud blowing-in-and-out sounds to better smell the invaders as they paused to examine our tent from just a few feet away. The last sounds I remembered that fine night before I drifted off to sleep were the ripping sounds bear make as they tear apart the flesh of the fresh-caught salmon.

Dawn came early, finding Larry and me busy about camp. I fixed breakfast (fried Spam, eggs, and sliced spuds) while he prepared to boat downstream and start hauling up loads of equipment and a zillion two-by-fours and weir pickets (six-foot-long by one-inch hollow aluminum poles). We had been assigned to build a fish weir, which is nothing more than a picket fence with three-legged weighted supports every fifteen feet, built across the stream. Well, it is a little more than that once you build the supports, nail the weir pickets on the two-by-four frame every inch apart, fill the sandbags to hold each supporting section in place against the flow of the stream, and build a platform on which to sit in the middle of the whole damn contraption. Our fish weir was built across 160 feet of stream. The purpose was to stop all fish migration upstream to the spawning grounds. The salmon would build up in large numbers below the weir, and periodically we would go out, sit on the small platform built into the middle of the weir, pull up four or five weir pickets, and let the fish come flooding through. In so doing, we would get an accurate count of spawning numbers, get blood samples from some fish and scale samples from others, and recover tags from tagged fish. But I am getting ahead of myself.

Larry would make a run downstream to where the stream and lake met. Sitting there was a Grumman Goose seaplane full of lumber, tools, and other needed equipment. Larry would get a load of gear, balance it in the bow of the boat, and roar back upstream. Once at camp, we would unload the supplies and he would head back down for more. In the meantime, I would start building the weir. This activity went on for two days until we had accomplished our task. In the meantime, the bear got more and more used to our presence, and we became more accustomed to theirs. In fact, many times the bear would catch fish right at our feet as we worked, and no one broke the truce. Of course, it helped to be working in Katmai National Monument, a place where hunting was forbidden and the critters were not really afraid of humans—just curious and cautious.

After a time we had our weir ready for business and commenced our research activities. It was quite a learning ground. It got so we could identify thirteen individual Alaskan brown bear frequenting our fish weir. We even named them all, and sometimes I swear they recognized their names. We worked every hour of daylight, and in June that is a lot. But the work was fun, informational, and a new life experience, and I loved it. I developed a sense and understanding about the salmon that I would never have acquired without that time with them in the bush. It was deeply moving to see them struggling against all odds, having come clear from the ocean many hundreds of miles away without eating, then fighting to stay out of the way of those things that ate them, finding a mate, locating their natal streams, fighting through fatal infections of fungus that many times covered the entire fish, and facing many other dangers. Soon I found myself understanding the heart and soul of the salmon and began developing strong feelings about protecting them, feelings that were realized years later when I was a state and federal conservation officer. That understanding had not been lost on me if the number of salmon snaggers, gill netters, illegal commercial fishermen, those taking over-limits, and the members of various illegal commercial fish houses feeling the sting of the courts were any measure.

A Bear in the Tent!

ONE EVENING my partner left for more supplies after the pilot of the Grumman Goose had buzzed our tent to let us know he was back in the country. From there, the pilot would fly to the lake and land. Taxiing over to the shoreline, he would trundle up onto the bank (they had wheels they could lower once the landing in the water was over) and wait for the arrival of my partner. It seemed that just about every day when we got up, we had to repair our fish weir. A two-by-four fish weir just doesn't stop a determined brown bear when he or she is chasing a salmon. After a collision, a three- to four-foot hole was the usual result, finding us in almost constant repair status. My partner headed back downstream while I repaired what I could with natural materials and continued counting the fish passing through the opening in the weir. I recovered numerous tags by dip-netting the fish as they tried to pass through the opening in the weir, as well as blood samples and more fish scales for the aging studies.

That afternoon a terrible storm blew up, and my partner did not make it back for the night. Not too concerned, since he could sleep in the belly of the plane, I continued my duties until it was too dark to work. Crawling back into my tent, I took off my wet gear and commenced making supper, the usual canned beans and stew mixed together. Having nothing further to do and not wanting to sit outside the tent and watch the world go by because of the fierce squall, I crawled into the sleeping bag, and soon the outside noises disappeared into my dream world.

Rattle-clank-clunk went the pots and pans in our camp box, located just inside the door of the tent at the head of my bed. Waking up and realizing I had company, I *very* slowly moved to unzip my sleeping bag. Once that was done, I slowly reached over the side of my cot for my .348 Winchester. Feeling the familiar cold steel, I slid my hand down to the pistol grip, cocked the hammer, and slowly lifted the rifle to my bed. *Clink-clank-clunk* sounds continued unabated from the end of my cot, not more than three feet from my head. Slowly, oh so slowly, I turned and looked up into the eyes of a grizzly bear cub licking the pans in our grub box! *Damn*, I thought. That meant only one thing. This bear cub was one of Suzie's (a female with three cubs who was a common visitor to our weir). There is nothing worse than messing with a bear cub when mama is around—except maybe messing with a cow moose and her calf. Turning so I could look the little fellow in the eyes (almost literally, as we were now separated by about two feet of air), I said (quietly of course), *"Shhhusss, get!"*

That damn little bear did what I had not expected. Instead of running back to mom, he stood up, arched his neck, and went, *Urrrgh.* Gutsy little bastard, I thought. *"Shhhuss,"* I said one more time, and that did it. The cub, realizing there was something very close to him that he didn't understand, arched his neck like an adult bear in a fighting mode, went *Urrrgh*, and then stepped backward—*stepping back right off our cook-stove table and into our box of plates, cups, and other cooking items! Crash* went the cub and, scared by the noise, let out a squall to melt the heart of any mama bear! *Woof-woof-woof* went Suzie, who had been fishing in the creek not far from the tent. Starting to scramble out of my sleeping bag, I could hear her running through the stream toward the tent making *gump-gump-gump* sounds as she popped her jaws in warning. Getting to my feet, I saw a giant shadow fall across the side of the tent as Suzie came crashing through! Quickly realizing that shooting my rifle at three feet would do me no good, I dove for the back side of the tent. Figuring I would dive under the tent and escape out the back, I hadn't counted on one thing. When we erected the tent, we had staked it every foot to keep curious bears from sticking their noses under the tent, lifting up the canvas, and coming on in. Hitting the end of the tent as the rest of it blew up with a very mad female grizzly and a still squalling cub, I hammered into the ground doing at least a hundred miles an hour! Slamming out the rear of the tent, I realized I no longer had any clothes on ... the closely staked tent had pulled every stitch off me, and now there I stood in front of God and everybody, looking like an African mole rat. Hearing a screaming mad grizzly behind me as the tent folded in and around her, I took off running—no, sprinting—for a thicket of Sitka spruce nearby. Going like a house afire, I slammed into the largest tree I could find (not nearly big enough to hold my ample carcass, to my way of thinking) and started climbing it in record time.

Meanwhile, the sow grizzly, thinking the tent had her, commenced to make handkerchiefs from what had once been a damn nice tent. The tent collapsing around the bear probably saved my life because it slowed her down long enough to give me time to scamper up my somewhat precarious tiny spruce tree. But when she finished with the tent, *here she came! Wham,* Suzie slammed into the base of the tree, almost knocking loose my bear-hug grip (no pun intended). If that had happened, you wouldn't be reading these lines today. ... Not being able to reach me, she began biting great chunks of bark and wood from the base of the tree. Oh, great! I thought. She is going to mow down the tree with her teeth and get me anyway! Holding that thought in mind, I never moved or said anything for fear of renewing her wrath at what had scared her cub. Hell, I couldn't do much anyway except pee down the front of that damn small tree every time she shook it. The goddamned tree was only maybe eight inches through, hardly enough to take much more chewing, I thought. Realizing that, I kept my movement to zero. When she stood on her hind legs and swung at me with those dangerously long front claws, they were only maybe three feet from my hind end! So I really didn't have a whole lot of options.

Then the real problem hit! Remember, when I left the tent, it was without any clothing. I now had an aerial problem to add to the big furry one below! Every goddamned mosquito, no-see-um, deer fly, moose fly, and white-sock in the vicinity had located me! Since I didn't dare take a hand off the slim tree top for fear of being knocked loose, the flying critters had a ball. They helped themselves to just about every ounce of juice I had in my body ... and that problem was compounded by another one. Any of you readers who has been around a Sitka spruce knows just how prickly they can be. Millions of dead small limbs, rough bark, millions of live limbs, and needles that will grab you back if you grab them. Well, remember the chap who had just climbed such a tree with nothing on? You got it! My entire front had been scraped off (well, almost), and the flying critters were having a go at my unprotected backside. I was hurting so much that I even considered coming down that tree once Suzie had moved off to the remains of the tent and was destroying the same, picking up my Winchester, and having it out! Just about then, here she came again and recommenced ripping and tearing at the tree. I was not so sure I would outlast that onslaught. For some reason, all the biting bugs on my backside mattered little at that stage of the game.

Finally tiring of the game after having taught me a lesson, Suzie gathered up her cubs and ambled off into the willows below camp. Giving her some time to make sure she was gone, I finally slid down my tree (yeah, that was fun) and made a hasty run for the tent. Plowing through the remains, I dug out my .348 Winchester (unharmed), checked the .250-grain bullet in the chamber, and turned toward where Suzie had exited. If she came back now, her day was going to end in a not-so-nice manner. I had had about all I could take of that bear and the bugs and was now hell-bent on vengeance. Fortunately, she didn't return, and the constant whirring and biting of the bugs got my attention once again. Digging out some clothes from the tent's remains, I dressed and set about trying to restore some order to the mess on the creek bank. Then I heard my partner coming back. His tales of being marooned on the lakeshore with the pilot and his plane along with a good home-cooked meal, a dry place to sleep, and a nice visit didn't set too well with me at the moment. That changed when he produced a large tinfoil package containing several campfire-baked spuds, a rather large T-bone steak, and half an apple pie.

Fortunately, the pilot was still in country, and my partner was able to go back downstream and procure another tent from the stores located in the Grumman's cavernous insides. For the next week or so, things settled down and the run of salmon on Hardscrabble Creek began to peter out. We dismantled the weir, putting all the parts where the crew the next year could easily find them, and headed back to base camp on Grosvenor Lake.

I found it ironic that years later as the special agent in charge of the Denver office for the U.S. Fish and Wildlife Service, I found myself protecting grizzlies instead of lying in wait for them so I could end their life with a bullet. It is amazing how the old boy upstairs works his magic. I had learned more about that thing called "survival" in the great land called Alaska. As I said before, death was always around every corner in that country.

The Storm

LEAVING THE GROSVENOR LAKE CAMP, my partner and I headed for the south end of Coville Lake and another camp some twenty miles away. The old and by now friendly Cordova skiff fairly flew the distance, and upon landing we were greeted by several old friends from our earlier tagging crew. After dinner we discovered that we were in for another series of projects. This time we would be stationed out of the Grosvenor Lake camp (twenty miles back across the lake) and were going to continue netting late arrivals on the Grosvenor River. We were to leave the next morning, and five of us with two boats would comprise the netting crew. That night was spent getting reacquainted, eating good food, and sleeping without having to worry about a bear coming into one's tent.

The next morning the sky was an ugly gray, tinged with streaks of yellow, orange, and red. Some sort of weather change was on the way and as we hurriedly loaded two Cordovas, Larry grimly came out with the latest weather report. It seemed that King Salmon was undergoing some of the fiercest weather of the whole summer. Winds exceeding eighty miles per hour, intense, almost tropical rains, and dangerous temperature plunges. "If we hurry, we can beat it," Larry said. "They are eighty air miles away, but if we get it in gear and I can keep both engines running, we can get to our next base camp in fine style." The fellows in the first Cordova needed little prodding. Off they went and were soon out of sight, driven by two powerful 40-horse Evinrude outboards running at full throttle. Doug Sherve and I piled more gear into our boat, including a new 40-horse engine for one of our other boat crews farther down the line. When we finished our chores, Doug and I piled into the center of our heavily laden Cordova and Larry took the helm. We were carrying one thousand feet of net, a spare 40-horse engine, thirty gallons of white gas, all our personal gear, four five-gallon cans of outboard motor fuel, and several cases of outboard motor oil. As Larry cranked up the engines, I took another look at the skies, especially to the west. They were now yellow and gray—ugly and getting uglier!

Shoving off from the Coville camp, we sped down the Coville River and out into Grosvenor Lake on full step. Twenty miles of lake and we would be safely home in our next base camp. As we hammered along under the power of the two engines running wide open, I noticed that the lake was strangely like a piece of glass. That was not right, I thought as we sped along. Grosvenor Lake always had a chop due to its huge size. Looking back over the stern, I got the shock of my life! The ugly gray and yellow skies to the west had now turned to black, and there was a weather front like I had never seen (until I got caught in a typhoon in Asia) bearing down on us. The water just under the black front quickly approaching us was churning the glass flat lake surfaces up into twenty-foot rollers with white caps on the crests! "Larry," I yelled. "Look to the west!" Turning, he went a shade of gray I had never seen in him. He was pretty resolute under fire but had just shown his other side. Doug and I quickly put on our raincoats and rolled up our hip boots to hold out the approaching rain. Not one of us had a life jacket on or in the boat to wear. ... Who says twenty-year-olds are adults?

Grabbing the throttles, I held the Cordova on course while Larry hastily put on his raingear. By now a roaring of high winds having a fit with themselves was heard. It sounded like a thousand freight trains coming our way, all pissed at having to do so! The storm reached us before we had gotten a mile from shore. There was no turning back now. We were in it for the duration. *Wham*, a wall of wind and water hit us from the stern. Down went Larry into the bottom of the boat, and Doug and I were knocked off the center seat by the wind's force! Quickly regaining his feet, Larry grabbed the helm and the steady, well-built Cordova just hammered along. Doug and I, realizing the danger, quickly sat on the floor of the boat to lower our gravity as each of us untied a gallon bailing bucket from the struts. *Whoom*, two feet of water rolled over the stern, almost swamping the boat! We were now in a violent oceanlike situation. Twenty-foot waves with howling winds reaching eighty to one hundred miles per hour were now our bedfellows! Doug and I bailed like dervishes as waves poured over the stern and bow of the boat as if trying to drag us down. Larry, the ever-alert boatman, tacked us on a course that was less dangerous, but we were still in the middle of the storm. Our boat would race down the back of a huge wave and crash into the trough, and three feet of water would roll over the heavily loaded bow, almost burying Doug and me. We would bail like crazy while Larry fought for control as we climbed the next wave. When we reached the top of a twenty-foot roller, the wind was so strong that it would stop us as it lifted the bow! But thanks to the thousand feet of net in the bow, the god of the winds could not quite blow us over from bow to stern. Then down the back of that wave we would plummet, crashing into the trough, and in would come another three-foot wall of water. The energy of those waves would almost wash Doug and me right out of the boat! But we held fast by the grace of God and the lead in our asses, bailing as if our lives depended on it. And they did!

Larry, experimenting with our predicament, would reduce the engine power as we hurtled down the back of the waves and then give them full power after the wave broke over the bow. I think he had become aware of how far the sides of the Cordova caved outward and then rebounded with the impact upon hitting the troughs. The boat was built tough, but not that tough! With the sides moving outward every time we hit, it was only a matter of time before we broke up. It was one superhuman fight to stay alive! It was readily apparent that the three of us were pitted against the forces in Alaska that make it their business to take lives, not spare them. Soon we realized that the Cordova skiff would take the best hurled at us as long as we did the right thing, and we took heart, almost to the point that we relished everything the weather could throw at us. We felt almost cocky. It sounds a little crazy, but that was the way it was with death so close to our front door. All of us grimly fought on, realizing that to sink was certain death! Between the frigid water temperature and violent waves, our chances of making shore, even just yards away, were nil. Knowing that, we grimly battled on. By now the winds had picked up even more, and the Cordova many times stopped cold in its tracks when it reached the top of a wave. The only thing carrying us over the crest was the following wave, and on we went, but oh, so slowly. We could see the shoreline every now and then through the almost tropical downpour, but we sure as hell were not making much forward headway, especially given the nearly nineteen miles we still had to travel to reach safety. ...

After six hours of numbing cold, high winds, and now even higher waves, we faced another problem. We were getting low on fuel! Crawling back between the waves to the fuel tanks, I saw that we were dangerously close to empty in both tanks (I had seen them floating when each great wave broke over our bow). Knowing that to lose our engines would mean instant sinking and death due to loss of steering control, I yelled at Larry over the winds, "I have to change our tanks or we will run out!" Straining to see through squinted eyes due to the stinging rain falling in sheets, he nodded without taking his eyes off the course he had set. Pumping up the pressure bulbs in each new reserve fuel tank, I changed them one at a time. Then I had to tie the almost empty ones to the struts on the sides of the boat to avoid having them blown overboard. Crawling back to Doug, I again began bailing the boat, which now was acting as if it was almost too heavy to carry on.

Six hours later, we faced a *real* problem! Normally we could have scooted across that lake in an hour or less, using just a few gallons of fuel. We were now twelve hours into the storm and, like it or not, were low on fuel once again. This time we didn't have any extra tanks to just quickly switch over, and our spare regular boat gasoline was under the thousand feet of net in the bow! Realizing our problem, I grabbed a five-gallon tin of Blazo white gas and two quarts of oil (our engines were two-cycle) and poured one quart of oil into each of the two almost empty fuel tanks I had previously switched. Then, kneeling in the bottom of the boat in six inches of sloshing water, I poured the white gas into the first fuel tank. Doug, seeing what I was doing, dumped five gallons of white gas from another tin into his almost empty fuel tank. It took about fifteen minutes to accomplish our task, but we got it done. Not without further problems, though. Understandably, we were being thrown from stem to stern and having to bail between bouts of waves rolling over the boat. In the process, we spilled white gas and oil all over the bottom of the boat. What had been a difficult situation with just the weather got even uglier as slick decks made almost any kind of movement extremely dangerous! Sliding the full fuel tanks over to where Larry struggled with the throttles and steerage, I again pumped up the tank pressures and switched tanks. Those wonderful Evinrude motors kept on purring and never missed a beat, even with the burning of questionable fuel! Normally we burned leaded gasoline mixed with oil in the engines. White gasoline is unleaded. ...

As we realized that we had gone only one-third of the length of the lake on twenty gallons of fuel, the specter of refueling once again hit us. So between bailing like a couple of crazies, the two of us managed to refuel the almost empty spare fuel tanks with white gas once again. The only good thing about having to jury-rig our fuel as it was used was

that it made the boat about 120 pounds lighter. That difference was just
the ticket. After that we could see that when we hit the troughs, we
didn't sink so much. That lessened the wall of water coming over the
bow, so Doug and I didn't have to bail as hard. Thank God both of us
were in really good shape. After all, throwing gallon buckets of water
over the side for twelve hours does take some doing, especially when
one is soaked to the ass and colder than Billy Hell because of being
drenched in 35-degree water, motor oil, and white gasoline. Before
rounding the turn at the bottom of the lake and getting away from a
major portion of the storm under the lee of several mountains, we had
burned over thirty gallons of fuel and spent fifteen hours doing it. Fifteen hours under some of the roughest conditions of survival I ever had
the pleasure of experiencing. The other Cordova skiff from our crew
had made it just before the storm hit. They were lighter and had moved
out shortly before we did. Then they sat in their camp and prayed that
it would hold and that we would make it. Man, you talk about two
happy individuals to see us rounding the turn into camp!

The wind had blown so hard that all the rubber had been blown off
the backs of our raincoats as we had sat with our backs to the wind and
stinging bulletlike rain drops as we bailed! Both of Larry's eyes were
almost swollen shut, and it was several days before he really recovered.
His raincoat was also ruined, and his face looked like he had a good case
of the measles. It was fortunate that he wore glasses, or the damage
might have been worse. Rejoicing, we hauled our gear into camp, got a
roaring fire going in our plywood cook shack, and warmed up. The
other two guys fixed dinner that evening, and I don't think any of the
three of us got through it before we fell asleep out of exhaustion.

The next day a plane was going to fly into our camp with our supplies. We were low on food and looking forward to not only the food
but the mail as well. Getting up early the next morning to go outside
and attend to a call of nature, I was floored! I stepped out into a world
totally without sound! A thick fog densely covered the area, and I soon
found myself coughing as I tried to take a pee. Breathing was difficult,
and I thought, What the hell? Then I noticed I had left footprints! The
ground was covered with ash. There must be one hell of a forest fire
somewhere close by, I thought as I went back to bed. Come daylight,
or what was left of it the next morning, we awoke to a strange world.
The air was full of ash and the ground had at least a third of an inch
covering it. None of us could figure it out, and when we walked into

our cook shack, we were surprised to discover that everything inside was also covered with the white powder.

Checking in on our radio, we were surprised to discover that our airplane would not be coming out to resupply our camp. It seems that Mount Trident in the Katmai National Monument had just erupted and blanketed our area with tons of volcanic ash! Boy, you talk about the luck of the Irish. First almost being killed by a freak storm and now starving because of an eruption! Suffice it to say, we ate a lot of fish for the next three days before the airplanes could safely fly to the camps once more.

A Handful of Hair

DICK STRATEY, our field supervisor, stepped off the plane and greeted us all around. He was a great boss, and we always had a good time when he was in camp. Sometimes too good a time. ... He had just a little bit of the devil in him, and when getting together with any of his field crews, it all came out. So much so that on this occasion the devil *almost* got his due. ...

Our next assignment took us far down the Grosvenor River, right next to the Savanoski River, a fairly large and fast-flowing, murky glacier stream. It was also one cold mother, running about 34 degrees on a warm day. Thousands of salmon had holed up right at the confluence of the Savanoski and Grosvenor Rivers, and within those multitudes were hundreds of tagged salmon that Dick wanted us to catch in order to recover the tags. After going over our records and scale sheets, Dick informed us that he wanted to take a run down the Grosvenor to look at those schools of salmon. For some reason, most of the crew didn't feel too well after a recent chicken dinner. Having a cast-iron gut, I was fine, so I was tapped for the boat operator's job. The rest of the crew was told to stay home and mend the soon-to-be-used nets. Most were glad to stay behind because they didn't want to go far from the toilet at that particular moment in time.

The next morning I checked over my equipment for the day's outing. With Dick in the bow and me in the stern running the Evinrudes, off we went. That little Cordova literally screamed down the Grosvenor, and the two of us had an opportunity to enjoy some of Alaska's spectacular scenery and wildlife. Swans, ducks, geese, loons, brown bear, moose, a pile of river otter, wolverine, and the like abounded. It was one of those cool but clear early fall days, and the scenery was breathtaking. Flying down the river in that kind of majesty, we were both soon lost in our thoughts. It was one of those great days that produced a world of memories still with me to this day.

We arrived at the confluence to find that Dick was right on about the schools of salmon. Right where the two great rivers met were about five thousand salmon schooled in such thick masses that it was amazing to see. There was something else. Just below a point of land where the two rivers met was a giant whirlpool. It fluctuated from thirty feet deep to just four or five and was probably thirty-five yards across. Swirling around in it were logs, brush, a dead moose, and just about everything else a river system can scare up and throw away. The roar of that monster was somewhat like the sound of the storm I had just weathered. It kind of gave me a bad feeling. ... But that menace was yards away from our salmon concentrations, and Dick decided that we needed those fish and their tags for the project. With a wave of the hand, he headed me for home, again with Dick in the bow and me at the helm.

Roaring upriver, we were again greeted with Alaska's natural bounty. Critters and scenery were on display at every turn, and again the two of us quietly enjoyed God's bounty. Then Dick turned and frantically waved back to me. Turning, he pointed to a dark spot far ahead in the middle of the river. Being up on step (the boat was almost level to the water), I looked over his shoulder, and there swimming in the river was a huge brown bear. He was going like hell if the waves of water he was pushing were any indication of his desire to get to the other side and away from the fast-approaching boat. "Terry," Dick yelled, "get us close to the bear and I will grab you a handful of hair from his back for your girl friend back in the States."

Grinning and nodding, I poured the power to the engines so we could catch the bear before he got to shore. Dick, still in the bow, directed me from side to side as we got closer since I could no longer see the bear. I finally throttled the engines back a bit and in so doing raised the bow to where I could no longer see much of anything. Sensing that we were close, I throttled back even more, raising the bow even higher. Dick was still giving me hand signals when all of a sudden he made the motion to stop! *Thump* went the boat as I plowed right into the swimming bear! *Jesus, did all hell break loose!* The bear went nuts and showed his displeasure by roaring like all get-out! Dick, in the excitement of the moment, reached over the bow, grabbed a handful of bear fur, and gleefully held it aloft like a fur trapper with a fresh pelt in the days of old. I shut the engines way down and realized that the jagged steel runners under the boat had tangled themselves in the fur on the bear's back! Meanwhile, the bear was going nuts, and there was another problem: the weight of the boat was forcing the bear's head under water.

To avoid drowning, the bear made a superbear effort, raised himself and the boat up out of the water, and roared his displeasure. Then his head was pushed underwater once again by the weight of the boat, and all I could hear was angry gurgling. It was becoming apparent that *this bear was really pissed!* Not wanting to drown the bear, I shut one engine off and put the other in reverse, hoping the action would pull us free from the bear and settle our accounts with the somewhat maddened critter. ... Mistake! The bear was so powerful that even with the one motor in reverse, *he was dragging us to the shore!* Whirling around so I could start the other engine and have more power in reverse, I slipped and fell to the bottom of the boat. Getting back to my feet, I saw my boss still in the bow, working the bear over with an oar for the fun of it. All of a sudden Dick was jerked almost out of the boat as the bear clamped down on the oar being offered in a not-so-nice way. Dick pulled back on the oar, and it came up *bitten in half!* Dick turned and with a big smile waved it into the air like some damn trophy. Meanwhile, the bear had reached the shallow portion of the river and, with even more power than I thought believable, carried the many-thousand-pound Cordova skiff toward the bank on his back! Realizing we were heading for one hell of a wreck since I couldn't back away from this "hurrah," I began to strip off my hip waders so I could swim if I had to when the bear came into our boat. Notice I didn't say *if* the bear came into the boat. ... In the meantime, Dick was still banging the bear on the head with the stump of the oar like a crazy damn schoolkid.

The bear dragged us partially up on land and in a superbear effort tore free from the entangling steel runners under the boat. Dick, realizing we were in trouble (about time), turned to flee to the center of the boat just as the bear gained his footing, whirled, and started into the boat himself! I can't say I have ever seen a bigger set of teeth and jaws. ... Dick fell onto the floor of the Cordova as the bear began to crawl over the bow. I was about to go swimming ... but once again my two guardian angels kicked in. The boat still had one engine idling in reverse and still in the water. It had just enough power to slowly pull away from the shore. The bear stood on his hind legs and let out a roar I can still hear today. That bear was at least ten feet tall and had to weigh easily over one thousand pounds. Slowly, the boat continued idling backward into the river. Regaining my senses, I cranked up the other engine and we hauled ass as if nothing out of the ordinary had just occurred.

Once under way, Dick slowly got to his feet and moved back to his place in the bow so I could get the boat back on trim and step. Somehow lost among his thoughts was the handful of bear fur scattered and blowing all over the floor of the boat and the now useless oar clearly bitten in half by something of great force and power. Not surprisingly, neither of us mentioned this event when we got back to camp—Dick because he had come within feet of losing his life and I because I was kicking myself for being so damn stupid in helping him almost become a bear scat.

The Whirlpool

THE NEXT DAY the airplane returned and took Dick back to his office in King Salmon, but not before Dick left us with instructions to net those salmon at the junction of the Savanoski and Grosvenor Rivers. Our plan was simple: take two boats with a thousand feet of net and back into the mess of fish as we played out the net, forming a horseshoe. Once on the bank, get out of the boats, remove our tagged fish, get scale and blood samples, and be on our way to our next assignment. Well, it didn't happen quite as planned. ...

Down the Grosvenor River the five of us went, loaded for bear. One boat carried the entire net and the other all the supplies we would need to remove the fish and record the data. Keep in mind that the fish were never hurt (other than occasionally being gilled by our piece-of-crap net) and were quickly released. Everyone had recovered from whatever they had had the day before except Larry. He was still pretty weak and was more or less going along just for the ride and the company.

Arriving at our work site, the two boats circled the area of massed salmon and checked out the possible ways to attack the issue. Landing upstream from the pools of fish, we laid out our plans. Steve and I would take one boat and back up the edge of the Savanoski River, playing out our portion of the net until we reached the tip of the point of land separating the two rivers. I was to be his net man because I was the largest and strongest, and we figured the drag of the swift-moving Savanoski would really pull on the net. Once close to shore, Steve would kill the engines, jump out, and drag the boat up onto land. I would jump out in about three feet of water and drag the net onto the bank, closing our end of the horseshoe. Doug would man the net in the other boat with a fellow named Jim Dender, who would operate the engines. About the time our boat started backing up the edge of the Savanoski playing out the net, their boat would do the same as it moved up the Grosvenor. They would continue until they had the salmon encircled in their portion of the net and then head for shore. Once there, Dender would land the rear of his boat and drag it up onto shore while Doug would jump out into about four feet of water and drag his portion of the net up onto the shore. That way we would have our completed horseshoe of net.

Doug and I transferred half of the net into his boat. Keep in mind that the net was a continuous one thousand feet in length, with five hundred feet now in each boat. Thus, the two boats, bound by the net, would slowly idle together downstream. Once below the pool of salmon, Steve and I would back out into the edge of the Savanoski, playing out our net. Doug's boat would be heading upstream on the Grosvenor doing the same thing. There were several small problems, however. The Savanoski River was roaring along about twenty miles per hour. It was a glacier-fed stream, so we couldn't read the water for underwater hazards because of its milky color. Since we would be backing upstream playing out net all the way (meaning increased drag), my engine man would have to have both 40-horse engines going in *full* reverse! One engine had a broken reverse lock, so in order to keep that engine in the water doing its job, Steve would have to sit on top of it to keep the torque from raising its propeller out of the water. ... No big deal. We had worked like this a hundred times before. But keep in mind that by the end of summer, all the engines were showing the wear and tear common to boat motors used hard in Alaskan waters. Doug's boat had it comparatively easy. The Grosvenor River was a deep and slower-moving river. They should be able to lay out their net using only half the power their engines were capable of providing. But we still had that damn whirlpool some fifty yards below our work area. To go into that, for whatever reason, would not be a good idea.

Slowly the two boats motored into position below the pool of salmon. Once lined out, Steve began backing our boat into the edge of the Savanoski as I began playing out the net. Doug and his partner did the same on the Grosvenor. As Steve got farther and farther into the Savanoski, I could hear him applying more and more power to the engines to overcome the river's swiftness. However, we still had plenty of power, and I continued to lay out our net in a measured fashion so that when we reached the bank, I would still have some left. We were moving more slowly now, and Steve was really pouring the power to the straining engines. I was also having difficulty. As more and more net was played out, the drag increased. Soon it was all I could do to slowly lay out the net and not let the force of the river's current jerk it all out of the boat in one roaring swoop. *Wham* went one of our roaring engines as its propeller hit an unseen rock in the murky Savanoski River, breaking its shear pin. No shear pin, no turning propeller—no turning propeller, *no power!* The other engine continued under full power, but the downward force of the river in its run for the ocean was just too much for only one engine. Steve fought to maintain control with his one engine as I desperately began to drag the net back into the bow using every bit of my upper-body strength! However, we were jerked rapidly out into the river with such force that we began dragging Doug's boat backward from his spot on the Grosvenor River. I was making headway getting our net back into the boat when I heard Steve scream. Looking back to see what had happened, I saw him looking over my shoulder with an ashen face. Quickly looking up from my bent-over position, I saw Doug's boat, still being pulled backward by ours from the force of the Savanoski, *go over the lip and into the whirlpool!*

Before I could do anything our net was jerked violently from my hands as it was sucked into the whirlpool as well. I quickly latched the net on a bow spike and it stopped spilling overboard, but now our boat was being dragged into the whirlpool. Reaching for my sheath knife, I started to cut the net rope *just as we went over the lip and down into the whirlpool!* Yelling at Steve to try to keep us near the top (away from the logs and other debris swirling in the bottom), I again began hauling in my net. Once inside the whirlpool, I could see our net roaring along the side of the wall of water with us. Since we were whirling along with it at the same speed, I could more easily recover the net and frantically began doing so. Doug's boat was on the opposite wall, and I could see Doug bent over pulling in his portion of the net for all he was worth.

The roar of the whirlpool was like that of a thousand freight trains. The outer wall would swell to twenty feet in height and then drop to three or four feet in a second. We could hear great rocks and boulders being smashed around in the bottom of the cup and the crashing of entire trees as the force of the swirling water tore them to matchsticks. Thank God Steve and Dender managed to keep our boats on the lip or all of us would have been crushed in the cup by the boulders and trees!

At one point our boat began to dangerously approach Doug's. Not having the time to sweat that, I continued pulling the net like a dervish. "Look out," screamed Steve as our two boats crashed into one another. I just barely avoided the bow of Doug's boat, but Doug was not so lucky. The bow of our boat smashed into his shoulder as he bent over his bow pulling in his portion of the net. *Crunch* went the two heavy boats, smashing Doug in between! Down he went in the bottom of his boat, knocked out and with a dislocated shoulder, as we discovered later. Realizing all was just about lost, I once again tossed my net over the bow spike, keeping any more net on my boat from spilling out. With Doug out of commission, I now had to pull the net for his boat. If I didn't, it would spill out, increasing the drag. Even more importantly, it might entangle the propellers from our remaining motors, killing all chance of steerage. If that happened, we were dead men! I am here to tell you, the icy water, all of us wearing hip boots, and none of us wearing life preservers was a sure formula for a final ride.

Pulling the net like a crazy man and with superhuman strength (thank you, guardian angels), I hauled in most of the net from Doug's boat, *but not fast enough!* Doug's boat engines found the net on one of our crazy passes around the whirlpool, tangling and killing both of his engines. About that time our boats crashed into each other again, and this time, I cut Doug's net off from my boat. By now I found myself angrier then all get-out. Turning around, I screamed at Steve to gun our remaining engine and head downriver on the next pass when we were at the crest of the whirlpool. His grim nod told me he had gotten the message over the roar. With that, I lunged over the side of my boat, using my knees to hold me in, and grabbed Doug's boat by the side. *Roar* went the whirlpool as it dropped in size, almost dumping our boats into the cup of smashing boulders and tree chunks. *Roar*, it surged in height and fired us like a stone from a slingshot up from the bottom of the cup onto the lip. Steve, scared to death, tightened down the throttle of our sole running engine and cranked the tiller over, and over the top we went! Speeding down the back side of the whirlpool, we found ourselves in the mighty Savanoski River, flying downstream. Doug had come to but was in a lot of pain and wasn't moving much. Yelling at the top of my lungs, I said, "Thank you, Lord," just as our boats slammed into the tall riverbank cut out by the force of the whirlpool. Doug's boat still had that ten-foot tower anchored in it, and that caught in a bunch of exposed tree roots. The current pushed us sideways as the tower hung tightly entangled in the roots. Dumping Doug's boat sideways, a wall of water flooded in with such force that it tossed Dender headfirst into our boat. He landed with such force that it knocked him out colder than a cucumber!

I held on for all I was worth as the two boats began to fill with water. Knowing I couldn't let go because of Doug's condition, I put every muscle into my effort. *Ka-pow,* the tower exploded from its supports in the bottom of Doug's boat as if on a spring, lifted into the air, and fell into the river behind us, never to be seen again. With that, both boats quickly righted and began quietly floating down the Savanoski. Steve still had one engine running, and with that he steered us onto a sandbar, where both boats stopped. Jumping out up to my armpits into the icy water, I felt my heart stop in shock. Somehow I kept going and pulled both boats safely up higher, then just sat down. I was so exhausted, I was not sure I could get up even if another emergency arose! My arms and shoulders were on fire from the exertion and strain, and my throat was so dry that I could hardly swallow. Steve killed our motor and just sat in the bottom of the boat, saying nothing. Then Doug's head popped up over the gunwale of his boat, and he said, "Terry, come give me a hand. I have a dislocated shoulder, but you can help me fix it." I just sat there. I wasn't sure I even had the energy to move. But after a few more moments, I found the strength and staggered over to Doug. He was one tough son of a gun. He had been a paratrooper and wasn't going to let a little shoulder problem slow him down. I got him to his feet, and he showed me how to reset his shoulder. When I snapped it back into the socket, he passed out again. Laying him on the remains of his net, I yelled, "Steve, give me a hand. We need to fix the shear pin on our other motor and cut the net away from the two motors on Doug's boat."

Lifting our broken engine, we spun the Cordova sideways up onto the sand bar and fixed our shear pin. Now, by damnit, we have at least enough power to go back upstream and get home, I thought, still on an adrenaline high. About that time Dender came to, sat up, and just looked all around. He had had his bell rung like Saint Paul's in Rome, and it would be a while before he was worth a shit, I thought. But at least he was alive! Swinging Doug's boat around and up onto the sandbar, Steve and I cut away the net that had entangled their motors. That finished, we checked their shear pins, and they were fine. As we swung the end of their boat back into the deep water, I noticed that Doug was now back in our world as well.

Then it dawned on me. The last thing poor old Larry had seen from his position on the riverbank was the four of us in our boats being dragged into the whirlpool! That poor bastard must be going nuts with worry, I thought. Here he was, miles from any help, bears everywhere, and all his partners slopped into a whirlpool. I brought that to everyone's attention, and we got our boat gear squared away, started up our engines, and, using only one motor at a time on each boat with the other in neutral, headed back up the Savanoski. We moved slowly because we could not see the bottom. If we ran up on some rocks and broke another shear pin, we would be in deep trouble. With another engine running just in case, we could pop it into gear and continue to steer instead of drifting downstream out of control.

Leaving Dender with his head still ringing in Steve's boat, I took the helm of the other boat. Since both Doug and Dender were still somewhat under the weather, I thought we should put our best feet forward while going back up the Savanoski. We were still not out of the woods, and until we arrived back on the Grosvenor, we had our work cut out for us. Taking the lead, I headed out with Steve on my tail. Several times I could hear my propeller lightly hitting sand and gravel, but fortunately nothing busted my prop or shear pin. Steve broke one shear pin but quickly got the other running motor in gear and made it in with that engine.

Rounding the bend in the river, we scooted across the last of the murky glacier water onto the clear, deep-running water of the Grosvenor. Sitting on the bank with his head buried in his hands was our fifth partner, Larry. Upon hearing the outboards, he jumped up and began running around and yelling in happiness. If I had been the one sitting there all by myself after witnessing what had happened, I think I would have reacted the same way. Needless to say, we had some reunion on that beach. ... Calling it a day, we went back to our camp and anchored our boats. While Larry went to fix supper, Steve and I quietly dragged the net from our boat and laid it out on the grassy bank next to our camp. Doug, without saying a word and soon joined by Dender, began patching the net. Soon all of us were patching that net like nothing out of the ordinary had happened.

The next day, with Larry and Dender at the helms and Steve and I in the bows with the repaired net, we returned. This time without wearing hip boots (so we could swim if we had to) but wearing our flotation devices, we recovered those fish and carried out our assignment. ... The trip back to camp that evening found all of us silent and thankful. To my way of thinking, based on numerous such experiences, anyone who thinks we don't have guardian angels needs to think twice!

The Alaskan Brown Bear Who Came to Stay

BY NOW SUMMER HAD ABOUT run its course. It was early September and almost time for me to return to Humboldt State to continue my education in wildlife management. Some of our crews had already departed for the lower forty-eight, and as the remaining crews were combined, we began the annual cleanup of equipment and readying the outback camps for winter. There was some final cleanup work on the scientific end of things, and our little crew of four at the Grosvenor River camp continued along those lines.

The September mornings were crisp and cool, with some ice forming on the river, portending colder weather to come. There were still a few salmon in the river trying to get to their natal streams. It was kind of sad for those late migrants, however. At this late date, when they arrived on their spawning streams I was afraid they would find no one alive with which to spawn. The major spawning period had passed, and these late migrants had most likely made the long trip for nothing.

One evening after a long, hard day of reclaiming scattered field equipment and centralizing it in a major dump site, I took the time to just sit by the front door of our camp and drink in the sights. The Grosvenor River was less than twenty yards from our front door, and I could still hear the occasional soft *phlop* of the salmon migrating upstream. The insects, due to the very cool evenings, had all but disappeared, but the mournful call of the Arctic loon could still be heard from Grosvenor Lake. As I said before, Alaska is a very unique land, beautiful on one hand and deadly on the other. Tonight, with the advent of the Northern Lights, was one of those beautiful moments that created many memories of a summer gone and a life partially lived ... but the deadly was never far away.

Sitting in a homemade wooden chair that memorable evening, smoking a good cigar, I was surprised to see a large object coming my way across the river. When I first noticed, it was at the far side of the river. Now, in the fast-fading light cast by the Northern Lights on the smooth flowing river, it looked as if I might have a visitor. I couldn't tell if it was a large loon, beaver, or river otter, but it sure as hell was coming my way. Now watching with more than the average degree of interest, I was amazed when the thing turned out to be an Alaskan brown bear's head, and a big one at that! Before I could even react, the animal pulled himself up onto the bank on my side and shook himself off. Now, this was no wimp of a bear but a giant! He had to be at least a ten-foot specimen, weighing in at over a thousand pounds. The bears were normally not a problem, but here I was sitting in a chair, unarmed and with no place to run. If there were more than forty feet between us, I was a monkey's uncle. Realizing he was not alone, he began the typical brown bear "casting," swinging his head from side to side. I could hear him blowing out and sucking in great amounts of air as he attempting to identify his company. I just sat there, not moving. This damn bear was huge and could be upon me in less than two seconds if the mood suited him. Behind me I could hear my three bunkmates inside the flimsy plywood cabin, loudly discussing a rather hot ongoing poker game. I wondered if they would be so noisy if they knew who was outside the door.

The bear, still casting for information, began shuffling toward me with characteristic pigeon-toed steps. I decided that if he took two more steps my way, I would be up and inside our cabin in a heartbeat! At least I knew that I would have access to my rifle there. ... Taking one more step, the great bruin began swinging his massive head once again from side to side as bears will do when confused at what lies before them. Then he quickly turned and ambled off upstream in a typical ground-eating shuffle. Watching him disappear into the inky blackness of the Alaskan night, I quickly got up and entered our quarter-inch-thick fortress. Noticing my rapid entry, my three buddies all looked up questioningly. Those looks changed to real surprise when I grabbed my Winchester, levered a round into the chamber, turned, and faced the door. You never saw such a noisy poker game go so silent.

"What the hell is your problem?" asked Doug.

"Bear, *big bear*," I replied without taking my eyes off the only way in or out of our cabin. Without a word, Doug, forever the military man, got up, grabbed our bolt-action, 30-06 rifle, chambered a round, and faced the door as well. Steve reached over the stove into a makeshift cupboard and withdrew his .38 Colt revolver. By now you could have heard a pin drop inside that little cook shack. Bear, especially the really big ones, always seemed to have an axe to grind in our neck of the woods. I don't know why, but just about every time any of us came across a really big one, we ended up with a tale or two to tell. For several minutes no one spoke or moved. Then Doug slowly opened the latch to our door, letting it swing fully open. The light from our two happily bubbling Coleman lanterns blazed out the front door and into the night. Nothing moved or stood to be seen. Taking down one of the lanterns, Doug hung it on the end of his rifle and slowly ventured out the front door. I and the Winchester were in lockstep right behind. For a bear the size of the one I had seen, it would easily take every bit of the firepower we had to ruin his day, if you get my drift. Steve stayed inside the cabin. He knew his little old .38-caliber pea shooter would do nothing but piss off the bear. In fact, I think the only reason he had brought such a goofy firearm to Alaska was to use it on himself if a bear got him. Seeing nothing, I took Doug out to where the bear had pulled himself from the river in front of our cabin. There in the mud were numerous *enormous* footprints. One of his back paw prints (they are the largest) measured eighteen and a half inches at its widest! Shortly thereafter we went to bed in our nine-by-twelve canvas-covered framed tent. That night we moved an unused cot in front of the tent flap and all carried our firearms to bed with us. It was the very first time any of us had done so in this camp!

The next morning dawned clear, cool, and with more than a touch of frost in the air. Many of the deciduous trees' leaves were turning into their coats of many colors, and God, it was great to be alive. That was, until the four of us went to the riverbank and looked at those bear tracks in the daylight. If the size of paw prints meant anything, we had a monster in our midst. ... We followed his tracks a few yards upstream, and there he was! I only saw a bear that big one other time, and that was in the Bismarck Zoo. *That* bear weighed over 1,300 pounds upon his death. This one was bigger! *Lying down*, he was at least three and a half feet high. The bear moved his head slightly to acknowledge our arrival, then just laid his big head on his paws and went back to sleep. The four of us, as if previously instructed, walked backward to give this monster all the space he needed. Loading our boats with our day's gear and lunches, we set off for our day's work details. However, in each boat a fully loaded rifle (for the first time) rode "shotgun."

Returning that evening, we were all looking forward to a repast of fried chicken, mashed potatoes, gravy, and mounds of canned peas in butter sauce. Our work had been hard and unusually heavy, all done in a cold, driving rain. By the end of the day our light lunches hadn't done the trick, but such a dinner would. I had been designated cook and was raring to go. The supply plane had arrived the day before, and our permafrost larder (a hole dug down to the ice and covered with a sheet of plywood and a large rock) held not only fresh chicken but steaks, pork chops, and a mountain of hamburger. The plane would usually bring us enough fresh meat for a week. Then it was back to canned meats and vegetables. Roaring up to our homemade docks, we secured the boats. Three of the chaps went into the cook shack to light the lanterns and get the stove going. I headed to our permafrost larder for the chicken soon to decorate our plates and fill our empty guts. Walking up to Mother Nature's icebox, I was surprised to discover that the plywood lid had been left off the larder. Looking inside, I saw nothing! Something had discovered our larder (sprinkled liberally with handfuls of black and red pepper on top and inside to keep curious noses at a distance) and eaten everything, including the paper wrapping the meat. Not believing my eyes and never having had this problem before, I checked the ground for clues. *Damn!* There it was, the telltale footprint bigger than a dinner plate. That huge bruin from the night before had found our larder and helped himself to over thirty pounds of meat.

Walking back to our cook shack, I broke the news. Man, you would have thought I had cut every one of those lads' guzzles. After dwelling all day on a great meal after a hard day's work, they were pissed to find that the bear had beaten us to the punch. I think if we hadn't been in a national monument, that bear would have died that afternoon! Realizing the great amount of disappointment, I made up one hell of a nice stew with biscuits for dinner. That helped, but it wasn't my world-famous fried chicken.

From then, we had a problem with the bear who came to dinner. One of us would walk around the tent or cook shack only to discover he was face to face with a great big damn old brown bear from a distance of four feet or less! Then the bear took a liking to our crapper, which meant no more dreaming on the bench! When that call of nature arrived, you got your hands full of paper, ran to the crapper, did your business, and got the hell off because within a minute or less, you had company! At night you might leave the cabin for whatever reason and would almost step on a sleeping mound of bear two feet away. Fishing, well, that was a horse of another color. Fishing from the bank got you a partner ... and if you didn't hurry and catch a fish, the bear would approach to highly unsafe distances as if to hurry you along. Anything you caught was taken before you could get it to a frying pan. By now the bear had become so habituated to our presence that I think he thought he was just another person, which made him very dangerous. To beat the bank-fishing problem, we had to resort to boat fishing to get any fresh meat because the King Salmon office was slowly closing down all the field stations. The aircraft, normally our suppliers, were busy ferrying people back to King Salmon so they could catch commercial flights home. Grocery runs were in short supply and not too dependable, so we ate a lot of fish along with our canned things. But therein lay another problem. We would boat off to go fishing only to have our bear swim out to us if we were close at hand and try to crawl into our boat! To avoid that type of nasty encounter, we would boat out onto the lake, do our fishing, clean our fish, and head home. Upon arrival, here would come the bear at a fast shuffle, and if you didn't have a bag of fish and fish guts for his dinner, you never kept yours.

One morning as I stepped out the front door of our cabin within two feet of our sleeping monster bear, I noticed something unusual. On the middle of his back were three distinct foot-long marks (like jagged skids under a Cordova skiff would make) where all the back hair had been removed or torn out. Stopping in my tracks, I realized that this was the same damn bear I had run over with the Cordova skiff with my boss in the bow. I couldn't believe my eyes! Stepping quietly back into the cabin, I closed the door and told my partners of my discovery and the whole story of the boat and the bear. I also mentioned that the bear was just outside the door and to venture forth might not be a good idea.

Almost at the same time we all decided we were at a crossroad. We had a huge bear in our midst who was becoming more dangerous every day. We had to do something about the situation, so we did. ... That evening when we returned from fishing for our dinner, we held one bag of fish guts back from our dangerous mooch. Taking that bag of guts inside, we liberally laced it with ant poison, broken shards of glass, a box of roofing tacks (I don't know where those came from), and an entire eight-ounce can of red pepper. We lobbed that concoction outside, and our bear ate the entire mess, bag and all. We could hear him crunching down on the glass and nails with apparent relish! For the next two days he passed a little blood, but that was about all. In the meantime, he was getting bolder, trying to break into our cook shack when we were eating or coming into our sleeping tent at night! Something had to be done.

After Doug had turned the corner of our cabin to be confronted by a very surprised and angry bear, we ran out of patience. In our toolbox we always carried M-80 firecrackers to throw at bears when they got a little too aggressive. Realizing we had a problem that defied normality and needed a solution, we got aggressive ourselves. One morning after breakfast, we decided we had had enough. The bear had chosen to sleep right outside our door, making it impossible to leave the cabin without stepping on him! We formulated our plan and set it into motion. After taping together two giant M-80 firecrackers (fuses as well), we were ready. Doug took the 30-06, loaded it, and stood at one side of our door. I took the .348 Winchester, loaded it with the heaviest bullets I had, and stood on the other side. Steve took his pistol and sat right in the middle of the floor covering that section. Jim got the job with the M-80s.

Opening the door slightly, we took stock of our situation. As expected, the bear was sleeping right at our doorstep! Cocking the hammer on my rifle, I looked over to see Doug slipping off his safety. If the critter decided to come back through the door, it would be a costly decision. John took the M-80s, lit their fuses, held them for a second to make sure he had a good burn, and tried to toss them out the door. The M-80s were supposed to hit the ground at the bear's hind end. But in the heat of the moment, tossed short by a terrified thrower, they hit our floor and bounced up over the backside of the bear, landing squarely between his shoulder blades! Doug closed the door just as the bear started to get up with the burning bombs still between his shoulder blades. A second passed, and Doug, unable to stand not seeing what was happening, flung open the door. The bear was up on all fours and there between his shoulders smoldered the fuses on the M-80s. *Boom boom!* They went off in quick succession in a blinding flash, sending a shock wave that rattled our cabin.

The blast drove the bear's head and front end into the mud at his feet. Lunging back up and on fire between his shoulder blades, the bear, roaring fearfully all the time, made for the river. Hitting the water with a giant splash, he disappeared for a moment, and when he came up there was still a smoldering area on his shoulders, but the fire was out. Growling and popping his jaws as a bear will do when aroused or mad, he continued to swim across the river, pulled himself up the far bank, and charged off into a thicket of willow. For many minutes we heard the gnashing of teeth, tearing of brush, and growling and roaring of anger. Suffice it to say, none of us left the cabin, maintaining our ready position in case he came back. In fact, we decided that if he did come back we would shoot him in the river because once he reached the shore, we were sure he would have malice in his heart! Plus, if we killed him in the river, our problem would drift downstream and other bear would eat him there instead at our doorstep (yes, bear will eat other bear).

For an hour nothing happened. Still ready for bear, we loaded our boats and went off for work. When we came back that evening, no bear. Still alert and cautious, we went about cleaning up our gear and mending (a never-ending job) our net. Finishing dinner, I opened our door to go to the bathroom, and lo and behold, there was our bear lying by our boats! We grabbed our firepower just as he got to his feet. *Woof-woof* he went as he made several bluff charges. To our credit, we held our fire. Suffice it to say that for the next few days, things were a little touchy around camp. Everywhere any of us went, it was with another chap with a rifle. ... The bear, well, he was another matter. Between his shoulder blades was a nasty hole into the meat where the M-80s had blown a patch of skin and hair off his back the size of a grapefruit. You could tell the bear was in an ugly mood, and his evolving behavior attested to that fact. Everywhere we went, we were challenged. He was always just feet away, growling, bluff charging, or moaning as they will do. This went on for several more days, and then it was time for me to fly out to King Salmon and catch a commercial flight back to the love of my life and college. When the float plane arrived for me to board and leave, the bear even charged it! Hastily loading my gear, I said my good-byes to my friends and was gone from the land of the midnight sun.

Alaska had been not only a heady adventure but a life experience of the highest degree. I discovered that I had matured by leaps and bounds. That will happen if you are on your toes and willing to get involved and learn. If not, in Alaska anyway, you are dead. I had grown quieter and more circumspect, and my philosophy of life had evolved into one that, combined with later experiences, would serve not only me but those who worked for me as well. There is still a little bit of the grandness and magic of Alaska in my heart and soul today.

Doug had to kill our bear three days after I left. It came so close to getting him that he stomped right into the cabin, armed himself, stomped back out, and killed it with a single head shot. Within two days other bear had eaten their recently killed compatriot, leaving only bits and pieces of hair to mark his passage. However for whatever reason, I carry a bit of that bear in my soul, just as I do the other aspects of my time in Alaska. It was a brief moment in my life, a lasting memory in my soul, and a milestone in the essence of a budding westering man.

PART TWO
Milestones

13

The Tule Lake Snow Goose Shoot

IN 1966 I BECAME a California State Fish and Game warden, stationed in the northwestern part of the state in the coastal city of Eureka. My duties included enforcing the state's fish and game laws, not only in my captain's district but in other adjacent fish and game districts across the state as the need arose. One such assignment in the winter of 1966 took me to the Tule Lake area in far north-central California.

Tule Lake in those days was a migration mecca for damn near all the millions of ducks and geese frequenting the Pacific flyway. That area housed several major national wildlife refuges, which were surrounded by natural marshes and many thousands of acres of grain fields. If there ever was a natural and manmade attraction for hordes of migratory waterfowl, this was it!

Sad to say, forty years later most of the great lure and attraction is no more. Drainage, legal battles over the area's sparse water supplies, clashes between federal laws and farmers, and declining waterfowl populations have left the area passed over, neglected, and almost a muddy hole. Humankind sure has a way with natural resource destruction and a lack of understanding when it comes to history. Especially our own!

Captain Gray called me into his office one rainy November morning and asked what I had scheduled for the following week. Quickly checking off in my head what I had planned and deducing that most of it was minor in nature, I answered, "Nothing that can't wait. What do you have up your sleeve, Captain?"

"I need to send one man to work undercover in the Tule Lake area. The geese are in the area in large numbers, and from all reports, many shooters are taking advantage of California's liberal bag limits. Since you graduated from Humboldt and majored in waterfowl, I have decided to send you." At that time the limit was up to six geese per day.

"Yes, sir," I quickly replied, not wanting to set him off on one of his tirades if I didn't respond respectfully enough to his way of thinking (the captain and I didn't get along very well because of his drinking habits and my inability to stomach his behavior).

"You will leave tomorrow, and I expect you to give my counterpart a damn good effort or you will find yourself tagging fish in the hold of some fishing vessel when you get back!"

Ignoring his shot across my bow, I said, "Yes, sir; you will get a day's work out of me."

He just sat there in his chair like a large toad, staring at me through a set of bloodshot eyes, and then said, "You need to contact the local warden in the town of Tule Lake, and he will line you out. Take our undercover truck, and now, get out of my sight."

Realizing our "discussion" was ended, I whirled and left his office before he could see my spreading grin. I had hunted ducks and geese in the Tule Basin while attending Humboldt State College. It was one of those natural areas where the miracle of the world of wildlife would be in full display at this time of year, not only the millions of ducks and geese but the graceful swans and every other flying, water-loving creature! When the migration was in full swing, it truly was the world of wildlife on parade. However, it also had its dark side. Anytime you have Mother Nature's basket of goodies laid out in plain view, human predators will do everything in their power to take more than their share. Well, Tule laid out its goods in front of God and everybody on an annual basis, and everyone except God came. ... You would find a few remaining market hunters, game hogs, the decent sportsman, outlaw commercial guides, outlaw farmers shooting over-limits behind locked gates, those who couldn't count, the greedy not mentioned above, and in fact every black heart except perhaps members of the Women's Temperance Union scurrying around on those hallowed resource grounds! The lure of millions of grain-fed and fattened birds was just too much for the masses. They came in droves, the birds were killed in the hundreds of thousands, the shot-shell manufactures were happy, and no one blinked.

Hustling home, I told Donna about my latest assignment. Bless her heart, she just smiled and said nothing about another ten days of loneliness for her as I roared around doing my thing. But Donna was always a great one when it came to supporting her husband on his vision quest, and she did so during this adventure as well as the many others that followed. Her only questions were, was I taking Shadow (my Labrador), was there a contact in the area who could be reached in case of an emergency, and what would be the date of my arrival home.

Kissing my young bride good-bye the following morning, I loaded Shadow into the undercover truck, and away we went. It rained hard all the way from Eureka and over the mountains on Highway 299 until we reached Redding. Turning north on Interstate 5, dog and I hammered along until we reached the town of Weed. Hopping off onto state Highway 97, we drove north to the town of Dorris. Man, you talk about being in the middle of nowhere! From there I took a few of the many roads winding through the work area in and around the Lower Klamath and Tule Lake National Wildlife Refuges, checking the area out for bird concentrations.

It was now spitting rain and snow and getting colder by the hour. That was all right, though, because I was driving a three-quarter-ton pickup with four-wheel drive. It would have to get really bad before we called it quits with that combination, so dog and I continued our exploration in the land of the Modoc Indians. The air was alive with skeins of waterfowl of every make, model, and color, and just about every grain field I passed was full of hunters, feeding waterfowl, or both. In particular, great strings of lesser snow geese laced through the airways from every point on the compass. God, I must have seen at least a hundred thousand that afternoon alone—*just in the air!* And that didn't account for the many thousands of subspecies of Canada geese and the excellent-eating little Pacific white-fronted geese! If there ever was a moment to have your heart swell from seeing all God's bounty laid out for you to appreciate, now was the time. It was getting late and we were both hungry, so we sped into the little agricultural town of Tule Lake and got ourselves a room. Ever since Shadow had saved my life (see my earlier book *The Thin Green Line*, the chapter titled "Dogs"), she had slept in a motel room with me instead of in the front seat of a cold vehicle—and in the other bed, I might add. That was the very least I could do.

Four o'clock in the morning found dog and me quietly sitting in the front seat of the undercover pickup. I had called Robbie, the local game warden, the evening before and he had lined me out into the needed work area. He would work one side of the valley and I the other. Robbie was a tall drink of water and a damn good officer. However, he had a very hard area to work, especially when the birds and the gunners were in the valley. "Overwhelmed" would be the word most fitting his situation in those days. Hence the extra help throughout the year from his and adjoining Fish and Game squads. Dog and I had positioned ourselves in the middle of the barley-growing country below state Highway 161. The biting wind rocked the truck from time to time as it hastened on its way to the Sacramento Valley with a portent of more to come. Even at that god-awful hour, I could hear the occasional squadron of just-arriving migrating geese. They knew the Tule Lake area was somewhere below them but in the dark and flying snow were having a hard time locating it. God, those birds are tough! I thought. Sitting there with my window partially down, I listened to the winds and the *ping* of sleet as it beat against the metal of the truck. Better the truck than me, I mused as I pulled my head down into the warmer recesses of my coat. Dog was doing her usual thing: snoring! Any Lab owners out there will know what I am talking about. ...

Finally the light of dawn broke later than advertised, due to the inclement weather and scudding low, dark clouds. As soon as it did, the noise of gunfire added its two bits to the cornucopia of sounds. Moving toward the sounds of the guns as I had learned (where there was shooting, there was usually plenty of my kind of business), I began to strike gold. The first to fall were two shooters from a Shell Block (an old Humboldt State graduate) commercially guided group of hunters. They had sixteen snow geese over the limit and no excuse, just that they had gotten carried away. Shell had apparently dropped them off and gone back to the motel to get the rest of the hunting party. Upon his return he discovered that the shooting had been good (too damn good, some might say) for his first bunch of shooters and then had the chance to renew an old college "friendship." The rest of the morning and into the early afternoon was taken up by many smaller over-limits, several unplugged shotguns (capable of holding more than three shells), no hunting licenses, and hunters not in possession of a federal waterfowl hunting stamp (required of every migratory waterfowl hunter once he or she has reached the age of sixteen). Nothing major, but let's say I more than paid for the gas and oil for the entire trip with that day's labors!

Throughout the morning and afternoon I could hear the steady drumming of shotgun barrages to the south. Every time I tried to move to that quarter, I would run across another set of dummies breaking the law and have to take care of business. Then I slid off the wet dirt farm road on which I had been driving and got the truck stuck. By the time I got it unstuck, nightfall was upon me, and the shooting had ended for the day. Tired, cold, muddy, and hungry, I headed for the barn, some hot food, and a nice warm bed.

Four o'clock the next morning found me roughly in the same place where I had finished the night before. No, not in the mud hole. ... I was colder than all get-out and was happy to have the truck with its heater between me and the elements. The wind was still blowing, but not as hard as the day before. There was about two inches of fresh snow on the ground, and what had been mud the day before was now frozen harder than a bullet. Dog was doing her usual thing as I sat there with the window partially down, smoking one of those rotten, stinking little Italian cigars I loved so much. I had eaten a damn big breakfast of two hamburgers, two sides of fries, and a piece of pie. That should set me for the day, I thought. Dog had had two large cans of dog food to fend off the cold and was showing her appreciation by filling the cab of the truck with putrid gas! Again, any readers owning Labs can testify to personal experience. ...

A set of headlights came on in a large grain field to the southwest, catching me by surprise. I swung my binoculars to them just in time to see two gents throw double handfuls of snow geese into the back of what appeared to be a farm truck (I could tell by the spare fuel tank in the back). Hell, shooting hadn't even started for the day, and yet these lads already had some geese! The truck drove around the field as the two men threw dozens of snow goose decoys into the back. This continued until the lads had a bed full of decoys. Then the truck started working its way out of the field. Damn, I thought, Either they had slept in the field in their truck the night before (not likely due to the cold) or they had shot a large over-limit the day before and had brought in as much as they dared, leaving the remainder for pickup the following day. They had gotten into the field before I had taken my place and were now fleeing the scene. Well, either way, hell is coming, gentlemen, and the devil is riding a green Ford undercover truck.

I worked my way toward the pickup without using my headlights and with the cutoff switches thrown so that all lights on the truck were off, even the brake lights. I finally arrived on the dirt road that looked as if it would intersect my suspects' line of travel (all you young conservation officers reading these lines, note the value of getting there damn early. It will pay in gold many times in your career if you do). On one side of the road was a deep irrigation ditch and on the other a vast grain field. Figuring I had them, I ordered Shadow to lie down on the passenger floorboards so she would not be seen if she decided to sit up and look around. That way she could be a surprising ace in the hole if need be. I slowly inched out of the truck into the elements and walked down the side of the ditch for about thirty yards in the direction of my fast-approaching suspect vehicle. That way when the bad guys got near, they would see an empty truck blocking their exit. As they sat there in wonderment, I would approach from behind them and make my presence known before they could "take a dump or get off the pot."

Soon I could hear the sound of their truck engine laboring under a load as they slowly made their muddy approach. It sounded as if it were in four-wheel drive, low range from the sound of the high engine revolutions per minute. That's good, I thought, because if they try to escape, they won't be going so fast that I can't capture them either on foot or with my four-wheel drive. They finally arrived in line-of-sight distance, and I could hear their engine slow and then stop. They blinked their headlights onto the high-beam mode and just sat there examining my truck. Lying next to the ditch bank in the snow, I held my ground. They started up and moved a few yards closer to my truck for a better look, then moved up right beside where I lay and stopped again. They honked their horn several times, as if that would make an empty pickup move. Realizing that wasn't going to do it, they drove the remaining few yards past me to my parked truck. "What the hell?" I heard one of them say as he got out of their truck and walked over to mine. I crawled up out of the ditch and walked up to the rear of their truck's cab, standing there just behind the driver's door. "Hey," yelled the guy beside my truck.

Woo-woo-woo went the deep-throated menacing barking of Shadow as she came up out of her place of hiding and lunged at the driver's-side window.

"Goddamn!" yelled the man as he jumped back, stumbling, then fell off the road the three feet to the grain field below. Scrambling up, he ran out into the field a few more yards as if he thought the dog was after him. "Goddamn, that dog is as big as a horse and black as night!" he bellowed. Shadow was not quite that big, but she did weigh in excess of one hundred pounds, and most of that was solid meat and bone. "Only a goddamned game warden would have a dog that big," he hollered.

"Not likely at this time of the morning. Those bastards are still in bed," called back the driver as he got out of the truck. "Ho-ho-ho!" he yelled as he stepped right into my arms. "Who the hell are you?"

"Your loving, wonderful game warden who never sleeps," I responded smartly.

"Jesus Christ, what the damn thunder are you doing out here this time of the morning?"

"Checking duck and goose hunters getting a jump on shooting times," I replied. Then I quietly asked for some identification.

For a minute no one moved, then all of them slowly complied. Standing off to one side and still at arm's length, I identified myself with my badge and asked for their driver's licenses. "What for?" angrily growled the driver of their vehicle.

"Because I observed you folks loading handfuls of snow geese into the back of your truck. As a conservation officer, I have a right to inspect those birds. But more importantly, if they are fresh killed, you folks shot early. If they are stone cold, which I think they are, I suspect they were shot last night and left for whatever reason for pickup this morning. Either way, you folks will have a problem, that being birds taken before legal shooting hours or untagged birds. Your driver's licenses, please."

For a moment, they just looked at each other. Figuring I might be in for a "hurrah" with these three burly farm types (all of them over two hundred pounds), I dropped my hand to my .44 magnum pistol and unsnapped the catch. Sticking out my other hand, I said, "Your driver's licenses, gentlemen." Then all began digging for their wallets and their driver's licenses. When they made that move, I made mine. Taking two quick steps to my truck, I opened the door and let Shadow out. Out the front door she came, and I instantly had her sit, which she did in record time. Now, in their minds, it was two against three.

Stepping back toward the lads, I collected their driver's licenses. "Now, gentlemen, if you would, please take ten steps out into the grain field." Without a word, they obeyed. Once they were in the field, I stepped over to their truck and removed and unloaded each shotgun. Taking the empty shotguns to my truck, I locked them in the cab. "Now, gentlemen, let's see what is in the back of your truck."

"There is nothing there but our decoys," responded the one with a potbelly like mine.

"Would you bet a trip to the local jail if I found anything else like goose bodies?" I asked.

Silence from my three early risers ...

"I thought so," I replied. "Now, gentlemen, please unload the contents from the back of your truck."

Sixty-nine snow, Canada, and white-fronted geese later, my three grim-faced "sportsmen" stood down from the unloading job. Taking stock of all the stone-cold geese, I said, "Gentlemen, please load them in the back of my truck, and when you walk by the dog, stay at least four feet from her or she will take you!" You never saw three sets of eyes go from the size of quarters to that of silver dollars so quickly. "And when you finish that, you can do the same with the ducks," I coldly added. I had discovered fifty-two mallards and thirteen American wigeon in two gunnysacks in the back of the truck along with the geese. These chaps had been busy the day before, I grimly thought. That sure would account for all the shooting I had heard yesterday from this area of the barley field.

Once finished, I took each one singly to the front of my truck and, with almost frozen hands, wrote citations for possession of over-limits of ducks and geese, which were the easiest charges to prove. Then, standing the three of them in front of my truck, I said, "Now, gentlemen, let's go get the rest from yesterday."

The three just looked at one another, and finally the farmer and owner of the land said, "You ain't getting on my property without a warrant. I know my rights." The other two instantly made like statements. They were right; they had me ... without a warrant, I couldn't go on their curtilage (the enclosed land surrounding a house or dwelling) to fish for yesterday's ducks and geese without their permission. They knew that, and so did I. But I figured, what the hell. I had given it the old college try and fallen in the slop. But nothing ventured, nothing gained. I knew damn well they had a shit-pot load of ducks and geese somewhere, but without a warrant or permission, I was out of luck. My bluff had failed. ...

We looked at each other for a moment before I said, "All right, if you don't want to cooperate, I will just have to let the judge know you fellows didn't want to finish this affair honestly and square it away." With that, I had pretty much fired my last legal shot.

"You go ahead, asshole. The judge is my cousin. I am sure he will understand, especially since he likes to eat the ducks and geese I bring him," shot off the one with the potbelly.

"Thank you, gentlemen, and have a good day with what is left of it," I said. With that, I loaded up Shadow and we left the scene. I had fired my best shot and it appeared to have gone uselessly into the dirt. ... However, God loves little children, fools—and *game wardens*. ...

The rest of the week wasn't quite as rewarding, but I managed to scratch another dozen-plus shooters without valid hunting licenses or duck stamps, shooting after legal hours, or using unplugged shotguns to take migratory waterfowl. The Friday before I was destined to leave, the weather turned really sour and my luck blossomed! The wind howled like there was no tomorrow, the temperature hovered around zero, and the snow, although never heavy, steadily blew horizontal. It was the greatest kind of weather for a duck and goose hunter (or many times for a game warden). The birds are hungry and feed longer because it takes more calories to stay warm, and when they fly, they fly low to the ground and take the shortest possible route back to their roost areas to conserve energy. It is a formula for great hunting and, if it is in you, a time for big over-limits.

Sitting in an area central to a major portion of the hunting in another set of grain fields at four in the morning, I huddled in my coat for the warmth it afforded. Shadow was doing her usual snoring and stinking up the cab, so much so that I had to lower my window all the way. I alternately dozed and snapped back awake until daylight finally showed its sorry face. Damn, what a bleak and sorry-looking day, I thought. But it was just what the doctor ordered. If anyone was going for a good shoot, today would be the day! Already the air was full of the whistling wings of the always greedy mallards looking for some breakfast, and skeins of brilliant white snow geese peppered the menacing sky as far as I could see. The color contrast between the dark gray winter sky and the thousands of white specks was an almost overwhelming sensation! Only the good Lord could paint such a living canvas. Soon a large flock of snow geese began swirling like a white tornado over a large barley field to the north. Within minutes the area was swarming with other geese and ducks looking for a safe place to feed as well. Soon it seemed that every duck and goose was heading for one particular barley field. The vast area began to fill with birds, and soon there had to be one hundred thousand geese alone on the ground gathering up the high-energy grits left in the fields by the farmers. Seeing that spectacle unique to waterfowl, vehicles began to arrive along the boundaries of the field, and the soft popping of shotguns could be heard pass-shooting arriving birds as they tried to get into the large flocks on the ground. I looked over the hunting crowd around the geese, but nothing really caught my eye. They were killing a few here and there, but the birds were in the middle of a huge barley field and the shooters just couldn't sneak them with any thought of success.

Then four hunters caught my eye. A car dropped them off by an irrigation ditch that ran the full width of the field. The four hurriedly dropped out of sight into the ditch, and the car left. That alone told me those chaps were shooters of the most serious vein. These might be the fellows worth watching. Now I had two huge "grinds" of geese and ducks working both sides of the ditch. Birds were coming from every direction on the compass as well as flying back and forth between the major concentrations. Yet nothing was happening with my lads in the ditch. Setting up my spotting scope, I adjusted it to 25-power and aimed it toward the point where the ditch intersected the two huge flocks. By now there were so many birds feeding on the ground that I could hear them from my downwind position a mile away! Nothing out of the ordinary happened for the next half hour, so I let Shadow out of the truck to attend to the call of nature. Boy, back into the truck she came like a shot once the intense cold hit her in all the warm spots after she got her business done. Getting her settled back down in the truck, I took another gander (no pun intended) through the spotting scope.

Then I saw it! Some birds flying over the irrigation ditch began to rise as if something below were bothering them. Then about two hundred geese of all kinds rose up from the northern flock and flew toward the birds south of the ditch. Crossing over the ditch, all of a sudden they rose as one into a ball of frightened birds! I clearly heard a rattle of at least fifteen shots and counted thirty-one birds dropping like stones to the earth below! Damn, I thought. With a limit of six each, those four chaps were already seven birds over the limit! For a second I couldn't hear the two large flocks of birds as they quieted upon hearing the shots. Not seeing any visible signs of danger, they began feeding once again, and the goose talk recommenced, filling the airways.

With a grimace over what I had just seen, I sat straight up in the truck. If I hadn't spotted those few flaring birds just moments before, I might have missed that action on the killing field. Then another small flock of twenty-two birds lifted up, heading south. Quickly getting back on the spotting scope, I watched their progress. Crossing over the ditch in the same place and no higher than thirty-five yards off the deck, all twenty-two dropped to the sounds of twenty shots! Son of a bitch! I thought. That puts those lads at least twenty-nine birds over the limit! That dog isn't going to hunt any further, I thought looking through narrowed eyes. ... Cranking up my truck, I headed for the ditch where those chaps were raising such a stink. Not being able to drive right up to them because of a locked chain gate across the lead-in road, I parked my truck next to some irrigation equipment, and Shadow and I took off on foot down the same ditch. Damn, you talk about brisk. ... It didn't take long to get the eyes watering and the snot flowing. But we were hot on a mission and had to hustle to avoid further bloodshed, extreme weather or not!

The shooting continued before me, but because of my position in the ditch, I was unable to count the dropping birds. Trying to hurry but not break too much of a sweat in the bitter elements, I pushed on. Shadow, realizing the hunt was on, kept tripping over the backs of my feet in her excitement. I was carrying my 10-gauge double-barrel to look the part in case I got too close to my targets, and now its thirteen pounds seemed to weigh a ton. ... Crawling in the snow and ice soon numbed my knees and hands, even with my heavy gloves. But dog and I kept going as the sound of the heavy barrage of shooting continued. Finally the irrigation canal dried up and I was able to walk along the bottom, making better time.

Whoops! Not forty yards from where I was walking out in front of God and everybody stood a lad looking right at me. All around his feet were mounds of geese, and he looked as surprised at seeing me as I was at seeing him. Dropping into plan B, I waved like an old friend and moved over to the far ditch bank like another hunter. From that side, waves of snow geese poured over not more than thirty-five yards high. Swinging my gun on a string of six, I picked out a Ross goose from the middle of the flock, killing it cleanly with one shot from my 10-gauge. I figured those guys knew I was there, so I might as well look the part. ... I purposely missed the next several shots as the shooting to my left diminished and then stopped, as if the lads were having a pow-wow regarding the intruder. The flocks of geese began swinging farther to the left of my suspects and me as I waved my hat at them to scare them off, but did so in such a manner that my shooters could not see what I was doing. Taking the geese moving out of gun range as an excuse, I began to horn into the space of my now aroused shooters of questionable ethics.

"Hey, asshole, go hunt somewhere else. This is our spot."

I just waved like another fellow dumb-ass hunter with a big grin and continued to shoot wide at geese way out of range. I was killing any chances they might have at killing geese, knowing they would either have to come over and run me off or gather up their birds and leave. Either way, they would place themselves in range for me to grab them.

Pretty soon a tall drink of water began walking down the ditch toward me with a mission written all over his puss. "Hey, asshole. Didn't you hear me? Go and find your own place to hunt."

Figuring I had better get in gear, I walked closer to him as if I couldn't hear what he was saying. He turned and said something to his buddies. Soon here all of them came with the bit in their teeth! I walked toward them as well, which seemed to confuse them. As I got closer, I could see many piles of geese and ducks in the area where they had been standing and shooting. No matter how you looked at this, blood would be spilled before the day ended—and it wouldn't be any more from the birds, I resolved.

Meeting the lads partway, I bade them good-morning. "Look, asshole, this is our hunting place, not yours. Why don't you go find your own place instead of ruining our shooting?" bleated the tall one.

"Yeah, we were here first. So get the hell out of our faces," growled a fat one with an ugly goatee.

I was beginning to enjoy this little get-together. It would be fun to see all those mouths stuffed with crow instead of snow goose once the cat was out of the bag. Starting off like a wimp, I said, "Well, I saw you guys getting all the shooting, so I thought I would join you. Surely there are enough geese to go around."

That gave that bunch of cowards more false courage, and here they came just like a German brown for a big gob of worms. "Look, prick, I don't care how big you are; if you don't leave us alone, the four of us are going to kick your butt!"

Using an old trick I had played on snow goose hunters near Tule Lake before, I set my plan into motion. "Well, as you guys can see, I haven't had much luck. I only have one bird. If you would give me a few of yours so I would have a limit, I would leave."

The four looked at each other as if to say, Who is this nut? Then the tall one strode back to their bird piles, picked up five shot-up geese, returned, and threw them at my feet. Acting more like a mouse than a man, I whined that they were pretty badly shot up. "Could I have some better ones?" I asked.

With that, the tall guy went ballistic! I surely could understand why. Here he had a wimp screwing up his hunting who was greedy as all get-out. "Why, you ungrateful son of a bitch," he shouted. Reaching over, he picked up all the geese he had thrown at my feet and said, "Suck on that, mister. Now, get the hell out of here or we are going to kick your ass. You want some geese, go get your own—but in an area other than this one. You ain't getting any of ours, so move it!"

Grinning, I pulled my coat back so the lads could see the Fish and Game star on my shirt and the .44 magnum on my hip. "Well, lads, since you won't share, how about I take all of them?"

"Mister, we aren't telling you any more. Move it or lose it!" the tall one continued. He hadn't yet seen the badge, but the horror on his buddies' faces said it all. Finally one of them tugged on the tall one's jacket and said, "Rich, look there!" He pointed to the star, and at that moment you would have thought the tall man had swallowed a squid! He just looked and looked through a set of bulging eyes.

I said, "State Fish and Game warden, lads. Let's gather up all those geese and throw them up on the ditch bank. But first, let's unload those shotguns one at a time, and watch where you point the muzzles. When that is done, I will need all your driver's licenses and hunting licenses."

With that, the four rather numbly emptied their shotguns. Every one of them ejected more than three shells, and as I had suspected when I heard fifteen shots in one barrage and twenty in another, all of the guns were unplugged. Then they dug out their wallets and handed me their hunting and driver's licenses. Leaving their shotguns up on the road, I had them pick up their dead birds and stack them alongside the road as well. Before it was over, I had four unplugged shotguns, four shooters without federal duck stamps, and four shooters with a collective fifty-nine snow geese and twenty-seven ducks over the limit and in their possession. Additionally, they had eleven Ross geese, for which in those days the bag limit was only one per person per day. That made another possession over-limit of a restricted species. Combined, they were facing a rather sizable fine before this meeting between the haves and have-nots was all said and done.

Taking two of the lads back with me to the truck so they could haul all the empty shotguns, I took a handful of geese in one hand and a handful of ducks in the other. As we drove back (they had the keys for the locked gate), my two tough guys were sure quiet. Back at the kill site as hundreds of geese milled overhead (to my way of thinking in celebration over the events unfolding below), I sat in my truck and issued citations while the shooters loaded all the ducks and geese into my truck, but not before gutting every one of them so they wouldn't spoil (fat chance of that occurring in the freezing temperature and howling wind).

As I looked at their licenses, I realized from the addresses that the tall man with the size 15 mouth and the fellow with the ugly goatee appeared to be the sons of two of the older men I had caught earlier in the morning loading up another haul of birds. I shook my head without any mention of that fact, but my sadness was supplanted by glee at having caught such fine, upstanding American "sportsmen." My, how the snow goose god had allowed me to catch the brass ring on this one, I thought.

All wanted to know what the fines would be, and I informed them that I was just a visiting game warden from Eureka. Since they all lacked a federal duck stamp, those violations would be processed in Sacramento in the U.S. District Court and would be $50 each. They would have to ask their local game warden for information on the other fines. Boy, that sure seemed to clamp all of them up as if I had fed them a dose of alum. "What?" I asked.

"He doesn't like any of us," the tall one mumbled.

"Who doesn't like any of you?" I asked.

"The local game warden," he responded.

"Well, it doesn't matter what your local game warden thinks. It depends on the evidence at hand, the bail schedule, and what the courts think," I said.

"Well, either way, our cousin the judge hates us as well," glumly reported the tall, mouthy one.

I had a hard time not laughing out loud. His old man had led me to believe that his crime would be a walk in the park with the judge his cousin and all. Now it appeared to be a cake in the face instead. To my way of thinking, it couldn't have happened to a nicer set of chaps. They had abused the ethics of the sport of hunting and had just slaughtered for the hell of it. Well, the devil would get his due, and in the end he sure did. My errant lads, both junior and senior, paid $1,000 each for the error of their ways. And that was in the days in which I made around $500 a month in salary before taxes.

When I got home my captain was pleased with my patrol. He had gotten word from the Tule Lake area captain that I had torn them up and had caught a hatful of local outlaws. That made my captain happy and kept me from having to tag fish in the hold of some damn smelly fishing boat. ...

The warm memories of episodes like these that I get on cold winter days now that I am retired are partly because of the thought that I gave the ducks and geese a little breather as well. Just a little ...

14

"Please Remove Baby"

I WAS PATROLLING the commercial fishing docks in Eureka one fine fall morning when my state radio crackled to life with, "154, this is base."

That was my call sign, so I keyed the mike and responded, "Go ahead, Eureka, this is 154."

"154, we have a call from 187 Princeton Lane on Humboldt Hill to remove a deer from a house. Can you assist?"

"Affirmative, Eureka. I am on my way. 154 clear."

Remove a deer from a house? I thought as I began working my way out of the city of Eureka toward the Humboldt Hill area. What next?

Turning the corner onto Princeton Lane, I saw a crowd of people at the end of the street in a small cul-de-sac. Driving into the area and parking, I was at once met by a frantic, wildly talking man and a bawling, screeching woman.

"Whoa—whoa," I said. "Let's not all talk at once. What is the problem?"

"Don't you dare tell him," the woman admonished her husband between sobs.

"I don't give a damn. This has gone far enough!" he said through gritted teeth. *Crash, ka-thump, crash* came loud sounds from inside a rather expensive-looking home near where we all stood. "See, Officer, that is what I am talking about. That damn deer! Ever since she brought him home to live with us, he has been a major problem and a pain in the ass! He has been expensive, hard to maintain, makes major messes, and now is destroying our home!"

"Roger, if you say one more word, that is it!" screeched the wife. Turning to me, the woman said, "Baby is just fine, Officer. All he needs is a little loving care and he will be all right."

Crash went breaking glass inside the house.

"I don't give a damn what she says. It is your job, Officer, to go in there and remove that damn deer before he destroys the house and everything in it!"

Crash, thump, thump, crash went breaking glass and other items being smashed to pieces inside the house. It sounded like a wrecking crew to me, not just one little deer.

"Wait a minute here, folks. You say you have a deer inside the house?"

"Yes," tiredly replied the man.

"How did he get there in the first place?" I asked in disbelief.

"Don't you say a word, Roger, if you know what is good for you," blurted out the wife in a threatening manner.

"I don't give a damn. He is going to find out what happened anyway, so the story might as well be told," he replied. "Officer, last spring my wife picked up a fawn not far from here and brought it home, and we raised it with the help of our local veterinarian. We've had to put up with major messes here and there over the year. But now the damn thing is sick and crapping green liquid all over everything. It has turned mean, and to be frank, I am a little scared of it now, especially the way it threatens us with its antlers. And this morning everything went to hell in a handbasket. It charged me during breakfast, sticking its antlers into the wall. That enabled me to get out of our kitchen–dining room area and slam the door shut. He is trapped in those rooms and, from the sound of it, is trashing the place.

"Get your ass in that damn house and get him out of there, and I mean now!" he shouted.

"First things first, folks," I replied, ignoring his demand. "To pick up and possess a game animal is not only against the law but pretty darn stupid. That is a good way to get yourselves killed. They don't call them wild animals just for the hell of it! Second of all, I am not going in there in an attempt to wrestle a deranged wild animal and risk my life, nor is anyone else. And if something is wrong with the critter, we can't just open the back door and turn this crazy animal loose in the neighborhood to hurt someone else. I will go in and try to knock the animal down with my night stick and kill it if I can. If not, I have no other option but to shoot it! Since neither the college nor the Fish and Game department has any means to tranquilize the animal, there is only one option, and that is a bullet, if I am not successful with my baton."

Boy, those words really set the wife off with a new and renewed volume of bawling and screeching at me. Ignoring the lady and her emotional state, I said, "What is it going to be, folks?"

Crrrasssh went a horrific sound of splintering wood and shattering glass to let everyone know the problem still existed.

"All right, please remove Baby. Kill him if you have to, but hurry up, will you?" quietly said the man.

"Sir," I said, "I am not carrying a mouse knuckle of a sidearm. I carry a Smith and Wesson Model 29 .44 magnum. It is a very powerful handgun and more than likely will go clear through your deer and out the other side into something in your house!"

"Oh, Jesus," the man said as he held his head in his hand. The deer still appeared to be having his way inside the house. "All right, all right, do what you have to do, but please hurry," he replied in a worried tone.

"Do we have an understanding here? Am I to understand that you will not hold me or the Fish and Game Department liable for any damages?"

"Yes, yes, yes," shouted the man. "Please remove Baby, and *do it now!*"

With that, I grabbed my baton from the back seat of the patrol car and trotted toward the house. Immediately following me were the street crowd and other homeowners. I stopped and asked everyone to remain where they were. I didn't need an audience or someone to stop one of my bullets if a shot went wrong. Quickly checking the back side of the house, I found it to be square against the hillside. Good, I thought. I will shoot in that direction if I have to, and if the bullet goes through the deer and house, it will lodge safely in the dirt bank. Then I trotted back to the door leading into the kitchen and peered through the window. God, what an awful mess met my eyes. The kitchen had been torn asunder as if a bunch of juvenile delinquents had trashed the house! If it wasn't smashed, it was trashed. Quietly opening the door, I carefully stepped around the litter so as not to alert the deer to my immediate presence and slowly walked toward the next room. Rounding the doorway, I looked left into the dining room. It was a big room, maybe twelve by twelve. Centered in the room was a huge mahogany table with a beautiful china setting for eight all laid out. There were also eight beautiful hand-carved wooden chairs, surrounded by three exquisite china cabinets. The floor was covered with a very plush white fluffy carpet, and a graceful chandelier finished the decor.

Quickly looking to the right, I gazed into the dining nook—or what used to be the dining nook! The table and chairs were tossed asunder,

and another everyday china hutch had been turned over, spilling its
contents onto the floor in a million pieces! Standing there looking at me
from the center of this destruction was a small Columbian black-tailed
buck deer. He was a spike buck and didn't appear to weigh more than
ninety pounds. You could count every rib, and it was obvious that the
animal was in pain. For a brief moment, we just stared at each other. I
will never forget those reddened, pain-filled eyes. They almost begged
for relief, but there was murder in them as well.

Then they changed to a look of fury, as if blaming me for the creature's discomfort. Lunging, hooves slipping on the slick hardwood
flooring, the animal lowered its head and charged. Grabbing my baton
tightly, I knocked him down as he came within range but was amazed
at the speed with which he regained his footing, only to charge me once
more. This time he really surprised me. He moved so fast he missed my
side by inches, driving his antlers into the wall behind me. Slipping on
the broken china and almost falling, I just barely avoided his flailing,
knifelike hooves. Ripping his antlers from the wall in a cloud of plaster
dust, he whirled, lowered his head, and charged once again. This time,
my baton blow and the energy from his attack sent him sailing across
that beautifully set dining table and into the china hutch at the end.
Crash went all the dishes set on the table into a zillion pieces, and
keraash went the deer into the hutch. Teetering for a moment from the
impact, the hutch fell onto the buck and the end of the table with a terrible, rending crash of glass, dishes, and splintering wood from the
hutch, table, and chairs!

I started to run around the mess to kill the animal with a blow from
the baton as it lay on the floor when, to my surprise, there he was
standing and facing me. Dropping the baton, I went for my pistol as
the animal jumped over the dining room table, gouging out great slices
of wood from the once magnificent finish and sailing headfirst into another china hutch alongside where I stood! Again, splintered wood,
flying glass panels, china, heirlooms, and everything else exploded
from the hutch as they too fell to the floor. Rising to his feet with un-
worldly speed and ability, the crazed animal turned and ran headfirst
into a .250-grain .44 magnum bullet. *Kaboom* went the handgun, and
the bullet sped true. Into the little animal's brain it went, and he felt
nothing after the first millisecond. However, the damage wasn't quite
done. That heavy bullet came out the other side of the deer's head and
drove through another china hutch, shattering much inside, then

passed out the back, through the wall, and into the dirt bank before ending its odyssey.

Standing there with the smell of gunpowder and fear in my nostrils, I was amazed at my speed in drawing and firing the weapon. As I slowly holstered the handgun, I watched the little animal kicking his last on the thick, expensive white carpet. The great masses of blood and brain tissue at first dotted and then slowly darkened the carpet with the contrasts of a wasted life.

Tasting my anger, I left the battle zone and headed out to the masses of quiet neighbors, upset husband, and bawling wife. "Is it all over, Officer?" Roger asked.

"Yes," I replied, "but your house is a mess." Looking him straight in the eyes, I said, "Who initially brought the deer home?"

"My wife did. Why?"

"Because she is going to get a citation for possession of a protected game animal, that's why," I quietly replied, holding back an urge to give her a real piece of my mind.

Expecting a damn good cussing from an outraged husband over those words, I was mildly surprised at what happened next. "Ha ha ha," loudly roared Roger. "Serves her right. I have told her a thousand times to leave the wild animals alone, and time and time again she has to drag the damn things home. I tell her that Mother Nature will take care of her own, and if she doesn't, then they were meant to die. Serves her right. Issue her the ticket, and I will personally see to it that she pays it!"

The wife just looked aghast. ... I think she was surprised that her Caspar Milquetoast husband had finally gotten enough sand to stand on his own two hind feet. Hardly another word was said except to answer my questions as I issued the citation for illegal possession of a protected game animal. She looked even worse for wear when I dragged the little deer past God and everybody and plunked him unceremoniously into the trunk of my patrol car for a ride to the rendering plant.

"Eureka, 154 is 10-8" (on duty).

"154, did you have any problems? Eureka clear."

"Eureka, this is 154. No problems, nothing out of the ordinary. 154 clear."

15

Earl "the Pearl" Dudley

IN MAY 1970 I RESIGNED my commission as a game warden with the California Department of Fish and Game and accepted a commission with the U.S. Fish and Wildlife Service as a U.S. game management agent. I was assigned to a new duty station in Martinez, California, in the San Francisco Bay area. My new district included the northwestern half of California, from Monterey north. As a game management agent I not only enforced the various federal wildlife laws but was also a deputized California State Fish and Game warden. In this new capacity, my job took me not only throughout my new district but anywhere else I was sent in the United States because I held a national commission when it came to enforcing federal wildlife laws.

One morning I was working in my office when the phone rang. It was Agent in Charge Jack Downs calling from his Sacramento office. Jack was the supervisory special agent for the Fish and Wildlife Service in northern California, and you wouldn't find any better man across the United States in that capacity. After exchanging the usual pleasantries, I asked, "What's up, Chief?"

"Terry, I need you to go to Nevada and spend a few days enforcing our waterfowl regulations. Ever since John Wendler retired, we haven't had much law west of the Pecos. Why don't you go over and work some of the waterfowl areas, especially the marshes in and around the Stillwater National Wildlife Refuge near Fallon? Those refuge folks have been complaining about sportsmen getting a little carried away, killing too many redheads and late-shooting waterfowl. Why don't you go over there and spoil Christmas for those inclined to break the federal laws?" John Wendler had been the agent in charge in Reno, and redheads were a protected species of duck.

Grinning at the opportunity to see some more real estate and the opportunity to "educate" some American sportsmen straying over the line, I quickly agreed.

Loading the gear for my new venture into my Dodge, I swung through Colusa (ninety miles east), where my family still resided (we hadn't been able to sell our home due to interest rates jumping from 4 to 13 percent in about sixty days—one result of our first OPEC oil crisis). Because of our geographic separation, my darling wife was not only Mom but Dad as well. All that in addition to teaching school full time and running the home front. What a gal! She still is after all these years, forty-three and counting as these words are written. After spending several days at home getting all the needed housework done, I finally headed out to my Nevada assignment.

Several days later I was concealed watching four duck hunters shooting over decoys in a marshy area near Fallon, Nevada. Their hunting had been pretty good, and they had killed numerous diving ducks. Then I saw one of them kill an American avocet, a slow-flying shorebird with a very long, upward-curving bill. The avocet is a totally protected migratory nongame bird. From my hiding place, I continued watching the shooter as he walked out to the floating dead bird, picked it up, and quickly realized it was not a duck. Knowing he was in the wrong, and probably illegal, he looked carefully all around to see if anyone other than his buddies had seen the deed. Satisfied that he was unobserved, he stomped the beautifully colored shorebird into the mud of the marsh. Figuring I would pay that lad a visit to show him the error of his ways, I started up the truck and headed toward my hunters. Just before I got to where their vehicles were parked by the marsh, I was surprised to see a Fish and Game vehicle suddenly whip in front of me, cutting me off as the driver sped into the parking lot. Braking sharply to avoid hitting the Fish and Game car, I thought, What the hell kind of dingbat drives like that? I was soon to find out!

Out of the vehicle strode a tall, lean older man wearing hip boots. He stomped straight out into the marsh, throwing water every which way, walking directly to my avocet shooter. Then he did something that surprised the hell right out of me! Reaching out, he forcefully grabbed the shooter by the collar, jerked his face to within inches of the officer's, and read him a riot act heard clear across the marsh! Man! I thought, stepping out of my truck. That certainly is not how one treats a member of the American public, violator or not! I could tell from his uni-

form and badge that he was a state Fish and Game warden. Still holding the collar of the avocet shooter, he led him to the place where he had
stomped the illegal bird into the mud. Grabbing the shotgun out of the
violator's hands with surprising force, the officer pointed to the muddy
area and made the shooter begin digging for the stomped bird. As I
walked out to the scene in the marsh, I began to hear the officer, who
was still reading the riot act to the shooter holding the bedraggled bird
in his hand. Man, did he ever get an ass chewing!

"You limp-headed son of a bitch. Don't you know you can't kill protected migratory nongame birds? Can't you tell the difference between
a duck and a shorebird? What the hell kind of hunter are you, anyway?" Those and other more colorful words aimed at the shooter continued to fill the airways as I continued my trek out to offer a fellow
officer whatever assistance might be needed. However, as I got closer
to the old-fashioned "wood-shedding," I could tell that I wouldn't
need to add my weight to the matter. Here was a game warden handling
an outlaw the way we used to in the days of old. To behave in such a
manner in the current day and age would get you a damn good ass
chewing from your supervisor, not to mention some time off. ... Ripping someone apart for an error just isn't done except under extreme
circumstances, and even then only in the oddest and most unusual sit-
uations. But right in front of God and everyone, here was a badge car-
rier who either hadn't gotten the message on how to professionally
handle our fellow humans or *just didn't give a damn.* ...

As I drew near, the officer asked, "Who the hell are you?" in a tone
meant to stop a freight train.

"Terry Grosz, U.S. game management agent, at your service, sir," I
replied with just a little bit of a flourish.

"Well, you're just a little late. I already caught the bastard!" he replied.

Grinning at the saltiness of my newfound "friend," I just shook my
head. "Yeah, I guess you could say that," I replied with a twinkle in
my eye.

"Well, then, stand aside. I have three more of these greaseballs to
check, and then we can take some time and jawbone," he said.

Jesus, I thought, where the blazes are this guy's manners?

"Come on, dingbat, let's go check your friends," said the officer as he
splashed off with his charge physically in tow to check the three other
shooters standing in a makeshift blind a few yards away. However, the
other three men, seeing their buddy in the hands of the game warden,

picked up their birds and were heading for the parking lot. Seeing what they were going to do, I cut across the marsh to meet them at their vehicles and make sure they didn't try to hide any birds if that was their intent.

We all arrived at the suspects' vehicles about the same time. As is more common than not with many duck hunters, they had two poorly trained and, to my way of thinking, useless dogs. They were peeing on everything, jumping up on me and the Nevada officer I now knew as Earl Dudley from the name tag on his shirt, boldly sniffing crotches, and the like. If my dog had behaved like those two, there would have been one hell of a hiding in the woodshed before all was said and done. I just didn't tolerate poor behavior on the part of hunting dogs, especially around loaded guns.

Earl barked out to all assembled, "I am Nevada Fish and Game Officer Earl Dudley. I am here to check your birds, the plugs in your guns, and your hunting licenses. This here rather large fellow standing alongside me with his thumb in his ear is a federal officer. He will check your federal duck stamps when I am through with you. Is that clear?"

Man, I thought, trying hard to suppress a grin. This Dudley fellow sure doesn't mince words!

There was some mumbling and shuffling of feet, and then the four men began digging out their hunting licenses and the day's bag of ducks. Earl began digging through their ducks as they tossed them onto the ground from inside their game bags. Earl quickly tossed nine ducks off to one side, and I figured he must think those were illegal for some reason. According to my identification of those birds in Earl's pile, the lads had a limit each of redheads (one apiece). The rest of the ducks in the pile were diving-duck kissing cousins, namely ring-necks (allowed five each in the bag per hunter), and all legal.

Earl checked their hunting licenses and then handed them to me to check their federal duck stamps. He could have done that, but I supposed he figured I needed to be doing something with my time. Satisfied with their licenses, Earl began in a more serious tone (if that was possible!), "Boys, we have a hell of a pile of illegal ducks here, namely redheads. If you didn't know, they're a species restricted to one per day."

Damn, my hair went straight up. There were only four redheads in the entire pile, or one per hunter, a legal limit! He had made a mistake on the identification of the ring-necks (which can easily be done if one is not careful). Before he could compound the problem, I said, "Earl, may I speak with you for a moment?"

Looking at me in disdain for interrupting his dealings with what he thought were all bad guys, he finally relented and walked with me back to my truck out of earshot. "This better be good, boy. I don't like being interrupted when I start in on a bunch of violating son of a bitch greaseballs."

"Earl, they only have four redheads. The rest are ring-necked ducks and perfectly legal."

"Are you sure?" he asked with a steely, doubting look.

"Yes, sir," I replied. "I have an extensive background in waterfowl identification, and trust me, there are only four redheads in that pile and the rest are ring-necks."

He continued to look sternly at me like a great horned owl looking over a mouse, then without a word whirled and stomped back to his huddled and befuddled charges. "This here federal agent tells me I made a mistake on the identification of those ducks. He says all are legal, and I believe him. However, none of you dingbats realized the difference, so shame on you as well. When you hunt ducks in the future, you damn well better be able to identify them and on the wing, or don't go."

I had to give Earl credit. He was a real man and professional enough to admit it when he was wrong. That took guts, I thought and a bucketful at that, after proudly making the four lads think they had violated the bag limit regulations.

"Now, lads, let's check those guns," he said.

"Need some help there, Earl?" I volunteered, thinking we could speed up the process if two of us did the work.

"Nope, I can handle it," he rather brusquely declared.

With nothing to do, I just stood there with my finger in my ear, in a manner of speaking. Grabbing the first man's shotgun, Earl checked it, and it was plugged. He did the same on the next two with practiced efficiency. When he came to the fourth man's shotgun, I noticed that it was some old, off-brand piece of junk. Not familiar with the brand, I looked over Earl's shoulder as he fiddled with it, trying to eject all the shells from the magazine. The more he fiddled trying to figure its workings out, the madder he got. After a few more moments, it was becoming readily apparent that his patience was wearing thin.

"Earl," I said, "can I give you a hand there so you can write up the other fellow for killing the avocet?" I figured putting my request that way would let Earl out of an embarrassing spot at not being able to figure out the gun. Then I would just ask the owner to unload it for me as

I watched. No big deal, and a better approach than continuing to look like a horse's hind end.

"Not on your *damn* life. I will figure out this piece of crap if it is the last thing I do," he replied through gritted teeth. *Boom* went the shotgun unexpectedly as the dirt and mud flew at Earl's feet! Jesus, I jumped like a bug on a hot rock, as did everyone else! The damn Rube Goldberg gun had gone off as Earl was trying to unload it.

Eeeooouu howled one of the dogs as he realized that Earl had just shot off most of his tail! The damn dog was whirling in circles, howling like a banshee and spurting blood over everyone from what had once been a proud and beautiful tail. Its howling was now hitting triple forte, and all the hunters, surprised as anyone, were talking excitably at triple forte as well! Goddamn, talk about embarrassing! Earl was standing there with consternation written all over his face. Nothing like shooting the tail off a man's dog, I thought. ... Even an untrained mongrel such as that dog was didn't deserve to lose a tail. By now the poor dog was dragging its bottom on the ground as if it had a serious case of pinworms and howling to the heavens as if his bottom was on fire! The owner was hollering at Earl and Earl was hollering right back about keeping one's dog out of the way, and on it went. Then Earl *really* vented his spleen on the poor unfortunate fellow who owned the offending firearm, and around and around the fracas continued! It occurred to me that these chaps were going to complain to somebody about this ugly incident, most likely their useless congressman. ... They wouldn't remember Earl (the one who did the damage), but they *would* remember the rather large federal agent standing beside him with his finger in his ear. ...

Oh, well, there wasn't much we could do for the poor dog. Before it was all said and done, Earl ended up eating the asses off the four hunters for everything from unsafe firearms to untrained dogs. I could hardly believe it! He had completely turned the tables from himself as the bad guy to those innocents standing before him before that "hurrah" was said and done! I just shook my head as Earl wrote the fellow a ticket for killing the avocet and then chewed out the other three once again for good measure. Boy, you talk about brass. Earl had a mineful!

As the hunters drove off, trying to figure out what the hell had happened, Earl turned to me and said, "Now, what the hell are you doing in my neck of the woods?"

"Well, I was sent over here by my boss to work waterfowl hunters, especially those killing too many redheads and shooting ducks after legal hours. I had set up on those chaps and was moving in to cite the lad who shot the avocet when you arrived. The rest is history."

Still looking at me like he wasn't too sure of me, my lineage, and my mission, he finally relented. "Well, if you are over here to work, let's get with it. Let's use your truck because it is unmarked, and that way those bastards I work for can't get me on the state radio."

"That's fine with me; let's do it," I said.

The rest of the day we tore the somewhat sloppy sportsmen in the countryside a new one! With Earl's knowledge of the terrain and the work ethics that we shared, we covered a lot of ground. During the next six hours we caught a Nevada Fish and Game commissioner with closed-season game birds, five individuals shooting hawks from a motor vehicle, three chaps for over-limits of redheads, one for theft of another man's property (his lawn mower), and two for shooting protected migratory nongame birds (black-necked stilts)—twenty-two of them! I came to know a little more about my new friend. It was clear to me that Earl was a black sheep. He was frank to the point of rudeness, brooked no nonsense, took charge of every situation, gave no quarter, and generally was hell on wheels. I spent most of our afternoon mending fences and replacing lips that had been torn off offenders for some minor infraction before a hungry magpie could find and eat them. But what a riot! Here was a man so totally dedicated to the natural resources of the state of Nevada that he took personal offense if anyone had the audacity to stray over the line in the world of wildlife, taking more than their share. ... I had never met such a man during my short time as an officer, nor have I met any more during my thirty-two years of service to the American people. Regardless of the fact that his manners were something to behold, I enjoyed working with someone who was a throwback even at that time. Regardless of his manners, the critters *always* got a fair shake from him.

Later that afternoon we stopped under some cottonwood trees, and I broke out some Italian salami, several types of cheese, crackers, cold drinks, and hot peppers. Earl eyed what I was doing and when invited for "lunch" more than obliged. "I always thought you federal son of a bitches were downright lazy as pet coons. And to be truthful, over the years I've found most of you guys about as useless as tits on a side of bacon. But Terry, you're an all right Joe," he said.

"Well, thank you, Earl, for including me among the living," I replied with a large grin.

Earl grinned right back through a mouthful of cheese and salami. It was the first grin I had gotten out of him all day.

From our place of concealment in the Stillwater Marshes, we watched three men going out into a great tule marsh just as everyone else was coming in at the end of legal shooting hours for the day. "Those son of a bitches don't know who they are messing with," hissed Earl from under the binoculars.

Pretty soon our shooters were about half a mile out in the dense marsh and began late shooting at fleeing and surprised waterfowl.

"Earl, since we know where their vehicle is parked and since we can watch and identify them from our place of concealment, let's let them shoot to their hearts' content and then lower the boom on them when they return," I suggested.

"The hell with that," he said. "I am going out into that stinking marsh right after those knuckleheads and beard them right in the middle of their late duck shoot. That ought to teach them a lesson they won't forget."

"Earl, how the hell are you going to do that? Once you leave the high ground, you will be level with those chaps, and if they move away from you in the dark in those dense reeds, they will be the devil to catch," I said.

"Don't make a whit of difference to me. I will run those dingbats to ground right out there in the swamp and make them wish they hadn't gone forth to do what they are doing in my state," he grumbled.

Well, that was fine and good except that I had torn my Achilles tendon running down a spotlighter who had blown a roadblock some four months earlier. There was no way I was going to don a pair of chest-high waders and plow several miles through a deep-water swamp chasing those young kids and expect the leg to survive! I explaining that to Earl, and he just snorted. "You didn't hear me asking for any help, did you? I plan on going out there myself and catching those bastards just as soon as it gets a little darker, and that is that!"

"Well, if your heart is dead set to run across that marsh in the dead of night, I got an idea. I have a Starlight night-vision scope in the back box of the truck. Why don't I hook you up with one of our handitalkies and let you go after the lads in the swamp, and I will crawl onto the top of the cab of my truck with the Starlight and direct you to them with the radio?"

Earl looked at me for a second and then said, "You know, that might work better than all get-out. Let's do it!"

Digging around in the back box of my truck, I dug out the Starlight scope while Earl put on his chest-high waders. By now it was pretty damn dark, and the lads in the marsh were banging away from within the deep covering reeds as if they were on a mission. Earl and I stood up in the bed of the truck and, turning on the Starlight scope, found our three miscreants very quickly in the lime-green field of the instrument. They were especially visible each time they shot because the gunfire left a bright light spot on the scope, clearly giving away their positions. Earl, looking through the scope for the first time, just squealed with delight! "Man, between this device and the portable radios, those bastards don't have a chance. Let me at them!" With that and a caution to keep his radio on and turned to channel 3, up over the bank he went and out into the pitch black and the methane stink of the marsh.

I had to marvel at Earl. We could have cut those lads off at the pass as they returned to their vehicles with one hell of a lot less effort. But no! Earl was going to track down the violators and catch them in their element. If my memory serves correctly, Earl looked to be in his early sixties at the time. He was a true, sterling member of the Thin Green Line. ...

Crawling up on top of the cab of my truck, I turned on my Starlight scope. The quiet whirring sound told me that the oscillators of the machine were up and running. Quickly locating my three outlaws and then Earl in the screen, I called him on the portable radio. He responded, and I told him to move another hundred yards to the west. In an instant, Earl made the change. By now a light wind had come up, and I noticed lightning splitting the sky off to the northeast. Not really a good idea standing high on the cab of one's all-metal truck in a lightning storm, I thought, but I too wanted these bastards. Damn, now Earl's language and way of thinking was beginning to rub off on me. ...

It took Earl about twenty minutes to get close to our late shooters. Between my directions and the noise of three shotguns shooting to their hearts' content, he kept moving closer to our prey. The use of the Starlight scope and my command of the high ground was the ticket. No matter which way the bad guys twisted and turned in the dense stand of tules, I had their number. By now the lads in the marsh realized there was someone on their tails! They had gotten together once that realization set in and as a group tried to flee into the dark and lose their pursuer. They would hurriedly walk about fifty yards and then stand very still. Seeing what they were trying to pull, I would get Earl on the radio.

"Earl, they are fifty yards off to your left. Head that way and I will guide you in," I would say.

"Ten-four," he would reply, and off he would go. Soon the bad guys would hear him coming and head off in another direction. Earl would stop, I would give him new directions, and off he would go once more. This went on for the better part of an hour. In the meantime, the lightning storm had moved over the marsh, and here I was standing on the cab of my truck as lightning danced all across the sky as only a thunderstorm in the Great Basin can do! Talk about stupid! But I found myself feeling like Earl. It was a do-or-die effort with these dingbats in the marsh, and unless I was swept off the cab of my truck by a bolt of lightning, they were ours.

Soon the lads in the marsh were dying on the vine. Earl was almost running these three shooters, who appeared to be at least thirty years younger than he, to ground. Their running distance was getting shorter and shorter each time. Finally Earl was less than twenty yards from the lads, who chose to sit down in the marsh in the hope that he would walk on by. Directing Earl right to the lads, I told him to turn on his flashlight and they should be sitting right in front of him. On went his light, and they were caught! Boy, you talk about being slicker than cow slobbers; this Starlight scope and handi-talkie were a sure-fire combination.

Half an hour later, Earl brought the three lads back to their vehicle, where I was now sitting. He broke out the cite book, and as he was writing up the lads, I heard them talking. "There is no way that old man could have found us. It must have been the flashes from the lightning that gave us away." I just sat there (with my finger in my ear, according to Earl), grinning in the realization of what a little technology and some get-up-and-go could do.

Earl finished with the lads by giving them a damn good ass chewing. There were a lot of hangdog looks among the three men as Earl saw to it that they would never forget this night.

After the thoroughly whipped trio disappeared into the dark of the night, Earl turned to me and said, "For a fed, you aren't half bad. It would have taken me most of the night to chase those knotheads around in the marsh. That toy of yours is really the ticket."

Grinning, I said, "Hell, Earl, you would have caught those guys in half the time if I hadn't muddied the waters for you with that damn scope." I was joking, but what followed really took me by surprise.

"No, I think I learned something tonight. The time for a man such as me is almost gone. Like a gunfighter, I am having trouble realizing that the days of my kind are coming to an end. I find that very sad." Without another word, Earl asked me if I would take him back to his patrol car. Man, I must have really struck a nerve. He said nothing more for the more than thirty minutes it took me to return him to his car.

"Thank you for the day, Terry. It was a good one, and one I will long remember. Speaking of remembering, you need to do the same. Remember, someday you will be like me, an anachronism or a piece of history, nothing more. Replaced by a bunch of young kids and women who won't have an ounce of common sense, life experiences, or the heart and soul needed to do the job. Replaced by those asking if they get overtime just because they have to work more than an eight-hour day. Replaced by those who really don't have the guts or moxie to do this job. Like the gunfighter of old, you won't have a job anymore and won't be needed. Enjoy your grace."

With that, he was gone. I never had the fortune to work with Earl again. A new agent arrived in Reno, and I was no longer needed to pinch hit. Maybe that was the beginning of what Earl said about being a piece of history.

Today I am retired after thirty-two long years of service to the American people and the critters. As Earl once said, I am an anachronism and no longer needed. In fact, the agency and profession have changed so much that if I was still on the line, I wouldn't fit in.

Wherever you are Earl, you were right. But during my run, I did as you advised. I enjoyed my grace.

16

To Shoot a Coyote

IN 1974 I WAS promoted to senior resident agent (first line supervisor) and moved to Bismarck, North Dakota. I was in charge of North and South Dakota's Fish and Wildlife Service law enforcement team, supervising three officers. Not long after arriving, I discovered that the Dakotas were a veritable hotbed of just about every kind of federal wildlife law violation imaginable! You may be thinking, "The Dakotas? The land of perpetual heat, humidity, mosquitoes and freezing cold? The land of constant winds and about 600,000 peaceful and quiet dirt farmers?" Yep, that's right. I soon discovered I had more law enforcement problems than you could shake a stick at! Both Dakotas are loaded with wildlife of every kind. To be frank, the wildlife resources in those two states are some of the best-kept secrets in the nation. And any time you have natural resources of that magnitude and people intermixed, you will have major enforcement problems. If that were not problem enough, the Division of Law Enforcement had no money, and it always seemed that I had even less! But you learn to do the best you can with what you have, and we did.

One of the many problems I had was dealing with violations of the federal Airborne Hunting Act, a law that had been passed to prevent those so inclined from illegally gunning down wildlife with the use and aid of an aircraft. It doesn't take more than a millisecond to realize the unfair advantage given by the use of a airplane when chasing wildlife. With the Dakotas being as flat as a plate of piss in most places and full of fur-bearing wildlife, a golden opportunity awaited the outlaws. With the tremendous rise in fur prices in the late 1970s, that golden opportunity was sensed and plucked like a ripe grape. Soon the outlaws in their aircraft were taking their deadly toll, out and about chasing animals from the air until they couldn't run anymore, then gunning those exhausted critters down by shooting heavy loads of lead shot down through their backs and into their vital organs. Once they were killed, the planes would direct someone on the ground to follow the path of the airplane so the carcass could be picked up and later sold. Many of the pilots were good enough that they would land almost anywhere with the aid of large balloon tires on their aircraft, pick up their fresh kill, and fly off looking for more. Soon fur prices went as high as $600 for a coyote (in the round—not skinned), $700 for bobcat, $1,000 for lynx, and about $200 for all species of fox. The new gold rush was on!

One of the last cases I was involved with was that of an illegal aerial gunner in Montana. He was using a helicopter and shooting fur bearers within the vast confines of the Charles Marion Russell National Wildlife Refuge. During just the last month of operation before agents from the Fish and Wildlife Service caught him, he made $209,000! I think the problem, in part, may now have become clearer. I say "in part" because that is just the tip of the iceberg. Aerial gunners in short order will remove most of the mammalian predators from an area. In so doing, they upset the ecological balance between predators and prey, creating an overabundance of many lesser forms of wildlife. In addition, the element of fair chase is lacking—and it is illegal!

Soon the complaints regarding illegal aerial gunning began rolling in. Reports from farmers, cattlemen, public-spirited citizens, and sportsmen flooded across my desk and the desks of my officers. According to the complainants, the air was full of aircraft illegally gunning wildlife on the ground! When you consider that there were only four of us in the Dakotas to enforce all the federal wildlife laws, and that we had to chase aerial gunners and their airplanes with simply a vehicle on the ground (one without four-wheel drive because they cost too much), you can begin to see the problem. Throw into that formula the fact that we had to call our head office in Kansas City to get approval every time we purchased a tank of gas because of budget constraints. Now you can see just how hard it was to catch those aerial outlaws. But go after them we did because it was a good fight, and one that had to be fought. In fact, before all was said and done, the four of us in the Dakotas seized between eight and sixteen airplanes a year in violation of the Airborne Hunting Act. And those aircraft seizure figures would have been higher if we could have seized our own agency's aircraft, flown by our own Animal Damage Control Division pilots, for violating the law as well!

One fine November morning, I kissed my wife good-bye and headed for the western portion of North Dakota to investigate an illegal drainage problem on a Waterfowl Production Area (like a mini national wildlife refuge, whose land was fenced and owned in fee title by the Service). Arriving about nine in the morning, I began my investigation into the illegal ditching and drainage on Service lands. I had barely started documenting the damage with my camera, when off in the distance in the nearby foothills I heard a very distinct *varoooom*. It was the classic sound an airplane makes when pulling out of a dive under full power. No big deal, though. A lot of ranchers in the area used aircraft for all manner of things, and I quickly forgot the sound in light of my work at hand. *Varoooom, boom, boom, boom* went the sounds of an aircraft again pulling out of a steep dive, this time followed by the unmistakable sounds of a shotgun being fired. Spinning around, I thought, That can only be one thing—aerial gunning! Quickly scanning my mind for any permits that might have been issued to aerially gun in that vicinity, I came up blank. One could get a permit to use aircraft to aerially gun mammalian predators, but only under very strict circumstances. First of all, state or federal agencies, acting within the scope of their official duties, could procure a federal permit to protect farmers and ranchers from damage to livestock; protect wildlife; or protect land, water, crops, or human life. In addition, states could provide subpermits to landowners for protection in the above categories if they wished to use their aircraft in the process. However, there was a reporting requirement that most gunners did not want to mess with. Hence, they tended to just crank up the airplane and do their gunning, the state administrative process be damned. Sport hunting with the use and aid of an aircraft was prohibited. This prohibition included anyone helping the aerial gunner on the ground, so if an illegal aerial gunner was working the critters over from the air and had a helper on the ground to pick up the carcasses, that helper was breaking the law as well!

Grabbing my binoculars from the seat of my sedan, I quickly scanned the rolling hills to the northwest in the direction where I had last heard the aircraft. After a few moments, I heard the signature *varoooom* and saw an airplane pull up steeply out of a draw. Then I heard two more shots. Damn, they were aerially gunning just as sure as God made green apples, I thought as I jumped into the car. Cranking it over, I hurriedly pointed it in the direction of the offending aircraft, all the while mentally running through my mind where the nearest road would be that would give me access to the action area. Now, keep in mind that this is not an easy kind of case to make. The chap in the aircraft has a height advantage and can see for miles. That advantage also includes seeing any vehicle entering the area other than his pickup person and vehicle on the ground. Once he spotted a suspicious vehicle in the vicinity, a pilot could just call down to his helper on the ground and alert them to the presence of the intruder. Then it was a hop, skip, and jump and he was in the next county. And so much for your case ...

Once I reached the foothills near the aerial action, I pulled into an abandoned farmyard as if I belonged and got out my Big Eye, a spotting scope, and in this particular instance a zoom sixty-power one. Focusing in on the area where I had last seen the plane, I was soon rewarded. *Varoooom* went a red-and-white aircraft as it roared up and out of a long coulee to the east. Quickly snapping back around, the plane dove back down and out of sight into the same coulee like a man on a mission. *Boom-boom-boom* clearly rang the sounds of three shots being fired. *Varoooom*, up from the coulee came the aircraft, and then it lazily circled the area as if waiting for someone. Soon I saw a Ford truck working its way over a far hill as it headed for the bottom of the coulee. The airplane continued circling and soon made a low pass over the coulee, probably to show the pickup person in the truck the exact location of the dead animal.

Then the aircraft scooted over to the next coulee and began checking out the brush-filled draw for likely targets. Soon I once again heard the sound an airplane makes under full power and the strain of dangerous flight. *Varooom*, up out of the coulee he came, this time with a vengeance. Back into that same coulee he went, and this time I heard *boom-boom-boom!* then a pause, and then *boom-boom!* *Varoooom*, up from the end of the coulee came the aircraft, then into a very tight turn and back down into the draw. *Boom-boom-boom-boom* went his shotgun. Turning tightly, back into the coulee he went like a banshee. He must have gotten into a mess of coyotes, I thought as I continued gluing my eye to the spotting scope. About that time, into the scope lumbered the Ford, and I could see a woman driving the vehicle. It was probably the wife of the pilot. That is all right with me, I thought. I can just as easily pinch the whole family as not! *Varoooom*, up from the coulee came my outlaw pilot and outlaw gunner in the red-and-white aircraft I now identified as a Super Cub. Turning tightly and hanging dangerously for a second, the pilot stormed out of that turn and dove to the battleground in the coulee below. Looking hard at the tail of the plane, I couldn't make out his identification numbers. He was moving so fast that they were a blur. All aircraft are numbered and registered, so in a situation like this, you try to get the numbers for later use in court. However, in this instance I just couldn't read the numbers off the tail or wing. I knew my eyes are not as good as they used to be, but by dang, they aren't that bad either! I thought. Getting as close to the spotting scope as I could (as if that would help), I waited for the next opportunity when the plane reappeared. *Varoooom,* up from the bottom of the coulee he came, and this time my eyes were riveted on the wing and tail. No matter how hard I tried, I couldn't get all the goddamned numbers read before he was on his way into the draw once again. *Varoooom,* down he went like a house afire into the coulee at what had to be full throttle. *Boom-boom-boom-boom* went the shotgun, and then a loud *craaaaash,* sounding like someone had emptied a trash can full of empty cans! *Jesus Christ,* I thought, *the damn fool crashed!* He must have fixated on the ground in his intense desire to kill a coyote and augered the screaming aircraft right into the deck!

Cranking up the car, I blew through a four-strand barbed-wire fence with a metal-rending crash, speeding cross-country to the crash site at a velocity my sedan was not meant to go. Dodging and weaving through all the obstacles, I gritted my teeth at my supervisor's lack of interest in providing those of us in the prairie states with four-wheel drive (they now all have them—it became my first order of business when I became supervisor of that district in 1981). Their wonderful reasoning was that we couldn't afford them, plus only game wardens drove pickups. Getting on the state radio as I hammered cross-country, I informed the Bismarck dispatcher of the crash, gave its approximate location, and requested an ambulance. Continuing across the prairie like a madman, I forgot about my investigation into the violation of the Airborne Hunting Act and focused on the well-being of the aircraft crew. Saying a quick prayer to the old boy above, I kept the hammer down.

Topping the edge of the coulee, I spotted the wreckage of the red-and-white aircraft at the lower end. Running along the top edge of the coulee (I couldn't cut across because I lacked a four-wheel drive), I continued at a breakneck pace, smashing into many things both large and small. Hitting the bottom of the ridge and now stopped by a deep draw, I hurriedly jumped out of the sedan and began running to the crash site. By now the Ford had rumbled up to the crash site, and even from where I was running, I could hear a woman screaming as if her guts were being ripped out. ... I could see her running to the plane, or what was left of it, screaming all the way. There didn't appear to be any sign of fire, so I kept running for all I was worth. But to no avail!

Both the pilot (an older man) and the gunner (probably his son) had been completely crushed by the impact of the speeding aircraft. The bawling woman walked away from the cockpit as I shooed her away and attempted to find a pulse on either of the men. There was none, and given the terribly crushed bodies, I did not expect one. Then I couldn't find the pilot's wife. Quickly looking around, I spotted her back by what was left of the tail—*bawling for all she was worth and pulling tape off the aircraft numbers!* Those bastards had taped over the numbers on the aircraft so, if discovered breaking the law, they could not be correctly identified. For example, she was tearing off the tape from a number 3. The tape had made it into an 8! Crying all the while, the farmer's wife had the presence of mind to remove all the illegal evidence before the law and reporters arrived. ... However, not before someone from the official community had seen it. This taping of aircraft numbers was a common trick of the trade for those involved in the illegal aerial gunning of wildlife.

Walking back to my vehicle, I talked the emergency vehicles racing around the countryside in to the wreck site. Once there, it was an hour or so before they were able to get the men's bodies out from under the twisted wreckage. They really needed body bags for this one. ... While at the site, I casually walked over to the Ford and discovered thirteen freshly killed coyotes in the back! Yeah, they had been on a killing spree all right. That was, until the great god of the coyotes had gotten involved. ...

As fate would have it, a neighbor was an insurance salesman, and it just so happened that his company held the insurance policy on the aircraft I had been watching breaking the law when it corkscrewed itself into the bottom of the coulee. Some time after the accident, it seemed that the pilot's wife was trying to collect an insurance policy connected with the aircraft. After discovering that I had been involved in an investigation into the illegal use of that aircraft, not to mention the violation of a Federal Aviation Administration regulation (taping over the aircraft's identification numbers), the insurance company balked at paying out for the loss of the aircraft. After threatening a lawsuit, the wife backed off and withdrew her claim upon hearing of the federal investigation at the moment of the crash. Honor is a gift humans give themselves! There is no honor in aerially gunning wildlife for sport or profit. As someone once said, it doesn't pay to mess with Mother Nature.

17

The Value of Training

IN EARLY SPRING of 1975, I decided to provide a forty-hour training class to the refuge officers in North Dakota. Refuge officers in those days had one of the most dangerous jobs in the federal government: alone for the most part in the country's outback, with zero equipment, no backup, and little or no training from an agency that had a decided lack of respect for and understanding of the wildlife management tool called law enforcement! No matter how you cut it, it was a surefire formula for disaster.

Having worked a year in the states of North and South Dakota as the senior Service law enforcement official, I had a firsthand opportunity to witness the ethics, courage, and skills of the refuge officers in those areas. They were outstanding! Always ready to help one another and with more guts than a slaughterhouse, they were dedicated to the resources of the land, possessed vision beyond their years, and always looked upon a challenge or setback as an opportunity. With that kind of talent, I decided I had better make sure they had at least a smattering of law enforcement training, even if the Service didn't agree. It was important to me that men and officers of such quality had the opportunity to come home to their families every day when the work was done.

Not having enough money in those days for any kind of enforcement activity (I once sat in a hotel parking lot all day waiting to get approval to replace a tire because the district was so broke), I had to really scrounge my way to the planned training. Getting together with Jim Gritman, the area manager for North Dakota, I presented my idea for training his refuge officers. "Great idea, Terry! When do you want to start and where?"

"I will start when I can raise the necessary funding for travel and per diem for my officers who will act as instructors," I responded hopefully with my hat and tin cup in hand.

"No problem. We have more money this year than we know what to do with. Have your guys submit their travel vouchers through my secretary, and that is that!"

Good old Jim. He was a man of few words, but when he spoke the whole state of North Dakota as well as the office of the secretary in Washington, D.C., listened. Jim was in charge of a pivotal resource-rich state with a world of related legal problems. He and his people were making history that is still looked back on and respected to this day as a legal base in the realms of cattle trespass, wetland easements, and just about every other imaginable type of resource problem. That North Dakota bunch was truly the most unique group of individuals I ever worked with. All you had to do was point them in the right direction and it got done, and well.

"I also need the conference room in the regional office for the morning lecture sessions. Then in the afternoons, we will use the office grounds for the practical training where the lads [there were no women refuge officers in the Dakotas in those days] can apply what they learned from the morning's lectures."

"Sounds good to me. If you have any problems and I am not around to square them away, get hold of my assistant and he will help you get them solved."

"Yes, sir," I said, and out the door I went before he changed his mind. Jim was the kind of man who took the bull by the horns in almost every situation. In this case, the dividends would be beyond belief.

Calling John Cooper, special agent in Minot, I laid out my training plan. John was an outstanding young officer, and it didn't take but a moment for the awareness of the value of such training to sink in. "Count me in, Chief. What do you want me to teach and how much time can I have?" I filled him in on what I wanted him to teach and the time I felt would be necessary to get his message across. "Perfect, Chief! Can do!" was his typical, energy-filled reply.

Next I called Special Agent Joel Scrafford, who also resided in my hometown of Bismarck. Joel could be a grouchy old son of a bitch, but what a good agent he was. He had come to the Fish and Wildlife Service from the National Park Service, and that agency, unlike the Service, had early on realized the value of training. Joel was a chip off that old block when it came to training and was raring to go. I told him what I wanted him to teach, and he quickly agreed.

Last but not least, I needed a man like Senior Resident Agent Ed Nichols from Jefferson City, Missouri, for the respected base of realism he brought to the table. He was in another Service region, but we quickly worked that problem out (especially since Jim Gritman was picking up the tab). I now had my team, all experienced instructors, excellent field men, experienced in practical law enforcement, and believers in providing field training to our refuge counterparts.

Putting out the word to my refuge counterparts in North Dakota regarding the upcoming training, I waited for their responses. Man, you talk about overwhelming! It was unreal, which really spoke to the problem of little or no previous training. I had limited the class to twenty officers, doing so because we four instructors would have our hands full with that number. The type of training I envisaged was to lecture on the most basic law enforcement concepts (laws of arrest, rules of evidence, arrest techniques, review of the regulations, elements of a crime, field interviewing, etc.) in the morning and then put those elements into practice in the afternoon. That way the learning curve would be reinforced by timely practical instruction.

Come the first morning of training, we four instructors arrived to find not twenty refuge officers present but *thirty-eight!* What pandemonium awaited us on the staff! I could already see that we were going to get worked over *but good* because we would be using ourselves as training dummies for the officers to practice on. Have you ever been handcuffed fifty times in one day? It sure does wonders for the wrists.

Just to give a glimpse into the preparedness of those officers—hang on to the willows on this one—there was only one model 1917 .38 Special handgun (without any holster) among the entire group of officers! Sixteen had real badges, and the rest had little blue cards that said, "I am an officer for the Fish and Wildlife Service." That was it in the way of enforcement equipment! The four of us just looked at each other in utter disbelief. We could not believe our eyes! And we were assured that that was par for the course for the rest of the refuge enforcement wing in North Dakota ... an enforcement wing that was responsible for refuge enforcement for 150 National Wildlife Refuges and over a million other acres of wetlands administered by the Service! And in those days the refuge division had more money than it knew what to do with.

At the end of what turned out to be an enthusiastic week of training, we had four tired and worn-out instructors. We also had thirty-eight partially trained officers with a lot more confidence returning to their fields of battle. In addition, we had the area manager ordering the right amount and quality of law enforcement equipment for the entire contingent of refuge officers for his state for the very first time. Man, you talk about excitement on all sides.

Reporting to my boss in Kansas City the following Monday, I got a surprise. First of all, he was happy! It took a miracle for Special Agent in Charge Chuck Hayes to be happy. Then came the bombshell! He said, "The area manager in South Dakota heard from Jim Gritman what a wonderful training program you presented to his men in North Dakota. He wants you to bring your instructors down to South Dakota and train his people as well. And I have agreed since he is picking up the entire cost of the program. That means what resources I would have had to use for you guys can now be diverted to your counterparts in other parts of the district." In those days the word of the special agent in charge was the law west of the Pecos. If you disagreed, you found yourself being transferred to such lovely places as Bowlegs, Oklahoma. I think you get my drift. ...

The following week found my somewhat tired but recovering crew teaching the refuge officers in South Dakota. On the first day of class we found that there were a few more handguns present, a few Remington 870 pump shotguns (used by officers nationwide), handcuffs, and some flashlights. The officers were still woefully deficient in the right kind of equipment, but they had more than the last class! Again the regimen of lectures in the morning and practical application of the law enforcement concepts in the afternoon was our model. As during the previous week, we instructors used ourselves as the "tackling dummies" for the realism it added, and by the end of that week we were bruised, bloody, and whipped to a frazzle. We not only had the entire contingent to contend with (forty officers this time) but it was hotter then the hubs of hell! Heat was a real killer to those training hard in the out-of-doors. Throw into that mix the cowboy refuge officers from Nebraska who worked on the National Bison Range (Nebraska was in the South Dakota area manager's district), and the practical exercise portion became a real experience. Those guys were tougher than a horseshoe nail! Hell, they had to be, working with bison and longhorn cattle all the time.

With my hind end dragging, I called my boss the following Monday with a battle and casualty report. The class had gone exceptionally well, partly because I had great instructors and in part because the refuge officers had really gone tooth and nail after the training. They were so happy to have someone teach them the right way to do things that they just about consumed their instructors in the process. I informed Chuck that my guys and I were beaten to a frazzle but happy with the outcome.

"That is great," he responded. "Plan on going to Missouri next. The area manager over there is a good friend of law enforcement, and he wants the same type of training for his guys."

For a moment I didn't speak, just sat there. Then I said, "Boss, my guys are shot. This training is killing us because we let all the refuge lads practice on us. Hell, I have sixteen-inch swollen wrists as we speak and can hardly hold the phone!"

"All right, I'll tell you what. I will call the area manager and inform him that you guys are going to take a week off and then be on Squaw Creek National Wildlife Refuge the following week to train his guys."

My heart just sank. It wasn't as if I didn't have plenty of administrative work to do and investigations to conduct. But his word was law, and when I told my partners about the conversation, they all just groaned.

Two weeks later found the four of us going through our training program in the middle of the summer heat and humidity of Missouri. This time there were fifty-eight refuge officers in the class! I could see nothing but bloody stumps for wrists when this class got through with us, I thought grimly. It was in this class that we had our first signs of trouble. Two of the students who just happened to be powerful refuge managers did not support this "law enforcement thing." For two days the class was atypically sullen and without any questions. Then, during a practical exercise involving a car stop, the two anti-law-enforcement refuge managers drew the car-stop straw. Their approach was all wrong, they thought the exercise was funny, and one of them had the audacity to stop and light up a cigar before he backed up his partner.

Sensing now what the problem was, I stopped the exercise. "What all of you have just seen is how not to execute a proper car stop. If I catch any more of you approaching these exercises like a couple of ding-dongs, count on losing your ass along with your credentials!" I think everyone got the message that I was pissed! Then it really hit the fan. "The two of you who find this work so funny are excused from any further classes, and if you show up for any reason, I will call your area manager and tell him it is either you out the door or the training! Now, get the hell out of here."

They were so surprised at my outburst that they just stood there for a moment and then left out of supreme embarrassment. I didn't care! We were giving our all to teach those officers the right way to do things, and by damn, I wasn't in any mood to put up with a couple of clowns. After their departure the class got typically lively and really into the mood of things. I found out later that those two clowns had warned all their people not to cooperate with us because after we left, they would go back to doing things their way.

The following Monday, now wearing a roller skate on my bottom to keep it from dragging in the dirt and wearing out my jeans, I called my boss. He was extremely happy over our most recent refuge officer law enforcement program, as was the area manager. "Terry, I know you don't want to hear this, but the Area Manager in Salt Lake City wants the same kind of training for his officers. It seems that someone higher up has discovered that the Service is mandated to provide basic training and in-service training for their refuge badge carriers or they are breaking the law. By pure luck and foresight on your part, Terry, you are the only guys providing those managers some relief until formalized refuge officer training can be initiated."

Boy, you talk about a sinking heart. ... I had really had a gutful of training. I had hardly been home, I had a faithful Lab dog who appeared to be off her feed, and my body was a mess. I was sure my fellow instructors were not much better off. "Yes, sir," I said. "When do we go?"

"You have to be there next week. That is the only date that fits into their schedule."

"Yes, sir," I replied mournfully.

The following week found us on the Bear River National Wildlife Refuge near Salt Lake City, Utah. Talk about heat and humidity! I had thought Missouri was bad. And now we had millions of bugs and the summer stink of their rotting bodies (after mating) to contend with. Walking into class that first morning, we looked over a sea of faces. The strong suggestion of no more than twenty students had apparently fallen on deaf ears once again. I also noticed a smattering of complete sets of law enforcement equipment scattered throughout the class. Brand-new handguns, batons, flashlights, handcuffs, shell holders, and Sam Browns (leather gear to hold all the law enforcement gear) matched the grins on many expectant faces.

We worked our magic again that week. Again the instructors reached deep within to give their very best, and the students took in every bit of information, leaving not a crumb on the table.

Wearing a wheelbarrow on my bottom to keep everything from dragging, I made the Monday-morning call to my boss. By now he had swelled up to my size over all the accolades he was receiving for a refuge officer training program that had been so well received. For ten minutes all he could do was rave about the program. During that time it was all I could do to look at the small mountains of mail scattered all over my office.

"Terry, I know you don't want to hear this, but the area manager in Montana wants the same kind of training for his guys. ..."

By now nothing surprised me. I just sat there in my wheelbarrow and waited for the other shoe to drop.

The following Monday found me and my very tired instructor core barely wiggling. In fact, we were about five minutes late getting to class, something I normally found unacceptable. Ed Nichols walked ahead of me into class and instantly turned back with a look of surprise and resignation. Ed was one tough individual. He had been a sailor on the battleship *Missouri* when a Japanese kamikaze pilot had hit the side of the ship, killing many men. He had also been a wildlife officer for a million years in a pretty tough state. Not much shook him up, but something in that first look into his class sure had! Stepping past his large frame, I looked at the roomful of students, and my jaw must have dropped a foot! Sitting there quietly were forty new students. Each was in a crisp new uniform, and *every one of them was completely outfitted with all the required law enforcement equipment!* There was a grim "can do" look on their faces, and it was obvious that this group of officers was deadly serious about the business at hand. I can't think of a time when I took such a beating from a bunch of officers so intent to learn! Those Montana cowboys came looking for bear and would not be deterred until they found one. ... God, that was one outstanding class. Their grades on their final exams all ran in the 90s.

The following Monday I somehow made it into my office for my weekly report. Holding the phone in a hand that was very sore from all the handcuffing by forty aggressive Montana cowboys, I called my boss. Suffice it to say, he was pleased, and this time he held no more training assignments up his sleeve. Some time later, all of us instructors received a special achievement award for our labors. *But it didn't end there. ...*

Six weeks later I was sitting in the quiet of my office catching up on my mail before I went into the field. The phone rang, and something told me that this was a very special call. Picking up the phone, I heard, "Is this Terry Grosz?"

"Yes, it is. How may I help you?"

"Terry, do you have a few minutes?" the quiet voice asked.

"Sure do. What can I do you in for?" I asked once more.

"Terry, this is Refuge Officer Bill Jones [not his real name] on the Charles Marion Russell National Wildlife Refuge in Montana. I recently attended your training class in Billings, and one thing you said just before we finished was when in extreme danger, a situation in which the bad guy is going to kill you, to keep talking. You said if you can keep talking, he will be listening. If he is listening, you are not dead yet and can formulate a plan to survive. Remember saying that?" he asked.

"Sure do," I replied.

"Well, this last weekend we had a rape committed on the refuge. The lady came into our refuge headquarters and reported it. She described the man as a tall hippie with a beard and an ugly red scar on his right cheek. She also told us the man was driving a red Volkswagen van with Montana plates. Well, we called the local deputy sheriff, who was too far out of position to immediately respond but said he was on his way. Since we didn't have many officers at hand and didn't want to lose the man responsible, we divided up. I know you said it was better to work in pairs if possible, but that just wasn't the case in this instance. There were only three of us, so each of us took an exit and staked out the road. Pretty soon I saw a red VW approaching my exit point. I waited until he passed my hiding place, then made a car stop just the way you guys taught us. Since rape is a felony, I got out with my shotgun at the ready and, taking cover behind my door, ordered the man out of the vehicle.

"Sure as shooting, out stepped a tall, bearded hippie-looking fellow with a large, ugly red scar on his right cheek. Staying behind my door like you guys said for the cover it offered, I told the man to put his hands on the side of the van, step back two paces with his hands still on the van, and spread his legs. Once he was off balance, I approached with my shotgun in the strong hand like you taught us and spread his legs apart even more to really get him off balance. I began to search him with my weaker hand, all the while holding the shotgun in the middle of his back where he could not reach it. I had just finished searching when all of a sudden a *huge* German shepherd jumped out of the van as if he was going to attack me. In reality he just wanted out and was a gentle dog, but I didn't know that at the time. Taking my attention off the bad guy for just a moment, something you told us never to do, I quickly checked the dog out to see if it was a source of danger. Seeing everything was all right there, I turned back just in time to see an elbow coming right at me, and it hit me right in the nose. The force was so great that it smashed my nose, knocking me to the ground. The hippie whirled around and grabbed my shotgun off the ground, pointed it at me as I lay there in a gushing pool of blood, and said, 'You are a dead man!'

"Boy, my heart just stopped as I waited for that charge of buckshot to rip through my chest! But then I remembered what you said! Keep talking, and if he is listening you can come up with a plan to get the hell out of a bad situation. I drew my pistol and pointed it right at him. I then told him to drop the shotgun or I was going to kill him! It worked! He dropped the shotgun, got back on the side of the van, and assumed the position! I jumped up, got the shotgun, and took command of the situation once again. Finishing my search, I handcuffed the man and brought him and the dog into the refuge office just as the deputy sheriff arrived. Off he went to jail. I still look like a mess with a red and swollen nose and two black eyes, but I am alive!" (That man would later get fifteen to twenty-five years for rape and for assault on a federal officer.)

I just sat there, stunned. The lad had told his story like he was eating a bowl of corn flakes, as if to say, no big deal. He was pleased that he had gotten the training when he had and thanked me for not only saving his life but fulfilling the first order of law enforcement, which was to come home every night! Then he had an incoming phone call, thanked me again, and was gone as if nothing out of the ordinary had happened.

Sitting there in the cool and quiet of my office, I had time to think over his story. He *had* done everything he had been taught by a bunch of battered and bruised special agents, and the teaching had brought him home. Well, that and the grace of God. ... After sitting there for the better part of an hour quietly reliving his story, I just smiled, not only with my face but also in my heart. ... All of a sudden, those hours of hard work and the beating we had taken at the hands of those eager students was more than well worth it!

While I was gone during those training exercises, my Labrador and constant companion for eleven hard years in enforcement had gotten sick and died. I am having a hard time, even after all those years, writing these lines. Perhaps if I had been home, I could have saved her. After all, she had once saved my life! That call from Refuge Officer Jones seemed to help the hurt I was still feeling from my recent loss of Shadow. Losing a "best friend" is always tough, but to lose a fellow officer because he is not equipped with the right tools to do the job would be even worse.

18

A Very "Special" Taxidermist

ONE AFTERNOON while traveling through the small South Dakota town of Bison, I noticed a large sign on the side of the highway that read, "Ingerbretson Taxidermy—taxidermy work performed on all species of fish and wildlife. All species of birds our specialty." That last line caught my eye. A taxidermist had to have a federally issued license in order to work on migratory waterfowl. As part of the terms and conditions of that license, the taxidermist had to allow an officer, such as me, reasonable access to his license, records, and freezers. Being a special agent for the U.S. Fish and Wildlife Service, I turned onto the dirt road leading to Ingerbretson's place of business.

I noticed a fairly sizable taxidermy building on one level of the property and a large white home on an upper portion. Entering the taxidermy building, I waited at the front desk while an elderly man finished up what he was doing in the back room. "Can I help you?" he said as he emerged from the back room, which appeared to be his working area.

"Yes, sir. My name is Terry Grosz, and I am a special agent with the U.S. Fish and Wildlife Service. If I could, I would like to check your federal license, records, and freezers." With that, I showed the man my badge and credentials, but he just stood there with his mouth agape. I said, "Is there something wrong, sir?" Again, it was as if my words had fallen on deaf ears. He just stood there and gaped at me! "Are you all right?" I asked, now a little worried at the man's strange behavior.

"Oh, I am sorry. I have never seen a person like you before. I mean, one with a badge and all."

With those words, I perked up. If he had never been visited by an agent, I wondered what he might have in his freezers in the way of illegal wildlife. Before that day was done, I would have one of the great surprises of my career, a surprise that would continue throughout the investigation that was to follow. ...

"I am pretty busy today. Could you come back another day?" he asked.

Now my interest was really up. Why would he want me to come back another day? I wondered. Was it because he had something to hide? "The inspection won't take more than ten minutes, I would wager, and then you can go back to doing what you need to," I replied. For me, the "hunt" was on! My senses told me there was something wrong, and I needed to get to the bottom of it!

"All right, but you must hurry. I have a school class coming here shortly and will need to be able to show them what a taxidermist does and answer their questions," he replied.

Walking around the counter, I stepped into his back room. There, laid out on a work table covered with newspapers, were *three golden eagles!* The species was totally protected, and I knew from the copies of eagle permits in my office that he did not have one! Ignoring the eagles for a second but not forgetting them, I asked for his federal taxidermy license. Again, I got that deadpan stare. When I asked one more time to examine his taxidermy license, he finally broke out of his stupor. "I don't have one," he quietly replied.

"Why not?" I asked.

"Just never took the time to get one, I guess," he replied casually. Looking into the back of the room, I spied three sixteen-cubic-foot freezers. Walking over to them, I asked if this was where he kept his specimens before performing taxidermy services on them. "Uh, yeah, I guess so," he replied.

"You guess so?" I asked.

"Well, yeah, I keep most of my specimens in those freezers until I am ready to prepare them," he responded.

To my way of thinking, that pretty much narrowed down the location of those critters waiting to be mounted. "May I look in the freezers, Mr. Ingerbretson?" I asked.

"Yeah, I suppose so," he replied.

"Is that a yes or a no, Mr. Ingerbretson?"

"Yeah, yeah, sure, go ahead. You can look in them if you like."

Taking that as consent to a search, I opened the lid to the first freezer and damn near fell over. *It was clear full of bald and golden eagle carcasses!* Finally regaining my composure, I turned and asked, "Where the dickens did all these eagles come from?"

"Oh, people bring them for me to use," he replied as if the eagles were so many sacks of wheat. The tags tied to their feet revealed the names and addresses of dozens of South Dakota folks. Even more disturbing were the names of several prominent colleges and universities from across the land. I discovered fifty-one eagles of both species, from numerous age classes, before I hit the bottom of that freezer! Every eagle was spoken for by either college museums or private collectors.

"Mr. Ingerbretson," I asked, "do you have any permits for the eagles?"

"No," he replied, and then, thinking better of it, spoke no more on the subject.

Freezer number two held even more surprises. Opening the lid, I found hundreds of protected migratory songbirds, wading birds, and shorebirds. I just stood there aghast! Plowing through this huge illegal horde, I again discovered numerous colleges, public institutions, schools, and private collections as future repositories for all those illegal birds if I was to believe the information on the toe tags. ... One thing for sure, I thought, this fellow sure keeps good records. Six hundred and ninety-one illegal bird carcasses later, I got to the bottom of that freezer. The whole time Ingerbretson just stood there as if I had just discovered nothing more than a pile of rocks out on the South Dakota prairie.

I thought I was immune to any further surprises, but when the lid to freezer number three swung open, my jaw about hit the floor. Lying on top of the carcasses in that freezer were seven carefully wrapped endangered peregrine falcons, and if that wasn't surprise enough, a live peregrine falcon stared balefully out at me from inside a corner of the freezer, where it had been left to freeze to death! By now I was getting a little pissed. No, a lot pissed! Carefully placing the live and crippled peregrine in a darkened cardboard box, I emptied that freezer. It had 412 birds of prey, including every kind of owl; rare and endangered species; migratory waterfowl; a ton of shorebirds; and every colorful songbird species in between! Once emptied out of the freezers, I stepped back and just looked with disbelieving eyes at the three mounds of birds sitting mournfully on the floor. Turning to Ingerbretson, I said, "Where the hell did you get all these birds?"

"Oh, people from all over the area just bring them to me for disposal," he replied. "Instead of just letting them rot along the highway, they bring them to me and I mount them."

"What about those tags identifying places of deposit such as banks, libraries, schools, courthouses, and a number of colleges?" I asked.

"I don't know," he blandly replied. *Lied* would be more like it, I thought as I stared hard at the gentle-appearing, almost fatherly taxidermist.

"May I see your books?" I asked. Ingerbretson shuffled across the floor to a set of file cabinets, opened up three file drawers, and then stood aside. Taking that as a consent to search, I walked over to where he stood, pulled a sheaf of papers from the top file drawer, and examined the very fine, almost methodical old-style writing on each and every document. Those documents showed that the birds in the freezers had been commercially consigned by the person submitting the bird to Ingerbretson for taxidermy purposes. Every document also showed that money had exchanged hands for the service to be performed! The second file drawer was full of nothing but college and university orders for species of birds! Hundreds of them! In every case, illegal orders from those institutions of higher learning that were supposedly steeped in legality! I found myself standing like a mop handle over my discoveries. Examining the papers from the third file drawer, I found documents showing several hundred sales, mostly to colleges and universities, of protected migratory and endangered species of wildlife. And those sales were only for the current year!

Man, you talk about floored! For once I didn't really know where to start. Finally gathering my senses, I seized all the file drawers of documents showing the illegal transactions and quickly loaded them into my truck so they wouldn't "disappear." Then I backed my pickup up to the front door and started loading the eagles (including the three he was working on). Then I loaded all the rest of the contents from the remaining two freezers, completely filling the bed of my truck and the inside of my cab. Finally, I loaded the live peregrine in the front seat. Returning, I sat down with Ingerbretson and informed him that he was in a world of hurt legally! I advised him to get an attorney because he would be needing one shortly, and left my card for the attorney to get in touch with me. I also told him I would be taking all those bird carcasses as evidence. I would sit down and figure out the charges that would be lodged against him for having such species in his possession without a permit. Then I gave him a receipt for the documents, 54 bald and golden eagles, 8 endangered species, and 1,103 assorted hawks, owls, shorebirds, neotropical songbirds, and waterfowl (most in spring plumage, meaning they had been shot illegally).

Ingerbretson stood as if in a fog over the information I was discussing. It was almost as if he didn't give a damn. *As if he held an ace up his sleeve.* ... Thanking him for his time, almost four hours' worth (the class of students never did show up), I loaded up my tired carcass and departed for Bismarck. On the way home, my mind was literally swimming! Never in my life had I seized so many birds and such a variety from one taxidermist in one fell swoop. And never in my life had I discovered such documentation showing individuals, corporations, and institutions of higher learning openly illegally dealing for restricted specimens on the black market! No two ways about it, I had the case of the century when it came to dealing with a crooked taxidermist! This guy had been supplying numerous major colleges throughout the nation with bird specimens that they could not legally, for whatever reason, acquire themselves. Here in the middle of nowhere, I had stumbled into a vast clearinghouse for specimens in the round or processed through the art of taxidermy. Specimens that had flooded across the country as the money had come flooding back!

As is often the case when dealing with serious violations of the law, I had unfortunately missed part of the evidence! An informant from the Bison area, upon hearing of the seizure, called my office and told me that Ingerbretson had three more freezers full of illegal wildlife that I had missed, located in his home. And of course, when I returned with those in mind, they were empty. One of the sad things about this investigation was that I never got one picture of all that contraband in the freezers or on his workplace floor. I didn't possess a camera! It seemed that the Division of Law Enforcement in my region didn't have enough money to operate, much less purchase cameras and film! So, like all my regional law enforcement counterparts, I didn't have a camera. Can you imagine that? Performing a law enforcement function without the use and aid of a camera! Shortly after this, Jim Gritman, area manager for North Dakota, bought me one out of his budget. What a hell of a way to run a program ...

Not having anyplace to store my seized birds and knowing that my boss would not authorize the purchase of freezers, since he could hardly afford a tank of gasoline, I took them to the Bismarck Zoo. Meeting with Mark Christianson, director of the zoo, I wangled a place to store the birds in some of his freezer space, with the promise that he could have the specimens (except the eagles and endangered species) to feed his critters if they were not carrying lead shot (taken illegally with shotguns—lead shot could be lethal to other animals if ingested). Mark took it upon himself to have the birds X-rayed for lead shot so he could plan on feeding some of them to his meat eaters in the zoo after the case was closed, only to discover that *all but fifty-one of the birds had been shot with shotguns or rifles!* That meant that someone was actively collecting birds for Ingerbretson's commercial market! Pretty damn sad commentary, I thought after Mark called me with the information. I wondered if the shooter was doing it for profit in light of Ingerbretson's brisk business with many institutions of higher learning across the land. With that many orders, there would be no way Ingerbretson could collect all those birds and still have the time to process them.

Sitting down in the quiet of my office over the next week, I worked on the Ingerbretson case report for the U.S. Attorney's office in Rapid City. Once finished with the narrative, I sat down with my evidence and looked at the potential charges. Before I was finished, there were potentially 54 possession charges under the Bald and Golden Eagle Protection Act, 8 possession charges under the Endangered Species Act of 1973, and 1,103 possession charges under the Migratory Bird Treaty Act! In short, he was looking at maximum fines potentially in excess of $775,000 if all charges were filed and a ton of jail time! And that didn't include all the potential charges against the individuals, corporations, and colleges illegally purchasing the illegal specimens. No matter how you looked at it, I had an investigation that was very complex, and getting more so daily.

There was obviously more to the case than met the eye. ... Approaching the U.S. Attorney's Office in Rapid City, South Dakota, with details of the investigation, I was met with incredulity and eagerness to receive the case report by my assigned attorney. Happy at my reception, I finished my case report a week later and sent it to my supervisor's office in Kansas City and to the U.S. Attorney in Rapid City. My agent in charge, Chuck Hayes, was so impressed with the investigation that he sent it to Washington, D.C., to the chief of law enforcement, Clark Bavin. Clark in turn sent it on to some of his buddies in the Department of Justice for their information and review. Then, nothing! For the next month or so I didn't hear a damn thing despite my repeated phone calls to the U.S. Attorney's Office in Rapid City for a progress report.

Then one day when I was in the Rapid City area working on another eagle-killing investigation, I stopped by the U.S. Attorney's office. Meeting with the assistant U.S. attorney assigned the Ingerbretson investigation, I was met with what could almost be described as a wet blanket! There was a lot of crawfishing and foot dragging, not to mention what appeared to be a newfound reluctance to prosecute! After getting over my surprise at this reluctance to pursue what I thought was the case of the century (easy to prove and monstrous in size), I questioned the motives of the government attorney. He was reluctant to get into the reasons why prosecution would be a problem and finally, after much prodding and threatening to break his legs if he didn't come clean, he did. It seemed that someone in the Department of Justice in Washington had a problem with the investigation. Not anything to do with my right to be there and conduct an investigation or the subsequent search and seizure, but something else. ... Unable to get that "something else" out of my prosecutor, I at least got a promise that he would reconsider and we would get together at a later date. Boy, to say I was less than pleased when I left the Federal Building that day would be an understatement! Some goddamned political hack in the Department of Justice needed his masculinity removed, I thought, and at that moment I was just the butcher to do it. I discovered later that the "someone" in the Department of Justice was leaning on the U.S. Attorney in Rapid City not to prosecute. I never did get any more information about that issue.

Returning to Bismarck, I called my boss and howled like a mad wolf at the outside interference. My boss was pissed as well at the news over what he considered to be a good case and, after a little time to think it over, blamed Chief Bavin for the hangup. Saying he would get the straight skinny or know the reason why, he hung up to call Bavin. Sitting back in my chair, I just shook my head. Sometimes the Department of Justice could be a real pain in the ass. ... Now we will get something done, I thought. Once my boss gets his teeth into an issue like this, something will get munched if it doesn't come off dead center.

Later that afternoon, my boss called back. "Terry," he said, "I don't know what the hell is going on, but that Ingerbretson is a heavy hitter in the Department of Justice. He seems to have someone who is high up in the organization listening to him, and that someone is really trying to derail the investigation. Not over the case itself; it is rock solid. But as near as I can tell, over something else, and no one is talking about what that is. It also seems that Clark owes this someone in the Department of Justice *big time* and is reluctant to make any waves to alleviate our situation. I don't know what to tell you, but get your tail end in gear and get back down to the attorney in Rapid City. See if you can free up the logjam from that end. If not, since they hold all the cards, I don't know what to tell you."

By now I was fit to be tied! I had a damn good case regarding a gross situation of illegal possession and commercialization of many species of migratory birds, endangered species, and eagles. I was determined to see this through! Making another trip to Rapid City, I again met with my assigned attorney. It was obvious that he was fit to be tied himself (he supported the investigation), but he would not discuss what was happening. To me, it was obvious that the U.S. Attorney himself was the nut to crack. I requested an audience with the man and was politely refused. "Terry, I am telling you, it won't do any good. There are a very special set of circumstances associated with this investigation, and if it moves forward, I will be amazed."

The office of the U.S. Attorney is the key to any federal prosecution. If they say no to your case, that is just about it if you want to pursue something criminally within the federal system. Bowing my head, I said, "All right, if you guys don't have the guts, I will pursue the investigation through the state courts." With that, out the door I stomped in a huff. What the hell is happening? I thought. A simple possession case on the grandest scale and I can't get it to first base within the federal system.

Well, my list of surprises was to get even more extensive. A trip to the county attorney with jurisdiction for the Ingerbretson investigation brought me to a screeching halt. The county attorney was already aware of the investigation and said he wanted no part in any prosecution of the matter! If I couldn't get it done in federal court, I shouldn't come running to him! What the hell? I thought. I had a perfectly legal right to file the charges against Ingerbretson in his county because the violations were against a series of state laws as well. "And I might add," continued the attorney, "that none of my judges wants any part of it either. In fact, I have been advised not to bring this case forth in their courts!"

I just sat there, stunned. What the hell had I gotten into? Somebody retired from the CIA or the NSA? Maybe someone under the Federal Witness Protection Program? Now I began to wonder why Ingerbretson had acted so calm and without emotion as I had seized the "ton" or so of evidence. He apparently did have an ace or two up his sleeve.

Not being one for standing last in line, I still had the U.S. Solicitor's office as a court of last resort. They couldn't do much for my Migratory Bird Treaty Act cases, but they sure as hell could civilly address my Eagle and Endangered Species Act cases! I had a case strong enough to go criminally with proof beyond a reasonable doubt, but since I was now heading for the Civil Division, all I needed was a preponderance of evidence, considerably less proof of guilt than in a criminal matter. With such solid proof, this would be a slam-dunk, I thought. So I set my sails and headed in that direction. I would show these gutless rogues in the Criminal Division at the state and federal levels how to work the justice system, I thought.

"No, we are not interested in civilly processing this investigation," announced Jack Little, solicitor for the region. Shocked, I asked why the hell not. "We just aren't interested, and that is that!" Jack could be a pompous ass when he so desired, and today, he *desired!*

Concealing a very strong urge to reach across his desk and squeeze him by the neck until he stopped wiggling, I cooled it. "Any particular reason why you won't process this case? After all, you are the Service's Civil Division, and that is your job. You certainly have more than enough evidence to proceed and win," I said.

"That is not the point, Terry. You have an excellent and very unique case. But my bosses in the Civil Division in Washington, for whatever reason, don't want this investigation to proceed any further. And that is that."

Slowly, I turned and walked away from killing Jack Little. It would have been a boon to humankind if I had, but they prosecute people in this country for that ... maybe not for a damn good bird case, but for killing some damn useless human.

When I got back to my office, where I intended to sit and quietly think over this investigation's disappointing course of events, I got a phone call. It seemed that my threat to take the case out of the hands of the federal system and into the state system had generated some damage control. I was informed that the U.S. Attorney's office had decided to prosecute my investigation after all—and *had done so!* "What?" I said. "Without my input or presence?"

"Yes, we proceeded in your absence since your case report was so complete and in the process took Ingerbretson's attorney's recommendation for settlement. *We settled out of court for $50, suspended the fine, and refused prosecution on all the rest of the charges!*"

I was stunned! "How the hell could you do that?" I yelled.

"Simple, we just did it," was his curt reply. "I suggest you let it go. We have, and as of now it is a dead issue. There is one good thing to come from the investigation: the Service gets to keep the birds. However, you need to return his records so he has them for tax purposes."

Tax purposes my ass! I thought. The bastard wants those documents back so he can continue filling those commercial orders from all over the country! "Wait a minute," I said. "There is still the matter of all those documents illustrating illegal sales and purchases."

"Oh, yes, that is correct. Those potential charges, if brought before us, will also be refused prosecution in federal court and probably in all the other avenues open to you as well!"

Sitting there stone cold at those words, I wondered if I had been transferred to Russia. What the hell had I gotten myself into? Seeing that further discussion was unnecessary, the phone went dead with no further explanation or good-bye. Leaning back in my chair, I just sat there for about an hour, running the case's events through my mind. I had obviously stepped into the Twilight Zone. Here was an old man out in the middle of nowhere, as simple appearing as a nobody but with an unseen source of power almost equaling that of the president of the United States. He had somehow single-handedly stopped my investigation and prosecution of a major case (one of the biggest involving a taxidermist I ever ran across in my thirty-two years of law enforcement) at two federal levels and one state level, with no more discernable movement than a five-toed sloth! I had had my feet swept out from under me before by the best of them, but never like this. ... You know, it is not nice to mess with Mother Nature or her minions, and the chase to find out why was on.

It took several months of investigation, looking behind all the angles and names of those involved, before I had my answer. It was fairly simple, and in one aspect beautiful! Bison, South Dakota, is out in the middle of nowhere. In fact, it is so close to the edge of the earth that the chickens out there have square faces. The one thing it did have was the Ingerbretson Taxidermy Shop. What the hell did that have to do with the price of crowbars in North Korea? Everything! There was nothing out there in those wide-open spaces to provide cultural events for the schoolkids. You may now have come to the conclusion that I had gone stark raving mad after having been out in the prairie wind too long, but stay with me. Ingerbretson for dozens of years had opened up the mysteries of his taxidermy shop to the kids and schoolteachers as a cultural event par excellence on their few and far-between field trips. After he showed the wide-eyed children the mysteries of taxidermy, the school usually received a mounted bird for their classroom, a highlight of the trip. Over the years, a beautiful collection was accumulated by each school.

Those kids eventually went on to become college professors, judges, attorneys (some at the highest levels in the Department of Justice), U.S. Attorneys, bankers, and politicians and entered just about every other walk of life as well. When those considerable forces (fifty years' worth of schoolkids) learned of my investigation into what may have been their one outstanding memory from the wind-blown plains, a gentle old man who took the time to entertain them, they were forcefully moved. When I drew my line in the sand, they rallied their minions through their many means and avenues, stopping me and any subsequent prosecution stone cold! It took almost a year, as I worked off and on through the events of that investigation, before I discovered how thoroughly those kids, so touched by Ingerbretson, were embedded in every level of our society. From out in the middle of nowhere, they were *everywhere*, as I was soon to discover! It really is a very small world. ...

Now you know why the statue of Justice wears a blindfold.

19

The Spring Sing

IN THE LATE FALL OF 1976 I was promoted into the headquarters office in Washington, D.C., as a senior special agent from my position as senior resident agent in Bismarck, North Dakota. That move from a line to a staff officer took a lot of internal examination on my part before I could decide to do it. I had always been a field officer and as such reveled in the great outdoors and the world of wildlife. Now I was heading for a major city, with gunfire in the streets at night, where I would have to stand in long lines just to go to the bathroom in public places, live in an area that cost more to live in than I made, ride buses everywhere I went, hear the constant noise of the city instead of that made by the "song dogs," hear the constant howling of sirens, and never be able to see the stars because of the constant light from the city at night. I think you can see why I felt some trepidation about moving to Washington.

However, those concerns aside, it was one of the best moves of my career. I was forced into realms of federal laws I had heretofore ignored; I had to write regulatory missives on a daily basis; I attended worlds of nonstop meetings of questionable value. I felt the frustration of never having my work be just that but something reviewed and changed by dozens of others in the "food chain" having not an ounce of law enforcement sense, or many times common sense, for that matter; of getting the toughest questions from the field officers, ones that they couldn't answer; of staying away from the dozens of constant office intrigues and love triangles; of trying to make ends meet economically and always riding those stinking buses to and from work for what seemed to be wasted hours at a time. But I also learned who the major players were in the Service, and they learned to know me. Perhaps the greatest lesson of all was how to work within the system, and how to work the system. Suffice it to say, I went to Washington a parochial wimp and came out a fairly savvy manager. Last but not least, I came away from that two-plus-year experience qualified within the Service's mandates for senior-level management as a special agent in charge.

One fine spring day in 1977 I was writing a law enforcement directive for the millionth time when in walked Special Agent Dave Kirkland. To my thinking, Dave was one of the Service's best undercover officers, if not *the* best. "Terry, what do you have planned for next weekend?" he asked pleasantly.

"Mow lawns, cut firewood for winter and do the weekly shopping," I replied.

"How would you and your oldest son like to go out to my hunting cabin in Pennsylvania and do some spring turkey hunting?"

Now, I had never hunted turkeys before, and my senses went on full alert. Here was a chance to get out of the concrete jungle where I lived and worked for a few days. I would have a free place to stay and a chance to hunt something I had never hunted before, in the process teaching my young son Richard some outdoor lessons as well. "God, that sounds great, Dave. However, I will have to ask Donna if we have enough money to buy an out-of-state license and the food and gasoline to do it," I replied.

"Why don't you check and let me know? No one else is using the family hunting cabin during that period of time, and the woods around our place are chock-full of fat turkeys," he replied with a smile. With that, Dave was out the door to another wasted-time meeting, leaving me to dream for the rest of the afternoon about calling in a big tom and making a clean, one-shot kill. That was followed with visions of a big wild-turkey dinner with all the trimmings. Yum! I thought.

Getting home that evening after a three-hour bus ride (it rained — that always made the D.C. drivers go nuts), I broached the subject with my darling wife. Since she was keeper of what few chips we had, she was the boss and always had the final say. Boy, when I mentioned the possibility of a turkey hunt in Pennsylvania, Richard's ears shot up like Spock's on *Star Trek*.

"Are just the two of you going?" she asked.

"As far as I know," I replied.

"How about asking Jerry Terry to go with you? That way gasoline only costs half as much," she shot back with a grin. Donna was something else. If there was a way to shave the buffalo off a nickel, she was the one to do it. But I have to admit that because of her shrewd business acumen, we went a lot further and did a lot more things than if I had been at the monetary helm.

Jerry Terry was a friend from our days in North Dakota, where we both had been senior resident agents, Jerry for the Secret Service and I for the Fish and Wildlife Service. We had gotten along famously then and, thanks to my wife, could possibly have another set of adventures if he could go. Jerry and his wife, Candice, lived in Winchester, Virginia, a short hop from where we lived in Fairfax. So a quick phone call and explanation found me with a partner for the turkey hunt.

We loaded up the car with all the hunting accessories, clothing, cooking pots (I was big into cast-iron cooking), every kind of food and drink imaginable, and some good chewing tobacco. I don't think Richard slept those few days before we left out of anticipation. Once on the road, we had a ball, chewing great gobs of chewing tobacco, drinking tons of soda pop, and seemingly paying a toll on the Pennsylvania Turnpike every twenty-six feet.

When we arrived at Dave's cabin in Pennsylvania, it was *Deliverance* all over again. We were so far in the outback that the chickens had square faces! Dave's cabin was something else. It slept at least twenty-six folks! It had huge, deep chairs for resting in after the hunt, beds everywhere, a kitchen built for a man my size to cook in, a place for my Dutch oven cooking, and much more! It was wonderful, except it didn't have a shower. ... But that was all right, I thought. We were going to be in the outback the whole time, with only the bears and turkeys to smell us as we ripened, so to hell with it! We unloaded the car, and out came great sacks of onions, bags of garlic, spices, lots of Dago Red wines, whiskey, thawing meats for cooking, and on it went. It didn't take me long to have that cabin smelling like a million dollars with my cooking skills hitting high gear. Everything I cooked was loaded with garlic, butter, and onions! Then in went the wines and spices from around the world. Since the weather was pretty warm, it didn't take long before the three of us happily smelled like all get-out between the sweating and the rich, well-spiced foods!

For the next two days, Friday and Saturday, the hunt for the turkey was on. After a lumberjack breakfast of eggs, bacon, spuds (heavily laced with garlic and onions), and Dutch oven biscuits each morning, off we went into the wilds. On the first day I called a turkey to within forty yards only to have some other unknown hunter ambush and kill it before it got to us. It was a great disappointment for Richard, who I was sure had great visions of bringing home dozens of the damn things. But we had a great time in the forests of Pennsylvania, and when we got back to the cabin we had more great eats, spiced to the heavens, heavily lathered up with gallons of cheap wine!

Come Saturday afternoon, we still hadn't killed a turkey, but boy, did we smell great! Like something that had been dead for a month and left out in the sun to slow cook! That evening's dinner was fried whole cloves of fresh garlic in olive oil, venison stew with a ton of raw garlic, cumin, and onions, Dutch oven biscuits, and a pie also from a Dutch oven. As I said, we ate well! About halfway through dinner, Dave arrived unannounced. Ever gracious, he accepted some dinner and several ice-cold beers. I could tell that something was on Dave's mind, but I knew he would let us know in his own time. When he did, we were floored! "Terry, you guys won't be able to hunt turkeys tomorrow. My wife expects you guys to attend our Spring Sing at church."

Man, you talk about sending Jerry and yours truly into orbit. I hadn't attended church since I was sixteen, and for Jerry it had been even longer. Rich got a big grin, knowing his dad was between a rock and a hard spot.

"Dave," I said, "I haven't been to church in years, and neither has Jerry! Crap, neither of us would know what to do."

"I know this is sudden, but she just told me this afternoon that it would be nice if you guys showed up since we had extended our hospitality to you for the turkey hunt."

Boy, were we in a bind. Not churchgoers, looking ratty as all get-out after several days of hunting, and smelling like the creature from the Black Lagoon! No matter how much squalling or wiggling we attempted, we were trapped. ... Dave left us instructions on how to get to the church and left. I was sure I saw what appeared to be a small glimmer of a sly smile pass his lips as he left. That sucker, I thought. If he is trying to sandbag us, I will rip his lips off and feed them to the nearest magpie! Suffice it to say, in light of the morrow's detail to the Spring Sing, we got roaring high on the cheap Dago Red that evening. After all, we needed something to give us the "sand" to attend the unknown looming before us. For me, it wasn't church itself. I had gone for years as a youngster because I liked to sing, and I was a good singer. It was the idea of going to another's church without knowing what it was all about. Especially out here in the backwater of Pennsylvania, smelling like a "dump." For all I knew, they practiced some kind of cult religion with rattlesnakes.

The following morning we loaded up on the smelliest food we could eat: garlic (raw), blue cheese, raw onions, more garlic, head cheese, and sourdough French bread. Between those food items guaranteed to get you any seat on the bus, we guzzled at least another gallon of cheap red wine to wash it down. With that, plus three days of hard hunting without a bath, we had to be the most "notable" lads in the woods.

Following Dave's map to the site of the Spring Sing, we made sure we arrived early enough to get a great seat in the church so no one would notice us. Smell us, yes, but we would remain unseen to the best of our abilities. We found a small clapboard building sitting back in a small hollow. It was painted white but in bad need of another paint job. The building was about seventy feet long and maybe twenty feet wide. The roof was covered with rusty tin, and no two ways about it, the house of the Lord looked like it had seen better days since it had been built in the late 1800s. Parking my car out of the way for a quick getaway, the three of us opened the unlocked front door and quietly walked in. The interior was somewhat darkened, with the only light coming from several small windows. The wooden floor was covered with rustic church benches, and there was a small platform at the front. Sitting on the platform was a piano that had to be at least a hundred years old. That was it! Something right out of the 1800s! Picking a bench seat alongside a window, the three misfits from the current century took our seats and waited for an imagined fate worse than death.

Soon we could hear automobiles arriving and a rustling at the front door. People started quietly filtering in, and we got the surprise of our lives! The men were dressed in suits and period clothing from the late 1800s, and the women wore even more elaborate costumes. Soon the church began to fill with folks right out of the previous century. Ostrich-feather hats, buckle-up shoes, flowing black dresses with hoop skirts, feather hand fans, stovepipe hats, strings of pearls, and the like soon filled the benches. It was all we could do not to stare in plain wonderment! And this wasn't dress-up for the day. The clothing appeared to be those folks' *normal* Sunday go-to-meeting clothes! These hill folks had just never gotten out of the late 1800s! You talk about open mouths; we had them. Jerry and I had a couple of old spinster ladies right in front of us. Jesus, I thought, our body odor and breath had to be something to experience. Those poor little old ladies! Getting all dressed up to come to a Spring Sing and finding that they are sitting in front of what smelled like a hog wallow. … On top of that, the place was now really filling up, not to mention that it was getting very warm inside with all those bodies jammed together! Soon the sweat was really beginning to roll off Jerry and me, and I was sure all the garlic was now flowing out from our pores in great smelly streams! Reaching over, I opened the window, hoping that would help. The warm spring air from outside just rolled in, adding to the heat and humidity in the room. Now I was really sweating, as was Jerry, and every time we breathed out, I could almost see the two little old spinsters in front of us nearly rolling off their bench seat from being "gassed." Oh, man, we were in the wrong place at the wrong time, I thought. People continued to jam into the church until it was overflowing. Everyone had to sit packed like sardines, and that made matters even worse. Soon the sweat was rolling off everyone as it would at an old-fashioned revival meeting under a circus tent in July in Georgia.

About that time a door in the front of the church opened and in strode a preacher looking as if he had just ridden in from the circuit, long black flowing coat and all. He was followed by an old woman who moved over to play the piano. She was followed by a fiddle player, two guitar players, one person on harmonica, and one carrying a five-string banjo. What the hell? I thought.

"Would you all please stand for the prayer?" said the circuit rider in a melodious voice, and the congregation rose in unison. The prayer was said and everyone sat down, packed tighter than a fresh-fed bunch of wood ticks. Grabbing a hymnal, the preacher spoke out to the crowd and said, "Today we will start with number 187, 'The Church in the Wildwood.'" Grabbing the songbooks from the holders in the back of the pews, Jerry, Rich, and I turned to page 187. I noticed as I thumbed through the pages of the songbook that it was the same one I had used as a boy when I had gone to the Methodist church! Jerry and I sang halfheartedly on the first song, still aware of being out of place and the terrible smells we had to be emitting. The second song was "The Old Rugged Cross," and this time, between the copious amounts of wine we had imbibed before coming to church and the surprising beauty of the singing, *we sang a little louder!* It turned out the songbooks were also the same ones Jerry had used as a kid. … And to be frank, the folks with the instruments were pretty darn good! Catching the spirit of the moment and forgetting where we were, Jerry and I discovered that we both sang tenor, and that we harmonized beautifully!

"What song shall we sing next?" asked the preacher, and before I knew it, I shouted out (fortified with the wine, I am sure), "Number 299, 'In My Heart There Rings a Melody'!" The preacher just smiled at the enthusiasm from a loud member of his flock. Stunned by my outbreak, I looked to see if anyone else had seen my strange behavior. It was then that I noticed Dave and his family sitting across the aisle from us, smiling at my antics. Suffice it to say that for the next three hours that little old church just rocked. As did the two visiting tenors, who by now were singing loud enough for even God to hear. ... The more Jerry and I sang, the better we harmonized, so we led that congregation in singing out our thanks. By now the whole damn gathering was just rolling in sweat as we sang our hearts out. What a wonderful experience that turned out to be! A memory for me that will live in my soul until I cross the Great Divide ...

Finishing the morning's Spring Sing, the preacher gave a final prayer for the safety of his flock and went to stand near the front doors of the church with the band members. Then the rest of the benches emptied as the congregation filed out the front doors, shaking hands with the preacher as they left. When it came our turn, the preacher gave us a particularly strong handshake and said, "You boys certainly brought the spirit of the Lord to our church this day. Anytime you two wish to return, you have my sincere blessing!" We mumbled our thanks for the praise, still aware of the garlic we were exuding, and headed out the front doors.

Pleased with ourselves as we stepped out into the bright sunlight, we were met by a congregation clapping in recognition of the music Jerry and I had made together (I guess). Embarrassed, Jerry, Rich, and I were led over to a long table that must have been set up in the front yard after we had arrived. Talk about a sight for sore eyes! It was loaded with some of the finest eats I have ever had. Creamy spuds swimming in real churned butter, roast bear, turkey, raccoon, and smoked hill-country hams. Potato salads by the score, greens, string beans, Jell-O salads, homemade breads of many kinds, muffins, country biscuits, bowls of some of the finest gravy I have ever eaten, fresh mushroom dishes, and green salads. Spaced throughout those dishes were jars of jams, jellies, cranberries, whipped butters, bread-and-butter pickles, sour pickles, spicy hot vegetables, and everything else under the sun! There were pitchers of lemonade, blood-red sassafras tea, and cold milk and quart jars of clear-looking liquid that was making the rounds as if it was something special. It was white lightning, and some of the best I ever tasted! At another table was every kind of homemade cookie, pie, tart, cake, cobbler, and brownie known to humankind. It was a hill-country feast fit for a king. After another prayer, we all fell to with an appetite fueled by our three hours of singing.

Richard and I still have very fond memories of that very first Spring Sing in our lives. We often recount our experiences during that day with many smiles, and it leaves us with warm hearts every time. It was a time when the very old and the new met on a common field and discovered that there wasn't really any difference between us. We all had good hearts and joyous voices, which we lifted up to God. What a fine and beautiful day it was and continues to be in my heart as these words are written some thirty years later. ... I just wish someone would ask me to go to another Spring Sing.

20

The National Wildlife Property and Eagle Repository

EARLY ONE MORNING my diminutive but absolutely top-of-the-line secretary, Debbie Lee, entered my office. Seeing that I was busy with some work on the budget, she waited until I was finished. "Good morning, Miss Alabama, what's up?" I said with a grin.

She smiled partly at my nickname for her and partly because of the close friendship we shared. "Dick Smith is on the phone for you," she said.

"Patch him through," I said, wondering what the hell I had done wrong now. Dick Smith was a throwback to earlier days and ways of doing business. Maybe even as far back as the days of the buffalo hunter. ... He was a rather large man, loud-spoken and overbearing, and could be a bully if you let him. To my way of thinking, he placed the Division of Law Enforcement's value in the "need for" and "respect of" category somewhere near the bottom of the Marianas Trench ... below whale dung. ... I didn't always see eye to eye with him or many of his edicts, but I kind of liked the old buzzard because, unlike many other Service higher-ups, he could and would make a decision. I had known him for many years and had learned how to deal with him. If he bellowed, I did the same. He would give me quick responses or decisions, and I would do the same for him. It was kind of like two bulls pawing up the middle of the ring. However, whether I liked him or not, he was still the Service's acting director, and I responded accordingly that morning.

"Good morning, Richard, what can I do you in for?" I asked.

"I need you to establish a National Wildlife Property Repository, and one for eagles as well. I don't care how you do it, but get it done and don't waste any time doing it," he barked in his usual "loving" style.

"That is fine and good, Chief, not to mention needed, but where do I get the money and positions to accomplish such a feat? I don't have enough money in my annual budget to pour pee out of a boot, and you know it. So I don't see how I am to mysteriously accomplish your directive unless I get some assistance," I responded.

"I just told you! That is all you need to know! I don't care how you do it, but get it done," he replied in his typical "Soapy Smith" fashion.

Shaking my head and planting my feet, I said, "With all due respect, Chief, no can do. Without some startup money, authority, an add-on to my annual budget, and at least four new positions to run the facility, you are asking the impossible."

"Oh, goddamn it, I will get a letter in the mail today authorizing the establishment of such a facility. As for the money and positions, you will just have to trust me."

"Trust you!" I said. "With your track record in dealing with the Division of Law Enforcement, how the hell can you say that?"

"Look, I don't have the time to verbally joust with you. Your authorization will be in the mail today. In the meantime, you get an outline to me on a repository annual budget, startup costs, position descriptions, and time frame needed to go on line. Now, I have to run." Click!

Sitting back in my chair after replacing the phone in its cradle, I just smiled. It was a characteristic Dick Smith operation: get it going and get it done. ... Knowing the tiger I had by the tail, I stepped out of my office and let Debbie know I was going to see Ralph Morgenweck, the regional director. In those days the agents in the field was directly supervised by the regional directors, and I had a great boss in Ralph. He was bright, visionary, supported law enforcement, and was always an outstanding sounding board. After filling Ralph in on my recent conversation with the acting director, I bounced a few of the ideas whirling around in my head relative to the project off him. As usual, he had some good suggestions and a lot of support. Returning to my office, I touched base with another entity in the chain of command. Calling my chief of law enforcement, who was a staff officer to the director, I filled him in on my conversation with Smith. As expected, he had not been informed in advance of my repository startup directive either. ... Hearing that, I assumed Dick, who did not like the chief, had bypassed him as he was wont to do, coming directly to me in the field. I just smiled. It was also typical of Dick to take the shortest route and get it done. And he could do it any way he wanted—after all, he was the acting director.

In truth, I supported what Dick was trying to accomplish. The Division of Law Enforcement should have had a central repository years ago for forfeited wildlife and eagle carcasses. The division's current method of centralization was to jam those responsibilities into our newly created National Wildlife Forensics Laboratory. It seemed to me that when the forensic facility was created (the only laboratory of its kind in the world), some of the opposition forces still upset over losing the argument regarding the need to establish such a facility dumped onto its "skirts" the forfeited-property and eagle responsibilities. It wasn't a very smart move because the forensics lab really needed all the space it had for its own rapidly expanding operations, and those operations didn't include serving as a storage bin for all the nation's forfeited property and eagles. I guess one has to live with the hairbrains as well as the visionaries.

The Division of Law Enforcement under its many federal statutes seizes all kinds and amounts of illegally taken wildlife and wildlife parts and products as a matter of course. Once those items have been forfeited to the U.S. government, they move in many directions. Some are destroyed if they are not fit for any use. Many are donated to a variety of public institutions for educational purposes. Some, by statute, go to the Smithsonian Institution (historical, archaeological, etc.). Others are used by the division for undercover operations as "show or flash" materials to lure in and convince the bad guys regarding our intentions as illegal dealers. A small amount is kept forever in safes or vaults because of its extreme value (such as rhino horns, some ivory carvings, medicines made from rare species, coats made from endangered species, and much more). But by and large, the major portion of the forfeited items is inventoried and sold to the highest bidder for resale or reuse. If it was illegal in the first place, how can it be resold and entered into commerce? Simple. Many parts and products enter the country without proper import documents. Since the importer or exporter of record violated U.S. laws just by lacking the proper documents, they are seized. A criminal or civil action is held, depending on the investigation's circumstances, and if the goods end up being forfeited to the Service, they can be resold. The money usually goes to the General Fund unless the court dictates that specific proceeds go to a special situation such as conservation of endangered wildlife or the like. Some federal statutes prohibit the sale of wildlife in every instance. One such statute, the Bald and Golden Eagle Protection Act, prohibits the sale of eagles or their parts and products.

That brings up the eagle issues. The Service routinely picks up dead and dying eagles from across the nation: eagles that are seized and forfeited as part of a civil or criminal action, road kills, those killed by ground strikes when they stoop on prey species, hitting the ground at a high rate of speed in the process, those killed by illegal poisons, and those shot, electrocuted, or trapped are collected, frozen, and saved. Their collective numbers may number in the hundreds annually. Once legally in the hands of the Service through such circumstances, they are centralized, inventoried, and mainly shipped to Native Americans for use in cultural or religious practices. Native Americans are prohibited from selling eagles or their parts and products but may possess or pass them from one native family member to another. That way the birds are not wasted and fulfill a cultural need.

Sitting back in my office with the repository question swirling around in my head like a dervish, I put on some music since I always thought better with a little "help" and let the creative juices flow. First of all, I decided I would only put together a facility that would accomplish the mission and allow for future expansion as the need arose. That is all fine and dandy, I thought, except that the Service is only going to provide you with a small amount of coin of the realm for the facility's acquisition, construction, and operation. So there went that first grandiose idea! ... Ah, but not quite. Having survived in the profession all those years without much support from the Service leadership, I had developed many of the qualities of a procurer or scrounger. It was either that, or you didn't survive and get the job done. There are lots of military resources in the Denver area, I thought. Perhaps I could scrounge a surplus building from the military since the Service is a federal entity. Then I could take the savings from not having to purchase a structure and put them into other aspects of the facility. Ah, the music was working its magic. Then it hit me! The Rocky Mountain Arsenal in Commerce City, just north of Denver, was in the process of being cleaned up and closed down. There had been talk of turning that facility over to the Service to manage as a National Wildlife Refuge. There were lots of excess buildings on that site. Plus that area was central to the air, rail, and trucking lines needed to haul the property and eagles from outside the area and to ship them back out. Later that morning I was in the office of John Spinks, deputy regional director.

John had his fingers in about every pie in the region, including the arsenal. We had been friends for many years since our stints together in Washington, D.C., and I trusted him. He was an east Texas rancher, born and bred, and an honorable man (even if he was a Texan).

As I ran my ideas by him, he just grinned a knowing grin. Hell, he was miles ahead of me. Picking up the phone, he called the base commander of the Rocky Mountain Arsenal. The next thing I knew, I was on my way with John to meet the colonel. After I described my ideas and requested a usable structure to house the proposed unit, the colonel just sat there looking deep in thought. "You know, a project of this scope and degree just might make the army look pretty damn good," he said thoughtfully. "Instead of a facility with a reputation of being full of poison [they had made mustard gas, rocket fuels, and other unmentionables at the arsenal], a facility such as you described might just be the ticket to partially rebuild our reputation. I think I can help and certainly have the authority to do so. By damn, let's do it! Do you have some time on your hands? Because if you do, we can go look at some available buildings right now."

For the next hour or so, we looked at abandoned building after abandoned building. Nothing I saw looked big enough, or if it did it would require a million dollars to fix it up. Figuring that the colonel might be holding out on some of his better buildings, I continued putting on the pressure about the wonders this type of a facility would do for the army's reputation. "You know, Colonel, this would be a one-of-a-kind facility. There would be none other like it in the world. You could always bring the visiting brass and other notables to the facility, and we would give them private tours anytime you needed."

Boy, I could see that got the colonel to thinking in spades. ... "Well, there is one building that could be used. We would have to move some Red-Eye bombs, but it could be done. Let's go and take a look."

A short drive found us by a huge all-brick building, one that was way too big for what I needed. But then the colonel had another officer open an iron door on the south end of the building. Walking into the cool and darkened space, I saw row after row of Red-Eye bombs (a chemical weapon) sitting there in awful silence. Fortunately, John and I had the proper security clearance to go into such a facility with an army escort. "What do you think?" asked the Colonel. My heart just skipped a beat as I looked over the building. Being brick, it had the level of security I would need to protect the millions of dollars' worth of property to be stored there. Walking around, I noticed dozens of overhead gas heaters used to heat the building. That would be great during the Colorado winters, I thought, trying not to show any enthusiasm. On the south side of the building were two large sliding doors with truck ramps leading to the outside. Perfect, I thought, for receiving large shipments of materials from all over the country. I really had to work now at hiding my smile. The floor was twelve-inch-thick reinforced concrete, another plus for security when storing many thousands of valuable parts and products. The area was also plumbed for water and waste, though no such facilities were installed. That was all right as well, since it would be fixable when office construction began. Looking up again, I noticed that the ceiling was covered with row after row of mercury vapor lights! By now the only thing quieter than the colonel and his crew were the Red-Eye bombs as he waited for my verdict.

Pacing off the interior, I discovered that I was standing inside a potential facility of approximately twenty-six thousand square feet! God, it was perfect! Suppressing my huge grin and desire to yell aloud in joy, I said, "Well, it looks all right. You would have to get rid of those bombs and make sure the area was clear of any chemical danger."

"That can be done," said an excited colonel as he ordered one of his men to make note of that concern. "What else?" he asked.

"Well, I can't afford to check and clean all those gas heaters in the ceiling," I said, letting my voice trail off in apparent worry.

"That is no problem," he quickly replied. "I have discretionary funds that can be used for that."

"And to be frank, Colonel, I don't have the kind of money either to supply those heaters with gas during the wintertime."

"That is fixable as well," he replied. "I can just leave them hooked up to the army's supply system, and it won't cost you a red cent!"

"How about those mercury vapor lights? Can your people check and clean them as well when they are doing the heating system?" I innocently asked.

"Piece of cake," he replied as he instructed the officer taking notes to record the same.

"Again, to be frank, Colonel, the Service won't be able to pay to operate all those lights. You may have to take some out or shut them off."

"Hell, Terry, I can use my discretionary funds to provide for the operation of those as well."

By now I had to bite my tongue to keep from smiling from ear to ear. Walking outside as if deep in thought, I looked up on the roof. It was one of those typical tarred roofs the Army had slapped on in haste during wartime. "Damn, Colonel," I said. "Do you know what condition that roof is in? If it started to leak on thousands of dollars' worth of property on the floor below, well ..." Within minutes of my question, the accompanying officer was scrambling up onto the roof. After a few minutes of inspection, he yelled down, "Colonel, it will need a new roof."

I looked at the colonel expectantly, but all I could see was one big frown. Maybe I had pushed him too far, I thought. "Well, this is a government building belonging to the army, so I suppose I could fix that as well—but that is it!"

Hell, that was everything I could have dreamed of or needed, I thought, but without showing any sign of emotion, of course! "Well, if that could be fixed, you would have yourself a deal, Colonel," I said. A big smile creased his face, leading me to believe I might have been able to push for a few more things. ...

When we walked back inside for one more look, it was hard to keep from jumping high into the air dancing a jig when I came down. I had just walked away with a promise of the use of a multimillion-dollar secure brick building, lit and heated by the army, and all under a new roof! I could hardly believe my luck. "How soon before those bombs are gone and we can move in?" I asked.

"Should have everything discussed here today done and ready to go in about four weeks," replied the colonel.

"Done," I said. Reaching out, I shook the colonel's hand and chanced a look over at my boss, the deputy regional director. He had a "for shame" look written all over his face for what I had just done. However, he had a smile on his puss as well, knowing I had just saved the Service a bundle of money, not to mention gotten the program heading down the road toward completion.

Now the work really started. Meeting with our Engineering Department (they had to draw up the plans for construction of the inside offices), I advised my friend "Big Ernie" Husmann that I didn't have the money to pay his division for conducting the necessary survey and drawing up construction plans. I told him I would gladly pay him when I got the money to do so. Ernie, a big and strong man in his own right, just looked at me, trying to decide whether he should accommodate me or throw me out of his office. "All right, you got a deal," he replied. I just saved another $10,000 to $15,000 for the moment, I thought. ... I did in fact pay him back the following year when I had a little extra funding.

Over the next few weeks as the bids were let for building the interior offices and the start of construction, I kept scrounging. Into our fold came a large walk-in freezer we had used for an undercover program, with a second free one being acquired from another region that didn't need it. I now had freezer space for all the eagles that would soon be arriving. However, the battle for funding and positions continued. I kept Dick apprised of our progress and the need for funding and positions. Finally, in true Dick Smith style, he descended on a couple of other hapless programs from other divisions, took their money and positions, and basically told them to lump it!

Swinging my hard-charging deputy Neill Hartman and crack administrative officer Grace Englund into action, I put them in charge of making sure all the nuts and bolts for the entire facility now came together. I almost had to laugh when I fired that shot. No better-matched pair of gunners did the Service ever create. When they went on line, things got done, and done well! Suffice it to say, the completion of the repository in record time was a done deal with those two!

As the construction folks finished up our offices and work areas within the huge space, more gold continued to poke its nose out of the gravel. Gregg Langer, a refuge officer and friend on site, and then-biologist Rich Grosz discovered all kinds of surplus heavy shelving. Soon about a third of the floor space was filled with shelving on which to place the wildlife parts and products soon to arrive. They also procured a surplus forklift that could be used to high-stack shelves. Things were looking up, I thought. Then in came our new security system and a series of automated cabinets for storing items of extreme value with their computer controls (thanks to Neill and Grace). The office areas were finally outfitted, and the processing room for the eagles was completed with all its stainless-steel tables, sinks, and finally a large air duct to whisk away the fumes from spoiling and rotting eagles. Many times when the eagles came into the repository, they were not in the best condition. In fact, some had lain out in the hot sun for many days before discovery and shipment. It is up to the eagle technician to salvage everything possible. Not only are the parts valuable, but there is a huge need in the Native American community for those eagles and their parts. Therefore, the Service always made every effort to save as much as possible so the items could be shipped to wanting Native Americans. Not junk, mind you, but the good parts, which many times had to be cleaned up, but it was done with caring understanding by Dennis Weist, the lead technician. Many times after watching Dennis work, I wondered if anyone knew more than he about those eagles and the cultures they supplied. He was a very intense and studious man, and the Native Americans truly benefited from his hands.

Along with all the activity constructing the facility, we were advertising for and hiring personnel to run it. Damn, we were flying toward completion day—and then we hit a snag. Grace Englund, my savvy administrative officer, had been canvassing commercial movers to see what it would cost to move all the eagles and wildlife parts and products from the forensics lab in Ashland, Oregon, to our new facility. The cheapest bid she got was a whopping $47,000! I did not have that kind of money.

Sitting there in my office late one afternoon after everyone else had gone home, I put some more music on my stereo, sat back in my chair, and let the wheels of imagination roll. For the longest time, I couldn't think of any way to get around the high price quoted to move the items from Ashland. *Then I got it!* The next morning, I called a staff meeting.

I said, "Folks, the lowest quote Miss Grace has gotten from the movers is $47,000 to move the goods from Ashland to our new facility in Commerce City. Yesterday I was trying to find a cheaper way to do it. I got an idea, and after checking it out, I think I can do it for less than half if I can enlist your support. I propose flying those of you on my staff who want to go to Ashland, and we will do the work ourselves!" Man, that created a ripple across their faces. "That is half of it. The other half is to get the moving truck from New Mexico Game and Fish along with one seized tractor-trailer rig of ours and to borrow another one from the refuge system. Three commercial-sized trucks and trailers should do it. We can use the drivers from New Mexico to drive their truck. One of our undercover officers holds a commercial truck driver's license, and I can get one more driver from Refuge Manager Royce Huber in Nebraska, which will take care of the second truck. Lastly, I can get Gregg Langer from the arsenal and one other refuge officer truck driver, and we will have it made for all three trucks. All the truck drivers are credentialed officers, so I will also have my security on board at all times protecting our cargo. We will use the forensic laboratory's forklift to load the pallets, and there you have it."

For the longest moment there was nothing, and then all at once everyone was talking excitedly. It didn't take long for most of my staff to sign on, and with the addition of Lori White, secretary from my Pierre Office, we were set. I arranged for the loan of the New Mexico truck through Agent Leo Suazo, who was from there, and obtained the other vehicles just as I had planned. Come moving day, my little crew met at the airport and off to San Francisco we flew. From there we flew to McKinleyville Airport just north of Arcata, where we picked up a couple of vans for the crew and our gear. Having worked in Northern California as a state and federal officer, I made sure the staff got a great "cook's tour" as we went: dinner at an old logging camp, a tour of a couple of beaches where those who had never seen the Pacific Ocean could soak their feet, and finally a back-way tour of the beautiful redwoods. By that time my staff all had a case of the "big eye" from the surrounding natural beauty.

The following day we arrived at the lab in Ashland, and my team was ready for bear. ... Now, keep in mind, I had six small women and one slightly built man from my office staff, Neill (my deputy), and myself. The ladies were not only tough but determined, especially after the lab staff told them they wouldn't be able to pack and move all the items in less than six days. I didn't say anything to the lab staff, but they didn't know whom they were talking to when it came to that crew! As for Angelo, he might have been slight, but he had a work ethic that was unreal. And Neill, my deputy, was a horse! Strong as a bull, quick as a cat, and not afraid of work. In fact, the only lazy and useless one on the whole crew was me. ...

The trucks had been sent on their way to Ashland several days earlier. Since it would take them three days to get there, they had to leave early to fit into my plan. I timed the arrival of my crew for one day before the arrival of the trucks. That way we would have a head start on the packing and have a mound of stuff for the truckers to load upon arrival. Once my crew arrived, off to the races we went. The women packed the loose items, of which there were thousands, into packing boxes (previously ordered), and Angelo, Neill, and I hauled. Man, those women may have been little, but the fur really flew. In fact, the three men were hard pressed to keep up with them! As the work progressed, various staff members from the forensic laboratory kept looking in on my hardworking crew. You could see they were not impressed, still thinking it would take six days to load all the wildlife items that were stored clear to the ceiling in the forensic laboratory.

Then our trucks arrived. I didn't think it was possible, but the women really turned it on, and man, we were hopping. *Nineteen and a half hours later, all the forfeited property was in the trucks, with all the shelving taken down and loaded and the floor swept clean!* You never saw such faces as those of the lab staff when they saw what a mountain we had moved in such a small amount of time.

Back to Arcata my tired but very pleased crew went. Me, I had problems keeping from popping off all my shirt buttons. ... Days later our trucks arrived in Commerce City, and that same crew, with help from the arsenal and regional office staffs, offloaded those trucks in exactly four hours! That included putting together all the shelving that had been removed from the Ashland building! Even the new deputy regional director, Terri Terrell, put on some old pants and a sweatshirt and pitched right in without any fanfare.

Bottom line, we were up and running in a short period of time, having saved the Service a bundle of money. Heck, instead of paying $47,000 for the move, I got away with spending just a little over $19,000 for my crew, and that included the special achievement awards to my staff for such an outstanding performance! You know, many American people hold the federal work force in low esteem. That is unfortunate because many fine people work for the government, and it shows in operations such as that one. Everyone from all divisions pitched in, and in a short time the impossible was done, and done well!

Within a week of this story being written, Interior Secretary Gail Norton will be on hand at the Rocky Mountain Arsenal to receive from the Department of Defense, the U.S. Army, America's newest National Wildlife Refuge. It is staffed by very capable professionals and has the potential to become an extremely important urban refuge, home to thousands of Canada geese, white-tailed and mule deer, and trees crowned with the symbol of America, the bald eagle. Among all that life and beauty on the refuge, secluded in a fairly new white building, are many thousands of animal parts and products. Broken bodies one and all, thanks to man's inhumanity to man. ... It is ironic that the National Wildlife Property and Eagle Repositories are located on lands holding such wonderful natural-resource potential for the American people. It is the kind of living hope that only a National Wildlife Refuge can hold.

About the Author

TERRY GROSZ was a conservation law enforcement officer for more than 30 years, initially for the State of California, and later with the U.S. Fish and Wildlife Service. His five previous books include *Wildlife Wars* (winner of the National Outdoor Book Award for nature and environment), *For Love of Wildness, Defending Our Wildlife Heritage, A Sword for Mother Nature,* and *No Safe Refuge.* Several of his stories were recently broadcast as a docudrama on cable TV's Animal Planet network.